WITHDRAWN
UML LIBRARIES

LOCATING
UNITED STATES
GOVERNMENT
INFORMATION

A Guide to Sources

EDWARD HERMAN

WILLIAM S. HEIN & Company
Buffalo, New York
1983

Copyright 1983 by William S. Hein & Co., Inc.
1285 Main Street, Buffalo, N.Y. 14209

All Rights Reserved.

FIRST PRINTING

Library of Congress Cataloging in Publication Data

Herman, Edward.
    Locating United States Government information.

    Includes bibliographies and index.
    1. United States--Government publications. I. Title.
Z1223.Z7H46 1983   [J83] 015.73   82-83991
ISBN 0-89941-182-7
ISBN 0-89941-245-9 (pbk.)

Printed in the United States of America

CONTENTS

PREFACE v

INTRODUCTION vii

CHAPTER 1
Item Numbers and Superintendent of
Documents Classification Numbers 1

CHAPTER 2
General Comprehensive Indexes 9

CHAPTER 3
Congressional Publications, Part I:
Tracing a Bill Through Congress 43

CHAPTER 4
Congressional Publications, Part II: CIS/Index 65

CHAPTER 5
Congressional Publications, Part III:
Additional Guides to Reports and Documents
(Serial Set), Hearings, and Committee Prints 77

CHAPTER 6
Indexes and Guides to Legislation and Regulations 109

CHAPTER 7
Locating Federal Statistics 147

CHAPTER 8
Census Information 169

CHAPTER 9
Locating Technical Reports 185

CHAPTER 10
Locating Maps and Audio-Visual Materials 197

CHAPTER 11
Using the Freedom of Information
and Privacy Acts 207

CHAPTER 12
Conclusion 217
Annotated Bibliography Section 218
Index Section 229

PREFACE

The purpose of this book is to provide a practical how to guide for locating United States government publications. Its workbook format incorporates illustrations from appropriate indexes and abstracts, plus questions and answers. College and University students—especially those studying social sciences and law, faculty, businessmen, market researchers, attorneys, and others who have need to consult government documents should find the book valuable. Both practicing librarians and library school students also have much to gain from this text.

Government Documents are defined in the Introduction. Their accessibility and problems associated with their use in libraries are also described. Two key concepts, item numbers and Superintendent of Document classification numbers, are considered in chapter 1. Item numbers identify depository documents, those distributed by the Government Printing Office to depository libraries. Superintendent of Document numbers are alphanumeric classification numbers used by most depository libraries for shelving government publications. General comprehensive indexes to Federal government publications, such as the *Monthly Catalog,* the *Publications Reference File,* and the *Index to U.S. Government Periodicals* are considered in chapter 2.

Chapters 3-6 cover Congressional publications, legislation, and regulations. The various kinds of Congressional documents are defined. Following that, significant sources used in compiling legislative histories are examined. To emphasize the similarities and differences between these reference tools, the identical bill S. 3295, which became Public Law 94-375, is traced through each source. The *Congressional Information Service Index* is described separately in chapter 4 because of its special significance. Again, S. 3295 is used as an example when discussing the *CIS.* The Serial Set and retrospective Congressional committee prints and hearings are considered next. Chapter 6 describes how researchers locate existing legislation and regulations.

Chapters 7 and 8 cover Federal government statistical publications. The most comprehensive guide to United States government statistics, the *American Statistics Index,* is explained. That is followed by a bibliographic essay describing quick reference sources, such as the *Statistical Abstracts.* Bureau of the Census programs and guides to census publications are also studied.

The remaining chapters consider other types of government information. Technical reports are covered in chapter 9. The following one deals with maps and other audio visual materials. The Freedom of Information and Privacy Acts are described in chapter 11. The concluding chapter summarizes with brief annotations the major sources noted in the book and provides a quick reference guide indicating what bibliographic tools are most appropriate to use under different conditions.

I am grateful to the many people who assisted me in this endeavor. Dr. Frederick Henrich, my former Department Head from whom I learned a great deal, offered many suggestions which enhanced the book's value. The editorial assistance provided by two friends, Ruth Gay and Mary Freedman, has been exceptionally useful. I am also grateful to the many students enrolled in the School of Information and Library Studies (SUNY at Buffalo) who read and commented upon the manuscript. Finally, I am especially grateful to my wife Linda whose support and encouragement has been invaluable.

INTRODUCTION

WHAT ARE GOVERNMENT DOCUMENTS?

Government documents are publications issued by governing jurisdictions, be they the United States Federal government, a state government, a municipality, or a local school district. Information published by international governing agencies are considered government documents as well.

Most laymen have an incorrect conception about the kinds of materials published by the United States government. They believe documents are limited to laws, regulations, court decisions, and loads of statistics. In reality, federal publications cover all subjects from A through Z. The National Aeronautic and Space Administration's volumes incorporate beautifully illustrated color plates of photographs taken from spacecrafts; the Air Force issues color posters of its airplanes; the Department of Justice publishes public opinion surveys about crime, and the House Government Operations Committee published hearings on the safety of intrauterine contraception devices. These too, and thousands more just as diverse, interesting, and informative, are also government documents. Moreover, much of the information published by the United States government is often the most recent available and is only on rare occasions available from commercial publishers. Hopefully, this book will be a key that helps researchers unlock the mysteries of these very valuable sources.

ACCESSIBILITY OF UNITED STATES GOVERNMENT DOCUMENTS:

United States documents are accessible through the depository library program, which is administered by the Government Printing Office (GPO). The GPO distributes gratis copies of government documents to institutions that have been designated "depository libraries." Depository libraries in turn are required to provide the public free access to these materials. Although Federal law allows for designation in the manner indicated below of 1,584 depository libraries, as of October 1980, 1,346 institutions were recognized as such.

DESIGNATION OF DEPOSITORY LIBRARIES

Under the present provisions of title 44 of the United States Code, the depository list comprises the following described libraries:

2 libraries for each congressional district to be designated by the Representative from that district (or at large in the case of undistricted States) 870
2 libraries to be designated in any part of the State by each Senator .. 200
2 libraries to be designated by the Resident Commissioner from Puerto Rico 2
2 libraries to be designated by the Mayor of the District of Columbia 2
1 library to be designated by the Governor of American Samoa 1
1 library to be designated by the Governor of Guam 1
2 libraries to be designated by the Governor of the Virgin Islands (1 on the island of St. Thomas and 1 on the island of St. Croix) 2
Highest State Appellate Court Libraries 52
State Libraries 50
Libraries of the land-grant colleges 71
Libraries of the executive departments in Washington 12

Libraries of independent agencies and of major bureaus and divisions of
   departments and agencies 125
Libraries of the U.S. Air Force, Coast Guard, Merchant Marine, Military
   and Naval Academies 5
Law School Libraries 194

Procedures for becoming a depository library are described in the *United States Code,* the official compilation of Federal law, Title 44, section 1905.

There are two kinds of depository libraries, regional and selective ones. Regional depositories are required to accept all materials distributed through the depository library system. Federal law limits the designation of regional libraries to two in each state and Puerto Rico. Forty-nine of the 1,346 depository institutions are regional ones. On the other hand, selective depository libraries have the option of electing to receive only those materials which fall within their needs, while bypassing publications that are irrelevant to them. A list of depository libraries appears in *Government Depository Libraries.* The list is also printed in the October 1981 *Monthly Catalog* and will appear in every forthcoming October *Catalog.*

While discussing the depository library system, it is important to note the difference between depository documents as opposed to those which are non-depository. The former are publications distributed through the depository system. Non-depository documents are those not distributed through the depository system. These materials comprise publications that are either printed and distributed by the issuing agencies, or if printed by the GPO, are made available only through the agency for which it was printed. Title 44 of the *United States Code,* section 1902, exempts three kinds of documents from depository distribution:

1. Those that were prepared for administrative purposes and thus have little or no educational value.

2. Those required for official use only.

3. Those classified for national security purposes.

The same section also requires that publishing agencies supply the GPO with a monthly list of their non-depository documents not classified for national security purposes.

Although this book is primarily aimed toward library users, it should be noted that United States documents are also available for purchase from the Government Printing Office. GPO requests that orders include titles, warehouse stock numbers (s/n numbers), quantities desired, prices and units of issue. Except for units of issue, which are explained and illustrated on the Government Printing Office's Order Form, the above information can be obtained from most of the sources considered in this book. All orders must be prepaid. The Printing Office welcomes Master Charge and Visa transactions. Documents can also be purchased in GPO bookstores located in the Washington D.C. area and major cities throughout the nation. The Public Printer has recently proposed those stores outside the Capitol area be closed, but final action has yet to be taken. Two commercial bookstore chains, Walden Books and B. Dalton, sell the more popular titles issued by the Federal Government.

Finally, government agencies will sometimes supply individuals with copies of their documents upon request. Two important sources are used to obtain agencies' addresses and phone numbers, the *United States Government Organization Manual* and the *Federal Executive Directory.* Most Congressional committees and their subcommittees are particularly cooperative in distributing gratis copies of their publications. The *Congressional Staff Directory* lists the names, addresses, and phone numbers of legislative offices.

PROBLEMS ASSOCIATED WITH THE USE OF GOVERNMENT DOCUMENTS IN LIBRARIES:

Government documents present many unique difficulties for library users. In most libraries, very few or sometimes none of the documents acquired are listed in the card catalog. Since the GPO is the largest publisher in the world, libraries simply cannot afford to catalog all or even some of its documents as they do other information.

The distinction between depository, as opposed to non-depository publications, presents serious problems. Because there is no central source of distribution for non-depository documents, it becomes extremely difficult to maintain bibliographic control over them. Although section 1902 of Title 44 requires agencies to supply the Government Printing Office with monthly lists of their non-depository documents, the agencies do not always oblige. The GPO cannot list many non-depository documents in its comprehensive bibliography, the *Monthly Catalog,* as it is unaware of their existence. It is a very difficult task for libraries to obtain gratis copies of non-depository documents as they do depository ones; few, if any institutions have the staff necessary to acquire copies of all documents from each of the publishing government agencies and their subordinate offices.

The designation of documents that fall within the three classes of non-depository publications cited above presents still further difficulties for researchers who depend upon the free flow of information. Decisions that certain titles have little or no educational value, or must be classified to preserve the national security are extremely subjective. What has little educational value to Joe might be very significant information to John. The Nixon Administration argued that release of the Pentagon Papers would violate our national well being; the Supreme Court disagreed.

It is hoped that this book will enable library users to overcome the problems associated with access to United States government information.

BIBLIOGRAPHY

Congressional Staff Directory. Indianapolis: New Bobbs-Merrill, 1959—annual.

Federal Executive Directory. Washington, D.C.: Carroll Publishing Company, 1976—bimonthly.

Government Depository Libraries. Joint Committee on Printing. Joint Committee Print. 97th Cong., 1st sess. Washington, D.C.: GPO, 1981.

Monthly Catalog of United States Government Publications. Superintendent of Documents. Washington, D.C.: GPO, 1895—monthly. Title varies.

United States Government Manual. National Archives and Records Service. Office of The Federal Register. Washington, D.C.: GPO, 1935—annual. Previously entitled: *United States Government Organization Manual.*

CHAPTER 1

ITEM NUMBERS AND SUPERINTENDENT OF
DOCUMENTS CLASSIFICATION NUMBERS

It is important to understand the purpose and significance of two numbers, the item number and the Superintendent of Documents classification number, before studying specifics of the various indexes.

Item Numbers:

The Government Printing Office uses item numbers as a record-keeping system to determine which documents selective depository libraries have elected to receive. Different kinds of documents are given different item numbers. When selective depositories choose the documents they wish to receive, they inform the GPO of those publications' item numbers. All documents that fall within the selected numbers are then forwarded to the appropriate libraries. As of October 1980, depository institutions were able to choose from among 4,127 item numbers. These are recognized in most indexes and abstracts by the heavy black dots, bullets (●), preceding them. Note that only depository documents are given item numbers.

Superintendent of Documents Numbers:

In most libraries, documents not listed in the card catalog are shelved according to Superintendent of Documents classification numbers or SuDoc numbers. Merely follow the alphanumeric sequence of the SuDoc number to retrieve information from the shelves. This system was developed by the Government Printing Office between 1895 and 1903. Many of the indexes described in this book provide library users with SuDoc numbers.

"HH 1.2:Eq2/4/v.1," the SuDoc number for *The Barriers To Equal Opportunity In Rural Housing Markets,* is a typical one. The chart below explains the alphanumeric sequence.

SuDoc Notation	Explanation of Notation	Discussion of Notation
HH	Department of Housing and Urban Development	SuDoc numbers begin with upper case letters or groups of letters which indicate the publishing agencies. For instance, Department of Agriculture documents are identified by "A," Department of Commerce documents by "C," and Department of Housing and Urban Development documents by "HH."
HH 1	Document was published by the Secretary's Office	The numbers following the initial letters indicate the division or bureau within the parent agency which published the document. The number "1" tells you that the publication was issued by the Secretary's Office of the Department rather than a subdivision. For example, documents whose SuDoc numbers begin with "A1" are those issued

by the Secretary of Agriculture, but others whose classification numbers begin with "A 68" are published by the Department's Rural Electrification Administration.

HH 1.2	Monographic or general publication	The numbers that follow the period indicate the kind of document or series of which the specific publication is a part. "1" represents annual reports and ".2" stands for monographs. For instance, "A 1.1" is the classification for the Department of Agriculture's annual report, while "A 68.1" is the classification for the annual report of that Department's Rural Electrification Administration.
HH 1.2:	All succeeding information in the SuDoc number, in this case EQ2/4/v.1, identifies the title of the document	The colon separates the more general information about the publishing agency and its various series of documents from the more specific information that relates to individual titles. "HH 1.2" tells you that *The Barriers To Equal Opportunity in Rural Housing Markets* is a monograph published by the Secretary's Office of HUD. The colon then warns you that "EQ 2/4/v.1" identifies the particular monograph in question.
HH 1.2: EQ 2	Keyword in title	Although the document in question is classified according to the keyword in its title, numeric, instead of alphanumeric representations are sometimes used to classify specific titles. For example, the SuDoc number for *Dairy Market Statistics,* the six hundred and first publication in the Department of Agriculture's Statistical Bulletin Series is "A.1.34:601."
HH 1.2: EQ 2/4	Fourth time this keyword was used for a monograph issued by the Secretary's Office of HUD.	Self explanatory.
HH 1.2: EQ 2/4/ v. 1	Volume 1 of this title.	Self explanatory.

Superintendent of Documents classification numbers vary greatly, depending upon the particular publications to which they apply. Consider, for instance, *John Brown's Raid,* a sixty-nine page pamphlet which is a part of the National Park Service historical series. Its SuDoc number is I 29.58/2:B 81. Note that in this case the slash precedes rather than follows the colon. The SuDoc number is still recognized by its alphanumeric makeup, combined with the period and the colon, regardless of where the slash appears. Using a second example, the Superintendent of Documents number for *Dairy Market Statistics,* the document mentioned above whose classification number is A 1.34:601, is still different. It has no slash. However, the alphanumeric sequence, together with the period and the colon, still enables you to identify the number easily.

Summary:

The item number, not the SuDoc number, indicates if a publication is a depository document. The various document indexes will ocassionally indicate SuDoc numbers for non-depository materials. In these cases, although the publication is not distributed by the GPO to depository institutions, the Government Printing Office still indexes and classifies these documents to make the public aware of their availability from the issuing agencies. Moreover, commercial indexes will often cite complete bibliographic information for documents, but will not indicate a SuDoc number. In these cases, the publishers of the indexes have become aware of a non-depository document with which the Government Printing Office is unfamiliar. Since GPO is the only office that can apply official Superintendent of Document numbers, private publishers will not attempt to apply unofficial numbers which might confuse the situation even more. Remember, an item number indicates if a document is depository or non-depository, regardless of the presence or absence of a Superintendent of Documents number.

Item Numbers and Superintendent of Document Numbers: Questions:

1. The following illustrations were taken from selected indexes you will encounter in this book. You now have enough information to distinguish between depository and non-depository documents and to recognize the Superintendent of Documents number. In each case, indicate the SuDoc number, whether or not the document is a depository one, and the item number. Why don't non-depository documents have item numbers?

Figure 1-1

80-19303

Y 3.J 66:13/(nos.)

Translations on USSR agriculture. Arlington, Va., Joint Publications Research Service; Springfield, Va., for sale by the National Technical Information Service.

22161

27 cm. (JPRS)

no. 1126, June 19, 1978; JPRS 71317.

●Item 1067-L-1 (microfiche)

Main series: United States. Joint Publications Research Service. JPRS

Continues: Translations on Soviet agriculture

1. Russia — Periodicals. 2. Agriculture — Russia — Periodicals. I. United States. Joint Publications Research Service. II. Series: United States. Joint Publications Research Service. JPRS.

OCLC 2370673

SuDoc Number _____

Depository _____ Non-Depository _____

Item Number _____

Figure 1-2

80-18406

E 1.28:SAND 78-0168

Gunderson, Donald O.

International safeguards for fast critical facilities / Donald O. Gunderson, James L. Todd, Sandia Laboratories ; prepared by Sandia Laboratories for the United States Department of Energy. — Albuquerque, N.M. : Dept. of Energy, Sandia Laboratories ; [Springfield, Va. : for sale by the National Technical Information Service], 1978.

5285 Port Royal Rd., 22161

68 p. : ill. ; 28 cm. — (SAND ; 78-0168)

Contract AT(29-1)-789.

Dec. 1978.

Includes bibliographical references.

pbk.

1. Fast reactors. 2. Nuclear facilities. I. Todd, James L., joint author. II. United States. Dept. of Energy. III. Sandia Laboratories. IV. Title.
OCLC 6394848

SuDoc Number _____

Depository _____ Non-Depository _____

Item Number _____

Figure 1-3

6784–7   UNION WAGES AND BENEFITS: BUILDING TRADES, July 3, 1978
Annual. Sept. 1979.
vi + 153 p. BLS Bull. 2038.
•Item 768-C-4. GPO $4.75.
ASI/MF/4
S/N 029-001-02389-8.
⁺L2.3:2038.

Annual report on 1978 survey of average hourly wage rates, supplemental benefit contributions by employers, and weekly hours for specified crafts and jobs in the building trades. Based on union minimum rates in effect July 3, 1978, in 65 cities with over 100,000 population.

Survey covered journeymen and helpers and laborers in 25 building, highway and street, and other heavy construction trades. Employer contributions are computed to cover 3 or 6 supplemental benefits: health and life insurance, pensions, vacations, holidays, savings funds, and supplemental unemployment benefits.

SuDoc Number _____

Depository _____ Non-Depository _____

Item Number _____

Figure 1-4

4044-2 **U.S. PUBLIC HEALTH
SERVICE ANNUAL REPORT
TO THE CONGRESS, FY78**
[1979.]   102 p. †
ASI/MF/4   *HE20.1:978.

Annual report for FY78, describing PHS programs and activities. Covers the following agencies: Office of the Assistant Secretary for Health, ADAMHA, CDC, FDA, HRA, HSA, and NIH.
  Contains a narrative chapter for each of the 7 agencies, presenting text statistics on numbers served, personnel, and expenditures.

Reproduced with permission from *American Statistics Index*, published and copyrighted by Congressional Information Service, Inc., 4520 East-West Highway, Washington, D.C. 20014

SuDoc Number _____

Depository _____ Non-Depository _____

Item Number _____

Figure 1-5

S321-13 **EXECUTIVE BRANCH
REVIEW OF
ENVIRONMENTAL
REGULATIONS.**
Feb. 26, 27, 1979.   96-1.
iii+504 p. † CIS/MF/8
●Item 1045.
*Y4.P96/10:96-H4.
MC 79-17529. LC 79-602197.

Committee Serial No. 96-H4. Hearings before the *Subcom on Environmental Pollution* to examine executive branch economic impact review of environmental regulations, emphasizing possibility of interference in the regulatory process and the undermining of environmental laws.

Reproduced with permission from *CIS Index*, published and copyrighted by Congressional Information Service, Inc., 4520 East-West Highway, Washington, D.C. 20014

SuDoc Number _____

Depository _____ Non-Depository _____

Item Number _____

Figure 1-6

H762–10   LEGISLATIVE PROGRAM OF
THE DISABLED AMERICAN
VETERANS.
Feb. 20, 1979. 96-1.
iii+10 p. ‡ CIS/MF/3

Committee Print No. 8. Contains Billy O. Hightower (Natl Cmdr, Disabled Amer Veterans) Feb. 20, 1979 prepared statement presenting organization proposals for 1979 legislation on veterans programs.

Reproduced with permission from *CIS Index*, published and copyrighted by Congressional Information Service, Inc., 4520 East-West Highway, Washington, D.C. 20014

SuDoc Number _____

Depository _____ Non-Depository _____

Item Number _____

2. Using the five examples above rearrange the SuDoc numbers into shelf list order—the alphanumeric sequence in which they would appear on the shelves, "A" being the first and "E" the final one. Note, one citation does not have a SuDoc Number.

A _____   D _____

B _____   E _____

C _____

ANSWERS: CHAPTER 1

1. Figure 1-1

SuDoc Number <u>Y 3.J 66:13/(nos.)</u>

Depository <u>X</u> Non-Depository___
Item Number <u>1067-L-1</u>

Figure 1-2

SuDoc Number <u>E 1.28:SAND</u>
<u>78-0168</u>

Depository ___Non-Depository <u>X</u>
Item Number <u>NONE</u>

Although the document in figure 2 has a SuDoc Number, it is still a non-depository one because it does not have an item number.

Figure 1-3

SuDoc Number <u>L 2.3:2038</u>

Depository <u>X</u> Non-Depository___

Item Number <u>768-C-4</u>

Figure 1-4

SuDoc Number <u>HE 20.1:978</u>

Depository ___Non-Depository <u>X</u>

Item Number <u>NONE</u>
(See explanation for figure 2)

Figure 1-5

SuDoc Number <u>Y 4.P96/10:96-H 4</u>

Depository <u>X</u> Non-Depository___

Item Number <u>1045</u>

Figure 1-6

SuDoc Number <u>NONE</u>

Depository ___Non-Depository <u>X</u>

Item Number <u>NONE</u>

The document in figure 1-6 is a non-depository publication because an item number is not indicated. It does not have a SuDoc number, since GPO never gave it one.

2. A. <u>E 1.28:SAND 78-0168</u>

B. <u>HE 20.1:978</u>

C. <u>L 2.3:2038</u>

D. <u>Y 3.J 66:13/(nos.)</u>

E. <u>Y 4.P 96/10:96-H 4</u>

CHAPTER 2

GENERAL COMPREHENSIVE INDEXES

General comprehensive indexes that provide access to documents published by all three branches of government are considered in this chapter. The *Monthly Catalog,* the first to be described, lists both depository and non-depository publications. In conjunction with this discussion, two supplementary indexes to the *Monthly Catalog* are noted, the *Cumulative Subject Index To the Monthly Catalog, 1900-1971* and *United States Government Publications. Monthly Catalog. Cumulative Personal Author Indexes 1941-1975.* The *Publications Reference File (PRF)* is the fourth source discussed. The *PRF* cites all documents available for sale from the Government Printing Office. The *Cumulative Title Index To United States Public Documents, 1789-1976* is described next. Following that, the *Index To United States Government Periodicals* is considered, along with two additional sources that list Federal periodicals, the *Monthly Catalog Serials Supplement* and *Government Periodicals and Subscription Services.*

Monthly Catalog:

The *Monthly Catalog of United States Government Publications* is the basic bibliography or catalog for United States documents available to the public. It has been issued on a monthly basis since 1895 under various titles.

Catalog of Publications Issued by the Government of the United States, January-March, 1895.

Catalog of United States Public Documents, April 1895-June 1907.

Monthly Catalog, United States Public Documents, July 1907-December 1939.

United States Government Publications: A Monthly Catalog, 1904-1950. Its current title was first used in 1951.

The *Monthly Catalog* consists of two parts, the bibliographic section which supplies information necessary to locate documents and six indexes for authors, titles, subjects, series report numbers, stock numbers, and title key words. The indexes are issued monthly and cumulated annually. Since 1977 semiannual indexes covering January through June have been published. Cumulative multi-year indexes to the *Monthly Catalog* are also available. In addition to the *Catalog's* supplementary indexes cited above, the Government Printing Office has issued five indexes covering 1941-1976.

United States Government Publications, Monthly Catalog: Decennial Cumulative Index 1941-1950.

Monthly Catalog of United States Government Publications: Decennial Cumulative Index 1951-1960.

Monthly Catalog of United States Government Publications: Cumulated Index . . . Three editions cover 1961-1965, 1966-1970, and 1971-1976.

Subject Index:

Suppose you are interested in locating information about the characteristics of residents of public housing units. Search the Subject Index for appropriate entries. Selected entries are reproduced in figure 2-1.

Figure 2-1

Monthly Catalog, 1980
Subject Index

Public housing — United States.
Social and economic characteristics of residents of public housing : instructor's guide., 80-18847

Social and economic characteristics of residents of public housing : participant's workbook., 80-18848

Public housing — United States — Security measures.
Household safety and security survey /, 80-18857

Public records — Law and legislation — United States — Periodicals.
Privacy act issuances., 80-18732

Refer to figure 2-1 when answering the following questions:

Are relevant documents listed?

Yes

Note their *Monthly Catalog* entry numbers—the numbers immediately following the citations.

_____ and _____

80-18847 and 80-18848

Bibliographic Section:

Use the *Monthly Catalog* entry numbers to locate the documents in the bibliographic section. Citations in that section are arranged in consecutive numerical order. For illustrative purposes, you are interested in document number 80-18848, the eighteen thousand, eight hundred and forty-eighth document listed in the 1980 *Monthly Catalog.* (figure 2-2)

Figure 2-2

Monthly Catalog, 1980
Bibliographic Section

```
      80-18848
1 ——————                HH 1.6/3:R 31/2/part. ———————————— 7
             United States. Dept. of Housing and Urban Development.
2 ————————Office of Policy Development and Research.
             Social and economic characteristics of residents of public
3 ————————housing : participant's workbook. — [Washington] : Dept. of
             Housing and Urban Development, Office of Policy Develop-
             ment and Research : for sale by the Supt. of Docs., U.S.
             Govt. Print. Off., 1979 i.e. 1980.
             20402
4 ————————— ii, 25 p. ; 28 cm. — (HUD-PDR ; 537-8) ——————————— 8
             One of 18 workbooks in a housing management curriculum
             developed by HUD and Center for Social Policy and Com-
             munity Development, School of Social Administration,
             Temple University.
             Feb. 1979.
             Bibliography: p. 25.
             ●Item 582-E ———————————————————————————————— 9
5 ——————— S/N 023-000-00583-2
             pbk. : $2.00
6 ——————— 1. Housing management — Study and teaching — United
             States. 2. Public housing — United States. I. Temple Uni-
             versity. Center for Social Policy and Community Develop-
             ment. II. Title.
             OCLC 6477723
```

1. *Monthly Catalog* entry number.	6. Price.
2. Issuing agency.	7. Superintendent of
3. Title.	Documents number.
4. Pagination.	8. Series/Report number.
5. Stock number.	9. Item number.

Refer to figure 2-2 when answering the following questions:

Document 80-18848 was issued by the Department of

————————————————————————————————————— , Office of

—————————————————————————————————— .

　　　Housing and Urban Development, Office of
　　　Policy Development and Research

This document has ———— pages.

　　　　　　　　　25 pages.

Does this document have a bibliography? If yes, on what page?

　　　　　　　Yes, page 25

The Superintendent of Documents number is ———————————— .

　　　　　　HH1.6/3:R31/2/part.

The *Monthly Catalog* entry number and the SuDoc number have two distinct purposes. Explain the objectives of each.

_____

_____

_____

_____

_____

The entry number refers you from the indexes to the main bibliographic section of the *Catalog*. The SuDoc number enables you to locate information on the shelves according to its alphanumeric sequence.

Author and Title Indexes:

When there is a reference to a specific document, it is easier to use the Author or Title Indexes than that of Subjects to locate the *Monthly Catalog* entry number. The Subject Index might refer you to many irrelevant documents before you locate the appropriate one. However, the Author or Title Indexes will refer you directly to the particular publication.

The publication illustrated in figure 2-2 appears as indicated below in the Author and Title Indexes (figure 2-3). Underline the appropriate citations.

Figure 2-3

Monthly Catalog, 1980

Author Index

United States. Dept. of Housing and Urban Development. Office of Policy Development and Research.
Annual housing survey: housing characteristics for selected metropolitan areas., 80-17909

Assistance in local government energy conservation in Massachusetts /, 80-18827

Budgeting procedures for housing managers : instructor's guide., 80-18819

Budgeting procedures for housing managers : participant's workbook., 80-18820

Personnel administration in housing management : participant's workbook., 80-18846

Pest control and grounds maintenance in housing management : instructor's guide., 80-18842

Title Index

Small business/labor surplus : report to accompany H.R. 7288., 80-19155

Small business size standards /, 80-19538

Small scale heater tests in argillite of the Eleana Formation at the Nevada Test Site /, 80-18419

Small vessel inspection and manning : report together with additional views to accompany H.R. 5164., 80-19194

Smithsonian year. Annual report of the Smithsonian Institution., 80-19023

Snow and ice accumulation around solar collector installations /, 80-17942

Social and economic characteristics of residents of public housing : instructor's guide., 80-18847

Social and economic characteristics of residents of public housing : participant's workbook., 80-18848

Pest control and grounds maintenance in housing management : participant's workbook., 80-18843

Professional career systems in housing management : instructor's guide., 80-18821

Professional career systems in housing management : participant's workbook., 80-18822

Resident participation in the housing management process : instructor's guide., 80-18849

Resident participation in the housing management process : participant's workbook., 80-18850

Residential security in multi-family housing : instructor's guide., 80-18851

Residential security in multi-family housing : participant's workbook., 80-18852

Social and economic characteristics of residents of public housing : instructor's guide., 80-18847

Social and economic characteristics of residents of public housing : participant's workbook., 80-18848

Supervisory skills for housing managers : instructor's guide., 80-18855

Supervisory skills for housing managers : participant's workbook., 80-18856

Targeting community development /, 80-18815

The social context of helping : a review of the literature on alternative care for the physically and mentally handicapped /, 80-18804

The social costs of unemployment : hearing before the Joint Economic Committee, Congress of the United States, Ninety-sixth Congress, first session, October 31, 1979., 80-19393

Social security financing : hearings before the Subcommittee on Social Security of the Committee on Finance, United States Senate, Ninety-sixth Congress, second session, February 22 and 25, 1980., 80-19413

Social security programs in the President's fiscal year 1981 budget : hearings before the Subcommittee on Social Security of the Committee on Ways and Means, House of Representatives, Ninety-sixth Congress, second session, February 21, March 17, 18, 1980., 80-19582

Social and Economic Characteristics of Residents of Public Housing was prepared for the Department of Housing and Urban Development by Temple University's Center for Social Policy and Community Development. The document is therefore listed in the Author Index under the name of the University, as well as under the Department of Housing and Urban Development, Office of Policy Development and Research (figure 2-4). Underline the entry.

Figure 2-4

Monthly Catalog, 1980
Author Index

Temple University. Center for Social Policy and Community Development.
Budgeting procedures for housing managers : instructor's guide., 80-18819

Budgeting procedures for housing managers : participant's workbook., 80-18820

Building exterior and interior maintenance and maintenance of equipment and lighting : instructor's guide., 80-18836

Building exterior and interior maintenance and maintenance of equipment
and lighting : participant's workbook.,
80-18837

Characteristics of the elderly : instructor's guide., 80-18825

Characteristics of the elderly : participant's workbook., 80-18826

Communication skills for housing managers : instructor's guide., 80-18823

Social and economic characteristics of
residents of public housing : instructor's guide., 80-18847

Social and economic characteristics of
residents of public housing : participant's workbook., 80-18848

Supervisory skills for housing managers :
instructor's guide., 80-18855

Supervisory skills for housing managers :
participant's workbook., 80-18856

Series/Report Number Index:

Agencies often assign report numbers to their publications which are not related to *Monthly Catalog* entry numbers or to SuDoc numbers. The
Series/Report Number Index enables you to locate citations to documents, providing the report numbers are known. This index was first issued in 1976.

Underline the part of figure 2-2 that tells us *Social and Economic
Characteristics of Residents of Public Housing* is report number HUD-PDR
537-8 (Department of Housing and Urban Development - Office of Policy
Development and Research). This title is listed in the Series/Report Index as
indicated in figure 2-5. Underline the appropriate citation.

Figure 2-5

Monthly Catalog, 1980
Series/Report Number Index

House report - 96th Congress, 2d session ;
no. 96-1104, 80-19214

House report - 96th Congress, 2d session ;
no. 96-1114, 80-19215

House report - 96th Congress, 2d session ;
no. 96-1138, 80-19216

House report - 96th Congress, 2d session ;
no. 96-1147, 80-19217

HRD ; 78-74, 80-18686

HS ; 2, 80-18028

HUD-PDR ; 475, 80-18827

HUD-PDR ; 510, 80-18817

HUD-PDR ; 527-2, 80-18857

HUD-PDR ; 537-1, 80-18854

HUD-PDR ; 537-2, 80-18853

HUD-PDR ; 537-3, 80-18839

HUD-PDR ; 537-4, 80-18835

```
HUD-PDR ; 537-5,   80-18823
HUD-PDR ; 537-6,   80-18830
HUD-PDR ; 537-7,   80-18824
HUD-PDR ; 537-8,   80-18848
HUD-PDR ; 537-9,   80-18856
HUD-PDR ; 537-10,  80-18850
HUD-PDR ; 537-11,  80-18832
```

Title Key Word Index:

Documents are indexed according to the key words in their titles in the Title Key Word Index. This index is ideal for locating publications for which you do not have exact titles. It should also be used when appropriate subject headings in the Subject Index cannot be located. Perhaps the concept(s) or term(s) at issue are mentioned in relevant titles. This index was first issued on an experimental basis in the July 1980 *Monthly Catalog.*

The publication in figure 2-2 appears in the Title Key Word Index as shown below (figure 2-6). Underline the citation.

Figure 2-6

Monthly Catalog, 1980
Title Key Word Index

pruned red spruce trees /, Growth trends in		80-17572
psychological aspects /, Stress; physiological and		80-18941
psychology of firesetting :a review and appraisal		80-17941
Public and private utilities.		80-18729
"	assembly., Saving money with energy conserv	80-18104
"	buildings act of 1980 :report of the Commit	80-19269
"	buildings, landmarks and historic sites of	80-18720
"	employment.	80-17892
"	fire education planning :a five step proces	80-18533
"	health :educational data project, 1974-1979	80-18798
"	health practices for improving children's o	80-18776
"	housing :instructor's guide., Social and ec	80-18847
"	housing :participant's workbook., Social an	80-18848
"	law 85-804—status as of July 29, 1979 :repo	80-18703
"	papers of the Presidents of the United Stat	80-18746

Stock Number Index:

GPO warehouse stock numbers, S/N numbers, are listed in numerical order in the Stock Number Index. It is important to include stock numbers on purchase orders when obtaining documents from the Government Printing Office. The stock number for *Social and Economic Characteristics of Residents of Public Housing* is 023-000-00583-2 (figure 2-7).

Figure 2-7

Monthly Catalog, 1980
Stock Number Index

```
022-003-94073-1 ,   80-18735
022-003-94084-7 ,   80-18736
022-003-94094-4 ,   80-18737
```

022-003-94099-5 ,   80-18738
022-003-94114-2 ,   80-18739
022-003-94119-3 ,   80-18740
022-003-94121-5 ,   80-18741
022-003-94124-0 ,   80-18742
022-003-94131-2 ,   80-18743
022-003-94139-8 ,   80-18744
022-003-94147-9 ,   80-18745
023-000-00548-4 ,   80-18827
023-000-00565-4 ,   80-18817
023-000-00581-6 ,   80-18857
023-000-00583-2 ,   80-18848
023-000-00584-1 ,   80-18856
023-000-00585-9 ,   80-18850
023-000-00586-7 ,   80-18832
023-000-00587-5 ,   80-18838
023-000-00588-3 ,   80-18834
023-000-00589-1 ,   80-18829

Monthly Catalog; Old Format:

The current format of the *Monthly Catalog* first appeared in July 1976. Prior to that date, the main bibliographic section was printed as in figure 2-8.

Figure 2-8
Monthly Catalog, 1973
Bibliographic Section

1
\

31159 Presidential campaign activities of 1972, Senate Res. 60, hearings, 93d
Congress, 1st session, Watergate and related activities.   ● Item 1009-A
L.C. card 73-602551   Y 4.P 92/4 : P 92/phase 1/bk. (nos.)— 2
Phase 1, bk. 1. Watergate investigation, May 17-24, 1973. 1973. v+456 p. il.
       * Paper, $3.00 (S/N 5270-01843).
Phase 1, bk. 2. Watergate investigation, June 5-14, 1973. 1973. v+457-910 p.
       il.   * Paper, $3.00 (S/N 5270-01962).

1. *Monthly Catalog* entry number.
2. Superintendent of Documents number.

These documents are part of a series consisting of at least two volumes.

Note:—the *Catalog* entry number was located along the left hand column and the SuDoc number was located in the lower right corner of the citation.

Three separate author, title, and subject indexes were first used in 1974. Prior to that date, the *Catalog* had one alphabetic index which was primarily subject oriented (figure 2-9).

Figure 2-9
Monthly Catalog, 1973
Index

Water vapor :
  heat and water vapor exchange between
  water surface and atmosphere, 31284
  vertical transport of water vapor, ozone
  and aerosols by thunderstorms observa-
  tions, 27800

Waterborne exports and general imports, 19012
Watercraft, *see* Boats.
Waterfowl, *see* Water birds.
Waterfronts:
   security of vessels and waterfront facilities, 16825
   urban river, staff proposal for waterfront development in District of Columbia, 23719, 25562
Watergate hearings, *see* Presidential Campaign Activities, Select Committee on.
Watergate investigation, 31159
Waterloo, Iowa:
   area wage survey, 26618
   housing and education, civil rights aspects, walk together children, 24257
Watersheds:
   annual streamflow summaries from 4 subalpine watersheds in Colorado, 23276
   computer simulation of snowmelt within Colorado subalpine watershed, 28966
   cost analysis of clearing ponderosa pine watershed, 28946

Cumulative Subject Index To The Monthly Catalog, 1900-1971:

The *Cumulative Subject Index to the Monthly Catalog of United States Government Publication: 1900-1971,* greatly simplifies the retrieval of older documents. This index provides access to all materials that appeared in the *Monthly Catalog* between 1900 and 1971 through a subject approach.

Suppose you are looking for information about the relocation of the Seneca Indians and do not know when the appropriate documents were published. Search the *Cumulative Subject Index* (figure 2-10).

Figure 2-10

Cumulative Subject Index to the Monthly Catalog, Volume 13

Seneca Indians (01) 10, 109, 132, 198, 507; (02) 421; (04) 180, 219; (05) 121; (07) 480, 540; (11) 342, 415, 441, 508
   constitution and by-laws (37) 1072
   fiction, legends, and myths (19) 572, 626
   fish and game (27) 438
      Allegany, etc., reservations (33) 618; (34) 807, 922; (35) 249, 271, 717
   money from leased lands –
      laws (50) 18296; (61) 18622
      reports (49) 19340; (50) 16450; (61) 14627, 16718
   morphology and dictionary (67) 13001
   New York commute annuities (48) 10714; (49) 9411
   Niagara River, hearing (15) 31
   ratification of certain leases (30) 1078; (32) 1085
   ratification of certain leases – continued
      hearing (31) 680
      report (31) 500
   receipts, from leasing lands, rp. (32) 1123
   relocation –
      hearings (64) 6359, 8448
      law (64) 17392
      reports (64) 6275, 8418, 17596

reports of Interior Dept. and Justice Dept. (15)
460
splint basketry (S 41-42) 1005

Relevant documents can be found in the 1964 *Monthly Catalog* under the indicated entry numbers. The 6359th entry is reproduced in figure 2-11.

Figure 2-11

Monthly Catalog, 1964

[Committee hearings], serial, 88th Congress. † ● Item 1023
Y 4.In 8/14 : 88/ (nos.)

6359   6. Kinzua Dam (Seneca Indian relocation), hearings before Subcommittee on Indian Affairs, 88th Congress, 1st session, on H.R. 1794, H.R. 3343 and H.R. 7354, May 18-Dec. 10, 1963. 1964. v+515 p. il. 3 pl. [These hearings were held in Salamanca, N.Y. and Washington, D.C. Includes list of selected references on Kinzua Dam controversy.]
L.C. card 64-60610

Its SuDoc number is Y4.In8/14:88/6. Y4.In8/14:88(nos), located in the top right hand corner of the illustration, tells you that all SuDoc numbers for hearings issued by the House Interior and Insular Affairs Committee during the eighty-eighth Congress begin with that notation. Entry number 6359 was the sixth document published in that series.

Citations in the *Cumulative Subject Index* which appeared in the *Monthly Catalog* prior to September 1947, refer to page numbers, not catalog numbers. The Government Printing Office did not adopt the consecutive accession number approach until that date. For instance, citations to publications about fiction, legends and myths of the Seneca Indians appeared on pages 572 and 626 of the 1919 *Monthly Catalog* (see figure 2-10).

The cumulative indexes published by the GPO which cover 1941-1950, 1951-1960, 1961-1965, 1966-1970, and 1971-1976 are arranged in the identical format as that covering 1900-1971.

United States Government Publications. Monthly Catalog. Cumulative Personal Author Indexes, 1941-1975:

The *United States Government Publications. Monthly Catalog. Cumulative Personal Author Indexes, 1941-1975* provides access by personal authors to documents listed in the *Monthly Catalog* between 1941 and 1975. The *Monthly Catalog* year and entry numbers, or when appropriate, page numbers, are indicated following the authors' names. For instance, Peter Hirs' *Discussion of the Slovak Theater,* part of the *Political Translations on Eastern Europe* series, was entry number 784 in the January 1963 *Catalog.* Hirs' name is listed in the index as seen below (figure 2-12).

Figure 2-12

Personal Author Index, 1961-1965

```
Hiner, R.L. and Marsden, S.J.. REF.62-06541
Hiner, Richard L. ................. 65-15189
Hines, Bob ....................... 63-17451
    ILLS.65-00619
Hinnov, E. et al. ............ REF.65-10173
    REF.65-17103
Hinshaw, L.B. et al. ......... BIB.64-13728
Hinshaw, Lerner B. et al. ..... REF.63-04503
    REF.64-05994  REF.64-05997
    REF.64-13734
Hinson, William C. and Strickler, Paul E.
    62-12929
Hinson, William F. and Falanga, Ralph A.
    REF.62-20137
Hinson, William F. and Foffman, Sherwood
    REF.64-03016
Hinson, William F. et al. .... REF.62-06280
Hintenberger, Heinrich and Ewald, Heinz
    LIT.63-01817
Hinteregger, H.E. ............ REF.64-20960
Hinteregger, H.E. and Hall, L.A.
    REF.61-08337
Hinteregger, H.E. et al. ..... REF.64-20965
    REF.65-10112
Hipp, Grace R. and Ateca, Harriet G.
    ASSI.63-03406
Hippolitus, Vincent P. ....... REM.61-04787
    REM.62-01572
Hipsley, Elmer et al. ........ TEST.62-23421
Hirakis, Emanuel C. .......... BIR.61-03752
Hirs, Peter ...................... 63-00784
Hirsch, Stanley N. ........... REF.62-17559
Hirschberg, Marvin H. et al. . REF.63-09152
Hirschfeld, A.B. ................. 61-09908
Hirschtritt, Moses and Lowe, Louise F.
    PREP.61-09037
Hirsh, N.B. ................... REF.65-20114
```

Readex Microprints of the Monthly Catalog:

Microprint copies of all documents listed in the *Monthly Catalog* are sold by the Readex Corporation. Microprints are six by nine inch opaque cardboards onto which images are printed, rather than filmed. This collection is separated into two parts, *United States Government Publications (Depository),* which covers 1956 to date, and *United States Government Publications (Non-Depository),* which covers 1953 to date. The microprints are filed according to the *Monthly Catalog* entry numbers instead of Superintendent of Documents numbers. The most recent issues of this collection include documents that had appeared in the *Monthly Catalog* approximately two years prior to the most current *Catalog.*

On-Line Availability of The Monthly Catalog:

Computer applications in libraries have proven to be very beneficial to researchers. Citations to documents indexed in *Monthly Catalogs* issued since July 1976 are available on-line in many libraries. Researchers are advised to consult librarians to determine how computer applications can be utilized to the fullest extent.

The GPO Sales Publication Reference File (PRF):

The *GPO Sales Publications Reference File* is the Government Printing Office's sales catalog which indexes documents available for purchase from GPO. It consists of approximately three hundred microfiche which are produced by computer. Revised editions have appeared bimonthly in January, March, May, July, September, and November since 1977. A supplement to the *PRF, GPO New Sales Publications Microfiche,* which generally consists of one or two fiche, is published monthly. Very often, the *PRF* and its supplements index new documents more rapidly than the *Monthly Catalog.*

The *Reference File* is arranged in three sections, numerically by GPO stock numbers, alphanumerically by Superintendent of Documents numbers, and alphabetically by subjects, keywords, titles, authors, and series. The supplement includes only the alphabetic section.

Fiche headers, index frames, and grids, which assist researchers in locating information, are described first. That explanation is followed by a description of the alphabetic sequence. Though it is the third part of the *PRF* it is still the *Reference File's* largest and most significant section. Most people would consult this section because stock and SuDoc numbers are usually unknown when attempting to locate documents. The stock and SuDoc number sequences are described next. Following that, the *PRF's* on-line availability is mentioned. The *Exhausted GPO Sales Publications Reference File,* a catalog of out-of-print documents which had been available for sale, is also discussed.

Headers, Index Frames, and Grids:

All fiche, regardless of the sections to which they belong, have headers and index frames. Headers located at the tops of the fiche include the *PRF* title, date, fiche number, and range of information covered on specific fiche, be it stock or SuDoc numbers, or alphabetical phrases (figure 2-13).

Figure 2-13
PRF, May 14, 1981
Headers

```
                    Stock Number Section

023-000-00574-3              GPO SALES              19 of 314
TO: 024-001-03159-1 PUBLICATIONS REFERENCE FILE MAY 14, 1981


                    SuDoc Number Section

HE 20.8302:A1 1              GPO SALES              61 of 314
TO: HH 12.2:P 94    PUBLICATIONS REFERENCE FILE May 14, 1981


                    Alphabetical Section

PROVING FEDERAL              GPO SALES              254 of 314
TO: PUBLIC LAW 96   PUBLICATIONS REFERENCE FILE May 14, 1981
```

Refer to figure 2-13 when answering the following:

The header reproduced from the stock number section indicates that the

fiche contains numbers _____ through

_____.

023-000-00574-3 through 024-001-03159-1

The fiche that illustrates the stock number sequence is fiche number _____

out of a total of _____ fiche.

19, 314

SuDoc numbers _____ through _____

appear on fiche number _____.

HE20.8302:A11 through HH12.2:P94, 61

In the alphabetic sequence, subjects, keywords, authors, titles, and series

falling between " _____ " and

"_____" appear on fiche 254.

"Providing Federal" and "Public Law 96"

Index frames enable researchers to determine on which grids appropriate information can be located. Grids are alphanumeric rows and columns that pinpoint specific microfiche frames. Horizontal rows are labeled A-O and vertical columns are labeled 1 through 18. For instance, "A1" represents row A, column 1, the first frame on a fiche (figure 2-14).

Figure 2-14

Microfiche Grid Arrangement

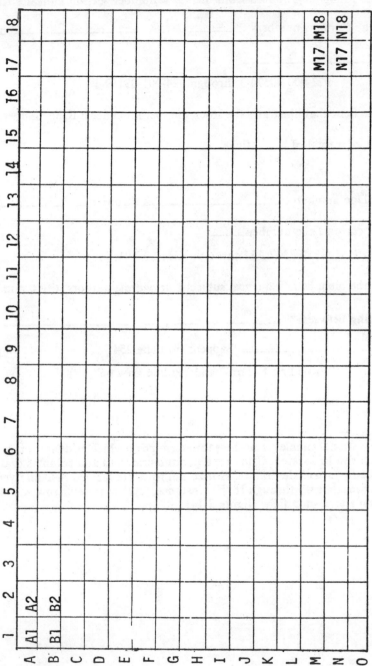

Most microfiche readers and reader/printers have grid keys adjacent to the trays into which fiche is inserted. These keys enable researchers to locate appropriate frames more easily.

The following illustrates typical entries from index frames (figure 2-15).

Figure 2-15
PRF, May 14, 1981

Stock Numbers	SuDoc Numbers	Alphabetic Sequence
A 1 023-000-00574-3	L15 HH 1.6/3:R 26/8	M 17 Public Health S
B 1 023-000-00576-0	M15 HH 1.6/3:R 26/8	N 17 Public Health S
C 1 023-000-00578-6	N15 HH 1.6/3:R 26/8	O 17 Public Health S
D 1 023-000-00580-8	O15 HH 1.6/3:R 26/8	
E 1 023-000-00582-4	A16 HH 1.6/3:R 31/2	A 18 Public Health S
F 1 023-000-00584-1	B16 HH 1.6/3:R 31/3	B 18 Public Health S
G 1 023-000-00587-5	C16 HH 1.6/3:Se 2	C 18 Public Health S
H 1 023-000-00590-5	D16 HH 1.6/3:Se 2/P	D 18 Public Health S
I 1 023-000-00593-0	E16 HH 1.6/3:Se 4/v	E 18 Public Health S
J 1 023-000-00595-6	F16 HH 1.6/3:Se 4/v	F 18 Public Health S
K 1 023-000-00598-1	G16 HH 1.6/3:Se 6/P	G 18 Public Health S
L 1 023-000-00600-6	H16 HH 1.6/3:Si 8	H 18 Public Health S
M 1 023-000-00602-2	I16 HH 1.6/3:So 4/2	I 18 Public Health S
N 1 023-000-00605-7	J16 HH 1.6/3:Su 6/P	J 18 Public Hearinas
	K16 HH 1.6/3:Ur 1/2	K 18 Public Hearinas
		L 18 Public Housing
		M 18 Public Housing
		N 18 Public Housing

Note that the index refers only to entries on its specific fiche. It does not provide cross references to other fiche.

Consult figure 2-15 when answering the following:

The citation to stock number 023-000-00583-2 is located on grid _____.

E1

(The first citation on grid E1 is 023-000582-4 and the initial one on F1 is 023-000-00584-1. Therefore, everything between these numbers is located on grid E1.)

SuDoc number "HH1.6/3:R31/2/part. is located on grid _____.

A16

Grids L18 through N18, reproduced from the alphabetic sequence illustration, includes information relating to _____.

public housing

Sometimes it is quicker to locate information on the *Publications Reference File* without using the index frames. Citations are arranged in vertical columns with the stock number sequence in numerical order, the SuDoc number sequence in alphanumerical order, and the alphabetical sequence in alphabetical order. That is, grid "B1" begins where "A1" leaves off, and "A2" begins where "O1" leaves off. Researchers can determine in which columns their information is cited by scanning the horizontal row "A." Suppose grid "A1" begins with the keyword "Car" and "A2" with "Census," entries about "Cats" would then appear in the first vertical row.

Publications Reference File Citations:

Characteristic *PFR* citations consist of thirteen parts that are useful to librarians and library users.

1. Stock Numbers: Stock numbers should be cited when ordering documents from GPO.

2. Stock Status: This notation tells researchers whether or not documents are currently in stock.

3. Key Phrases: Key phrases determine the type of entries cited, i.e. stock numbers, SuDoc numbers, subject headings, authors, titles, or series.

4. Catalog or SuDoc numbers.

5. Titles.

6. Personal authors.

7. Document sources or publishing agencies.

8. Imprint or the date of publication, pagination, and indications for illustrations (ill.).

9. Descriptions: Report numbers, contract numbers if the materials have been prepared by grantees, titles of series, alternate titles, Library of Congress card numbers, and item numbers are provided.

10. Notes: Weight of documents and supersession information are given.

11. Subject bibliographies: GPO's subject bibliography series cites basic document sources on three hundred topics of current interest. The *PRF* includes bibliography numbers when documents relate to specific lists. For instance, SB004 and SB280 in figure 2-16 refer respectively to bibliographies on *Business and Business Management* and *Housing, Urban and Rural Development*. The first is of questionable value to the subject at hand, "Public Housing," but the later could be a useful source to many studying the topic.

12. Binding.

13. Prices: "Discount" notations in the price section indicates that one hundred or more copies can be purchased at a twenty-five percent discount.

Each of the thirteen parts is indicated on figure 2-16.

Various parts of *PRF* citations are irrelevant to researchers. The "location" symbols below the stock numbers, and the status codes and dates in the upper left hand corner are meaningful only to Government Printing Office sales personnel.

Figure 2-16

PRF, May 14, 1981
Subject Entry

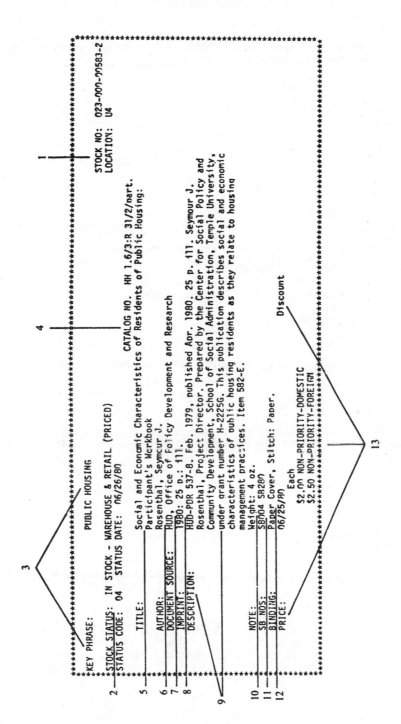

Alphabetic Section:

The citation to the document considered when studying the *Monthly Catalog, Social and Economic Characteristics of Residents of Public Housing: Participant's Workbook,* is illustrated in figure 2-16. Refer to that when answering the following:

The citation is listed in the alphabetic sequence under its key phrase, which in this case is the subject heading, " _____ ."

> **Public Housing**

Its SuDoc number is _____ and its stock number

is _____ .

> HH1.6/3:R31/2/part, 023-000-00583-2

The item number is _____ .

> 582-E

The author is _____ .

> Seymour J. Rosenthal

The location symbol, "U4," is (relevant/irrelevant) to library users.

> irrelevant

Underline the appropriate section of the citation that summarizes the document.

The alphabetic section also cites the identical document seen in figure 2-16 by its author's name and title. Each is indicated appropriately under key phrases in figure 2-17.

Figure 2-17
PRF, May 14, 1981
Author Entry

```
KEY PHRASE:           ROSENTHAL, SEYMOUR J              STOCK NO:  023-000-00583-2
                                                        LOCATION:  U4
STOCK STATUS:  IN STOCK - WAREHOUSE & RETAIL (PRICED)
STATUS CODE:  04   STATUS DATE:  06/26/80

                              CATALOG NO.  HH 1.6/3:R 31/2/part.
     TITLE:           Social and Economic Characteristics of Residents of Public Housing:
                      Participant's Workbook
     AUTHOR:          Rosenthal, Seymour J.
     DOCUMENT SOURCE: HUD, Office of Policy Development and Research
     IMPRINT:         1980: 25 p.: ill.
     DESCRIPTION:     HUD-PDR 537-8. Feb. 1979, published Apr. 1980. 25 p. ill. Seymour J.
                      Rosenthal, Project Director. Prepared by the Center for Social Policy and
                      Community Development, School of Social Administration, Temple University,
                      under grant number H-2225G. This publication describes social and economic
                      characteristics of public housing residents as they relate to housing
                      management practices. Item 582-E.
     NOTE:            Weight: 4 oz.
     SB NOS:          SB004 SB280
     BINDING:         Paper Cover, Stitch: Paper.
     PRICE:           06/25/80                                    Discount
                              Each
                              $2.00 NON-PRIORITY-DOMESTIC
                              $2.50 NON-PRIORITY-FOREIGN
```

Title Entry

```
******************************************************************

KEY PHRASE:     SOCIAL AND ECONOMIC CHARACTERISTICS OF RESIDENTS OF PUBLIC HOUSING    STOCK NO: 023-000-00583-2
                PARTICIPANT'S WORKBOOK                                                LOCATION: U4
STOCK STATUS:  IN STOCK - WAREHOUSE & RETAIL (PRICED)
STATUS CODE:  04    STATUS DATE: 06/26/80
                                                CATALOG NO.  HH 1.6/3:R 31/2/part.

     TITLE:            Social and Economic Characteristics of Residents of Public Housing:
                       Participant's Workbook
                       Rosenthal, Seymour J.
     AUTHOR:
     DOCUMENT SOURCE:  HUD, Office of Policy Development and Research
     IMPRINT:          1980: 25 p.: ill.
     DESCRIPTION:      HUD-PDR 537-8. Feb. 1979, published Apr. 1980. 25 p. ill. Seymour J.
                       Rosenthal, Project Director. Prepared by the Center for Social Policy and
                       Community Development, School of Social Administration, Temple University,
                       under grant number H-2225G. This publication describes social and economic
                       characteristics of public housing residents as they relate to housing
                       management practices. Item 582-E.
     NOTE:             Weight: 4 oz.
     SB NOS:           SB004 SB280
     BINDING:          Paper Cover, Stitch: Paper.
                       06/25/80
     PRICE:                    Each                              Discount
                         $2.00 NON-PRIORITY-DOMESTIC
                         $2.50 NON-PRIORITY-FOREIGN

******************************************************************
```

Stock and SuDoc Number Sections:

Stock numbers and SuDoc numbers are listed in numeric and alphanumeric sequences in their respective *PRF* sections. (figure 2-18)

Figure 2-18

PRF, May 14, 1981

Stock Number Section

```
KEY PHRASE:                         STOCK NO:  023-000-00583-2
                                    LOCATION:  U4

STOCK STATUS:  IN STOCK - WAREHOUSE & RETAIL (PRICED)
STATUS CODE:  04   STATUS DATE:  06/26/80

   023-000-00583-2

   TITLE:          Social and Economic Characteristics of Residents of Public Housing:
                   Participant's Workbook    CATALOG NO.  HH 1.6/3:R 31/2/part.
   AUTHOR:         Rosenthal, Seymour J.
   DOCUMENT SOURCE: HUD, Office of Policy Development and Research
   IMPRINT:        1980: 25 p.: ill.
   DESCRIPTION:    HUD-PDR 537-8. Feb. 1979, published Apr. 1980. 25 p. ill. Seymour J.
                   Rosenthal, Project Director. Prepared by the Center for Social Policy and
                   Community Development, School of Social Administration, Temple University,
                   under grant number H-2225G. This publication describes social and economic
                   characteristics of public housing residents as they relate to housing
                   management practices. Item 582-E.
   NOTE:           Weight: 4 oz.
   SB NOS:         SB004 SB280
   BINDING:        Paper Cover, Stitch: Paper.
   PRICE:          06/25/80                                    Discount
                   Each
                   $2.00 NON-PRIORITY-DOMESTIC
                   $2.50 NON-PRIORITY-FOREIGN
```

SuDoc Number Section

```
*****************************************************************************
*                                                                           *
*                                             STOCK NO: 023-000-00583-2      *
*                                             LOCATION: U4                   *
*  KEY PHRASE:      PH 1.6/3:R 31/2/part.                                    *
*                                                                           *
* STOCK STATUS: IN STOCK - WAREHOUSE & RETAIL (PRICED)                      *
* STATUS CODE:  04   STATUS DATE:  06/26/80                                 *
*                                      CATALOG NO.  HH 1.6/3:R 31/2/part.   *
*                                                                           *
*  TITLE:        Social and Economic Characteristics of Residents of Public Housing: *
*                Participant's Workbook                                     *
*                Rosenthal, Seymour J.                                      *
*  AUTHOR:                                                                  *
*  DOCUMENT SOURCE:  HUD, Office of Policy Development and Research          *
*  IMPRINT:      1980: 25 p.: ill.                                          *
*  DESCRIPTION:  HUD-PDR 537-8. Feb. 1979, published Apr. 1980. 25 p. ill. Seymour J. *
*                Rosenthal, Project Director. Prepared by the Center for Social Policy and *
*                Community Development, School of Social Administration, Temple University, *
*                under grant number H-2225G. This publication describes social and economic *
*                characteristics of public housing residents as they relate to housing *
*                management practices. Item 582-E.                         *
*                Weight: 4 oz.                                             *
*  NOTE:                                                                    *
*  SB NOS:       SB004 SB280                                                *
*  BINDING:      Paper Cover, Stitch: Paper.                               *
*  PRICE:        06/25/80                          Discount                *
*                    Each                                                   *
*                    $2.00 NON-PRIORITY-DOMESTIC                           *
*                    $2.50 NON-PRIORITY-FOREIGN                            *
*                                                                           *
*****************************************************************************
```

Online Availability of PRF:

The Publications Reference File is available online through the Lockheed system. Lockheed's Dialorder Online Ordering System can be used when purchasing documents from the GPO.

Exhausted GPO Sales Publications Reference File (EPRF):

The *Exhausted GPO Sales Publications Reference File* indexes documents no longer available for sale. It is arranged in three sections like the *PFR*. The *EPRF* published in 1980 includes one hundred and thirty-six microfiche which cover 1972 through 1978. The 1981 edition consists of seventy-six fiche covering 1979 through June 1980. GPO intends to issue this reference tool annually.

Further Information About The PRF and the EPRF:

For more information, consult *PRF User's Manual: A Guide To Using The GPO Sales Publications Reference File.*

Cumulative Title Index To United States Public Documents, 1789-1976:

The *Cumulative Title Index To United States Public Documents 1789-1976* indexes by titles all documents published between 1789 and June 1976 to which the Government Printing Office has applied SuDoc numbers. Entries are based upon the Public Document Library's shelflist. A shelflist is a card catalog arranged by classification numbers. That is, cards are filed in the identical manner as documents would be arranged on shelves.

Entries include titles, publication dates, SuDoc numbers and reel codes. Dates for selected citations are not given if the information is unavailable in the shelflist. Moreover, when identical titles have different SuDoc numbers, appropriate entries are listed as many times as necessary. The reel code refers researchers to the microfilm version of the shelflist, the *Checklist of United States Public Documents, 1789-1976,* which includes additional information about the entries. The code is shown with an "A" or an "I," representing the active or inactive parts of the file. The shelflist was separated into two parts by GPO. The active section is one in which cards are still being added, whereas entries are no longer being added to the inactive section. Tables located inside the front and back covers of each volume of the *Title Index* indicate on which reels the appropriate SuDoc numbers are located.

Index To U.S. Government Periodicals:

The *Index To U.S. Government Periodicals* is an extremely important reference tool because the coverage of government sources in most periodical indexes is very limited. The *Index* provides author and subject access to articles printed in over one hundred and seventy depository and non-depository journals. The editors believe that all periodicals indexed have information of permanent research and reference value. Press releases and other ephemeral materials are excluded. Though it has been published quarterly since 1974, the publisher has prepared four retrospective volumes covering 1970-1973. Each year's final issue is an annual cumulative bound volume.

To locate information on public housing, search the *Index* under appropriate subject headings. (figure 2-19)

Figure 2-19

Index To U.S. Government Periodicals, 1981
Subject Approach

1.—— PUBLIC housing   ┌──————————3.
2.—— HUD's crime prevention program. Lynn A. Curtis, ref ——————4.
5.—— Pub Health Rep 95 6 558 N-D 80-146
                          │   │   │   │   │
                          6. 7. 8.   9.   10.

1. Subject heading.	6. Volume of periodical.
2. Title of article.	7. Issue number.
3. Author.	8. Pagination.
4. References.	9. Month.
5. Title of periodical.	10. Microfiche identification.

All periodicals indexed are available on microfiche in the *Current U.S. Government Periodicals* series. They are accessed by microfiche identification numbers, 80-146 in the case of the above citation.

The following questions refer to figure 2-19:

The title of the article is _____ .

HUD's Crime Prevention Program

Its author is _____ .

Lynn A. Curtis

The title of the journal in which it is published is _____

_____ .

Public Health Reports

The article is published in volume _____, issue number _____, which appeared

in _____, _____.

Volume 95, issue 6, November-December, 1980

The identical article is also cited under the author's name. (figure 2-20)

Figure 2-20

Index To U.S. Government Periodicals, 1981
Author Approach

CURTIS, Lynn A.
HUD's crime prevention program. ref Pub Health Rep
95 6 558 N-D 80-146

Each issue of the *Index To U.S. Government Periodicals* includes a list of journals indexed, their abbreviations, and their Superintendent of Documents classification numbers. This information is printed on the verso of the covers in each year's first three quarterly issues and in the introductory section of the annual cumulative volume. (figure 2-21) The cumulative issue also lists the names and addresses of the publishing agencies whose periodicals are indexed and the names of their editors.

Figure 2-21

Index To U.S. Government Periodicals, 1980

Prologue—Prologue: The Journal of the National Archives,
    GS4.23: quarterlyx○ ———————————————————   *
Psychopharm Bul—Psychopharmacology Bulletin, HE20.8109:
    quarterly
Pub Health Rep—Public Health Reports, HE20.6011; bimonthly
Pub Road—Public Roads, A Journal of Highway Research and
    Development, TD2.19: quarterly
Q J Lib Cong—Quarterly Journal of the Library of Congress,
    LC1.17: quarterly
Recla Era—Reclamation Era, I27.5: quarterly
Record. See FEC Rec
Report Ser—Report Series, HE20.8215: irregular○
Reporter—The Reporter, Office of The Judge Advocate General
    the Air Force, D302.11: bimonthly

*The "X" indicates that a journal is a non-depository title and the "O" indicates that a periodical is unavailable from GPO, but may be available from the issuing agency.

Refer to figure 2-21 when answering the following:

The SuDoc number of *Public Health Reports* is _____ .

HE20.6011:

It is published every _____ months.

two

Additional Sources of Information About Periodicals:

The *American Statistics Index,* which is considered in chapter 7, is the only other source which indexes regularly large numbers of articles in government periodicals. The *Monthly Catalog Serial Supplement, Government Periodicals and Subscription Services,* and the *Publications Reference File* all cite journal titles, but they fail to index the articles printed in the periodicals.

Monthly Catalog Serial Supplement:

Titles of depository and non-depository periodicals are listed and indexed in the *Monthly Catalog Serial Supplement.* The *Supplement* was published semi-annually between 1945 and 1960 and has appeared annually since 1961. All citations in the *Serial Supplement* are indexed in an identical manner as monographs are in the *Monthly Catalog. Public Health Reports,* the document discussed above, was cited in the 1981 *Supplement* as indicated below. (figure 2-22)

Figure 2-22
Monthly Catalog Serial Supplement, 1981

81-8811

HE 20.6011:(v.nos.&nos.)

Public health reports (United States. Health Resources Administration)

　　Public health reports. [Hyattsville, Md. : U.S. Dept. of Health, Education, and Welfare, Public Health Service, Health Resources Administration ; Washington, D.C. : Supt. of Docs., U.S. G.P.O., distributor,

　　Supt. of Docs., U.S. Govt. Print. Off., Washington, D.C. 20402

　　v. : ill. ; 26 cm. (HRA)

　　$15.00 (U.S.) $18.25 (foreign) $3.00 (single copy, U.S.) $3.75 (single copy, foreign)

　　Began with Vol. 89, no. 4 (July-Aug. 1974).

　　Cover title.

　　Description based on: Vol. 94, no. 6 (Nov.-Dec. 1979).

　　Indexed by: American statistics index ISSN 0091-1658

　　Indexed by: Index to U.S. Government periodicals ISSN 0098-4604

　　Bimonthly.

　　●Item 497

　　S/N 017-020-80001-0

　　ISSN 0033-3549

　　Main series: DHEW publication ; no. (HRA)

　　Main series: DHHS publication ; no. (HRA)

　　Continues: Health services reports (United States. Health Services Administration) ISSN 0090-2918

As of 1981, the *Monthly Catalog Serial Supplement* cites sources in which the periodicals are indexed. Figure 2-22 indicates that *Public Health Reports* is indexed in both the *American Statistics Index* and the *Index To U.S. Government Periodicals*. Infordata International, Inc., who publishes the *Index To U.S. Government Periodicals,* hopes to cooperate with the Government Printing Office in expanding this feature.

Government Periodicals and Subscription Services (GPSS):

This quarterly publication, which is arranged alphabetically by titles, has been issued since August 1943. Between that date and November 1960, it was entitled *Government Periodicals*. Unlike the *Serial Supplement, Government Periodicals and Subscription Services* is limited to depository documents for sale through the Government Printing Office. However, *GPSS* has a significant advantage over the *Serial Supplement*. The former is available from GPO at no cost, while the latter was priced at $5.50 as of 1981. The entry for *Public Health Reports* is cited below. (figure 2-23)

Figure 2-23
Government Periodicals and Subscription Services,
Fall, 1981

●▶**POSTAL OPERATIONS MANUAL.** Subscription price: Domestic—$37.00; Foreign—$46.25.
[*PORM*]   P 1.12/8: trans.1
(File Code 1P)   S/N 039-000-81008-5

Subscription service includes updating transmittal letters for an indeterminate period. In looseleaf form, punched for 3-ring binder.
This manual sets forth policies for the internal operations of post offices. It includes retail services, mail processing, transportation, delivery services, and fleet management.

▶**POWER REACTOR EVENTS.** (Bimonthly.) Subscription price: Domestic—$8.00 a year; Foreign—$8.00 a year.
[*PREV*]   Y 3.N 88:
(File Code 2T)   S/N 052-010-80018-3

Presents summaries of selected events that have occurred at nuclear power plants.

▶**PUBLIC HEALTH REPORTS.** (Bimonthly.) Subscription price: Domestic—$18.00 a year; Foreign—$22.50 a year. Single copy price: Domestic—$4.50 a copy; Foreign—$5.65 a copy [5].
[*HSMHA*]   HE 20.6011:
(File Code 2N)   S/N 017-020-80001-0

Publishes scientific, technical, administrative, and analytical articles of interest to the public health profession.

▶**PUBLIC LAWS.** (Irregularly.) Subscription price: Domestic—$165.00 per session of Congress; Foreign—$206.25 per session of Congress; single copies vary in price.
[*P9701*]   GS 4.110 : 97/
(File Code 1L)   S/N 022-003-81002-1

A Public Law, often referred to as a *Slip Law,* is the initial publication of a Federal law upon enactment and is printed as soon as possible after approval by the President.
Beginning with the 88th Congress, 1st session, some legislative history references appear on each law.

Note, in figure 2-23, the bullet (●) immediately preceding *Postal Operations Manual* indicates that the publication consists of a basic volume or beginning group of materials which is provided as part of the subscription. The bullet, in this context, is no reflection of the document's depository status. Also, the arrow (▶) immediately preceding the other titles indicates that price changes have occurred since *GPSS* was issued previously.

Publications Reference File (PRF):

Periodicals available for sale through GPO are indexed in the *Publications Reference File* in the identical manner as monographs. *Public Health Reports* is listed as indicated below. (figure 2-24)

Figure 2-24

Publications Reference File, January 14, 1982

```
** Eng**

KEY PHRASE:         PUBLIC HEALTH REPORTS                    STOCK NO: 017-020-80001-0
                                                             LOCATION: UB
STOCK STATUS: IN STOCK - WAREHOUSE & RETAIL (PRICED)         SUB LIST: HSMHA
STATUS CODE: 04   STATUS DATE: 09/13/76

                                          CATALOG NO: HE 20.6011:

TITLE:          Public Health Reports
DOCUMENT SOURCE: HEW, Health Resources Administration
DESCRIPTION:    Bimonthly periodical. Subscription price covers issues for 1 year.
                Subscription service begins with the first issue after the order is
                processed. Copies of the latest 5 issues are retained in stock for
                individual purchase. Single copy, $4.50; foreign single copy, $5.65.
                Publishes scientific, technical, administrative, and analytical articles
                of interest to the public health profession. HSMHA. File Code 2H. Item 497.
SB NOS:         SB172
BINDING:        Perfect Binding; Paper.
PRICE:          11/02/81                                Discount
                     Subscription
                     $18.00 NON-PRIORITY-DOMESTIC
                     $22.50 NON-PRIORITY-FOREIGN
```

BIBLIOGRAPHY

American Statistics Index: A Comprehensive Guide and Index To The Statistical Publications of the U.S. Government. Washington, D.C.: Congressional Information Service, Inc., 1973-monthly.

Checklist of U.S. Public Documents, 1789-1976. Arlington, Virginia: United States Historical Documents Institute, 1976?.

Cumulative Subject Index To The Monthly Catalog, 1900-1971. Comp. by William W. Buchanan and Edna M. Kanely. Washington, D.C.: Carrollton Press, 1973-1975. 15 vols.

Cumulative Title Index To United States Public Documents, 1789-1976. Comp. by Daniel W. Lester et al. Arlington, Virginia: United States Historical Documents Institute, 1979-   . Completed series will include 16 vols.

Current U.S. Government Periodicals. Chicago: Infordata International Incorporated, 1975-current.

Exhausted GPO Sales Publications Reference File. Superintendent of Documents. Washington, D.C.: GPO, 1980-annual.

Government Periodicals and Subscription Services. Superintendent of Documents. Price List 36. Washington, D.C.: GPO, 1943-quarterly.

GPO Sales Publications Reference File Microform. Superintendent of Documents. Washington, D.C.: GPO, 1977-bimonthly.

Index To United States Government Periodicals. Chicago: Infordata International Incorporated, 1974-quarterly. Retrospective editions have been published for 1970-1973.

Monthly Catalog of United States Government Publications. Superintendent of Documents. Washington, D.C.: GPO, 1895-monthly. Title varies.

Monthly Catalog of United States Government Publications: Cumulated Index, 1961-1965. Superintendent of Documents. Washington, D.C.: GPO, [1976]. 2 vols.

Monthly Catalog of United States Government Publications: Cumulated Index, 1966-1970. Superintendent of Documents. Washington, D.C.: GPO, [1978]. 2 vols.

Monthly Catalog of United States Government Publications: Cumulative Index 1971-1976. Superintendent of Documents. Washington, D.C.: GPO, [1981]. 2 vols.

Monthly Catalog of United States Government Publications: Decennial Cumulative Index 1951-1960. Superintendent of Documents. Washington, D.C.: GPO, 1968. 2 vols.

Monthly Catalog of United States Government Publications: Serials Supplement. Superintendent of Documents. Washington, D.C.: GPO, 1961-annual. Published biennially between 1945 and 1960.

PRF Users Manual: A Guide To Using the G.P.O. Sales Publications Reference File. Superintendent of Documents. Washington, D.C.: GPO, 1981.

United States Government Publications (Depository). New York: Readex Microprint Corporation, 1956-monthly.

United States Government Publications (Non-Depository). New York: Readex Microprint Corporation, 1953-monthly.

United States Government Publications. Monthly Catalog. Cumulative Personal Author Index, 1941-1975. Ed. by Edward Przebienda. Ann Arbor, Michigan: Pierian Press. 1971-1972. Vol. 5 published in 1979. 5 vols.

United States Government Publications, Monthly Catalog: Decennial Cumulative Index 1941-1950. Superintendent of Documents. Washington, D.C.: GPO, 1953.

Monthly Catalog, Questions:

1. Suppose you are looking for a document that describes the costs of the Medicare Program during the mid-1970's:

   A. Is the relevant document indexed in the 1977 *Catalog?* _____

   B. If yes, what is the catalog entry number? _____

   C. Define: "catalog entry number."

      For illustrative purposes, you are interested in catalog entry number 77-2605. Questions D-I relate to that entry.

   D. What is the title of this document?

   E. Who is the author or issuing agency?

   F. How many pages does it have?

   G. When was this document published?

   H. What is the Superintendent of Documents classification number?

   I. On what page of the 1977 annual cumulative index to the *Monthly Catalog* does the Author entry for this document appear? _____

   J. On what page does the title entry appear? _____

   K. What is the *Monthly Catalog* entry number of report DOT HS 803-393? _____

   L. You are attempting to locate a document published in 1980 by the Department of Defense, which you believe is entitled *Television Systems Specialist*. After discovering that it is not listed in the Title Index, you then search the Title Keyword Index. What additional information about the document does the latter index provide?

2. You are looking for President Kennedy's statement about the October 1962 Cuban missile crisis that was published during that year. After consulting the 1962 cumulative index, you discover that relevant information is not included. You must now search the 1963 index because materials issued toward the end of one year will sometimes be listed in the following year's *Catalog*.

   A. Is relevant information cited in the 1963 index?

   B. What is the catalog entry number?

   C. What is the title of this document?

   D. What type of information does it include?

    E. How many pages does it contain?

    F. What is the Superintendent of Documents classification number?

3. Using the *Monthly Catalog,* compile a bibliography of four documents relating to any topic of your choice. For each document include:
   A) Title
   B) Author
   C) Catalog entry number
   D) Pagination
   E) Superintendent of Documents classification number
   F) Year of publication

Publications Reference File, Questions:

4. Using the most recent *Publications Reference File,* compute a bibliography of three sources relating to abortion. Include the publishing agency, the title, and the Superintendent of Documents number in your answer.

5. Is it possible to locate on the PRF documents relating to abortion available from the Government Printing Office at no cost?

6. A bibliography about the chemical and petroleum industry was published in 1967. Its stock number is 024-004-00148-8.

    A. Is this publication still available for sale from GPO? Locate it on either the *PRF* or *EPRF.*

       Available for sale _____. Unavailable for sale _____.

       PRF or *EPRF* fiche number _____

    B. Its SuDoc number is _____.

    C. The bibliography was compiled by _____ and

    _____ .

Cumulative Title Index to United States Public Documents, 1789-1976, Questions:

7. Locate the Superintendent of Documents number of a document published in 1973 entitled *Aerospace Human Factors Engineering, USSR.*

Index to U.S. Government Periodicals, Questions:

8. Lewis Sorley wrote an article published in 1979 about the ethical issues of the U.S. involvement in the Vietnamese Conflict.

A. What is the title of the article?

B. In what journal did it appear?

C. What are the volume and issue numbers, and date of the journal?

D. The article is printed on pages _____ through _____.

E. The microfiche identification number of

the journal is _____ .

F. The editor of this periodical during 1979 was _____ .

G. His address was _____ .

H. The SuDoc number of this journal is _____ .

Monthly Catalog, Answers:

1. A. Yes
   B. Entry numbers: 77-1855, 77-2443, 77-2605, 77-2606, 77-4204, 77-5008, 77-5389, 77-9176, 77-11049, 77-11837, 77-12722, 77-14144, 77-14255, 77-15639 and 77-15792 are probably the most likely choices. Other answers are not necessarily incorrect. Many citations can be interpreted as having a cost effect upon Medicare.
   C. The catalog entry number is the number used when referring from the *Monthly Catalog* indexes to the main bibliographic section. Citations in the main bibliographic section are arranged in numerical order according to entry numbers.
   D. *Medicare Administration Costs*
   E. Subcommittee on Oversight of the House Committee on Ways and Means.
   F. 239 pages
   G. 1976
   H. Y 4.W 36:M 46/16
   I. Page I - 356
   J. Page I - 931
   K. 79-18807
   L. The Title Keyword Index indicates that a series of documents are entitled *Radio/Television Systems Specialist*.

2. A. Yes
   B. 1577
   C. *To Protect The Peace*
   D. A speech by President Kennedy and excerpts from a speech by Adlai Stevenson before the United Nations Security Council.
   E. 36 pages
   F. IΛ 1.2:P 31/2

3, 4. Answers will vary, depending upon individual's choices.

Publications Reference File, Answers:

5. The *PRF* lists only publications available for sale from the Government Printing Office. Gratis materials are excluded from the *File*.

6. A. Unavailable for sale; *EPRF,* 1980 edition, fiche 14.
   B. I 28.27:8346
   C. Sidney Katell and William C. Morel

Cumulative Title Index to United States Public Documents, 1789-1976, Answer:

7. Y3.J 66:13/60419

Index to United States Government Periodicals, Answers:

8. Sorley's article is listed in the 1979 index. The author citation is found on page 833 and two subject entries are found on pages 380 under "Foreign Relations" and 912 under "Vietnamese War."

   A. "Review Article: 'Just and Unjust Wars'—Moral Responsibility and Conflict: A Post-Vietnam Perspective."

   B. *Naval War College Review*

   C. Volume 31, issue 3, Winter 1979

   D. Pages 88-94

   E. 79-114

   F. Cmdr. W.R. Pettyjohn

   G. Naval War College, Newport, RI 02840

   H. D 208.209:

CHAPTER 3

CONGRESSIONAL PUBLICATIONS, PART I:
TRACING A BILL THROUGH CONGRESS

Researchers are often concerned with the issues Congress considers and the laws it enacts. This chapter describes the legislative process, emphasizing the various kinds of published information about public bills and the many ways of locating this documentation. After summarizing how a bill becomes a law, detailed definitions are provided for the various kinds of Congressional publications. The section following that describes the various sources used in compiling a legislative history of a specific bill. This includes dates of approval or disapproval, the law number, and a list of relevant Congressional publications.

How a Bill Becomes a Law

To understand the various kinds of Congressional publications, it is necessary to review very briefly the legislative process. The following chart summarizes how a bill becomes a law and the various types of publications issued by Congress during each step of the process.

How A Bill Becomes A Law

The Legislative Process	*Publications*
1. Senators and Representatives introduce bills and resolutions into their respective chambers.	Bills and Resolutions
2. Bills are referred to appropriate committees for hearings.	Hearings
3. Committees report recommendations to their respective houses.	Reports
4. House bills are debated by the entire House, and if approved, are forwarded to the Senate for consideration. The process is reversed for Senate bills.	*Congressional Record*
5. Differences between House and Senate versions of a bill are settled by a Conference Committee consisting of representatives from both chambers.	Conference report
6. Compromise is forwarded to the respective houses and the bill is again debated.	*Congressional Record*
7. Bill is forwarded to President for his approval. A. President signs bill into law.	Slip Law*
or	
B. President vetoes bill and sends it back to Congress.	Veto message is published as a document.

*Although slip laws are published by the General Services Administration, rather than Congress, they are included here to illustrate continuity within the legislative process.

8. A two-thirds vote of each house overrides the   *Congressional   Record* and
   veto.   *Journals.*
                                                     Slip law is published if veto is
                                                     overturned.

     The above Congressional publications, plus others not directly involved in
the legislative process, are defined on the next chart.

Definitions of the Congressional Publications

Type of Publication	*Scope*
Bills	Bills are proposals for the enactment of new legislation or the amending of existing laws. Those introduced during each Congress are numbered in sequential order. S. 1500 represents the fifteen hundredth Senate bill introduced, whereas H.R. 7000 represents the seven thousandth House bill introduced. Various sessions of the same Congress maintain continuous numerical schemes. Suppose the last Senate bill introduced during the 95th Congress, first session, was S. 1479, then the initial bill the following session would be S. 1480. However, the first bill introduced into the Senate during the 96th Congress would be S. 1.
	Public bills differ from private bills in that the contents of the former are designed for the benefit of the entire nation, whereas the latter applies only to specific individuals, such as John Doe or Jane Smith.
	Although House bills are most often identified by H.R., they are sometimes cited by a mere "H."
Joint Resolutions	Like bills, joint resolutions are considered law after approved by both houses and the President. There is no practical difference between bills and joint resolutions, except that the latter usually deals with more limited matters. For instance, joint resolutions are sometimes used to correct errors in existing legislation, to provide for special appropriations, or to reflect Congressional foreign policy initiatives. House Joint Resolution 1145 and Senate Joint Resolution 189, two identical measures considered by the 88th Congress, are among the most significant ones ever enacted. President Johnson used these measures to justify the involvement of the United States in the Vietnamese War.
	Joint resolutions are numbered consecutively within each Congress and are identified as H.J.Res. (House Joint Resolution) and S.J.Res. (Senate Joint Resolution).
Concurrent Resolutions	These resolutions, identified by H. Con. Res. (House) and S. Con. Res. (Senate), deal with matters that affect the operations of both Congressional chambers. Concurrent resolutions must be ratified by the House and Senate, but do not require Presidential approval. They are consecutively num-

bered within each house. The term "concurrent" does not reflect simultaneous introduction and consideration in the Senate and House.

Simple Resolutions

Simple Resolutions reflect issues of concern to only one house and require neither ratification of the other chamber nor Presidential approval to become effective. They are numbered in consecutive order within each house and are identified as H. Res. and S. Res.

Committee Prints

Committee prints are studies prepared by either the Congressional Research Service of the Library of Congress, or committee and/or subcommittee staffs. They are intended for use by Congressmen as background information. These factual analyses are often the most objective materials published by Congress. However, Committee prints, until very recently, were difficult to locate because they were intended for internal use within committees and consequently, were produced in limited quantities. The more recent prints are indexed in the *Monthly Catalog,* the *PRF,* and *Congressional Information Service Index,* which is discussed in the next chapter. The *CIS* Committee Print Series on microfiche is the most comprehensive collection of retrospective prints. (see Chapter 5).

Hearings

These publications include everything said at committee meetings or hearings concerning pending legislation, topics the committees have been authorized to investigate, or programs the committees are charged with overseeing. Statements or testimony submitted by witnesses, who are very often officials or experts in various fields, appear in the printed transcripts or hearings. Additional material, such as journal articles, statistics, or letters submitted by the witnesses as evidence, are often appended to hearings. Hearings are indexed in the *Monthly Catalog,* the *Publications Reference File,* and the *Congressional Information Service Index.*

Reports

Reports are statements describing committee findings and recommendations submitted by committees to their respective chambers. This information sometimes includes section by section analysis of significant legislation, factual analysis of situations as seen by the committees, or minority opinions of committee members. The 1974 Congressional Budget Act, an attempt to streamline consideration of fiscal issues, mandates that reports on bills providing for new budget authority include the following:

1. The committees' assessments of the bills' inflationary impacts must be stated.

2. The Congressional Budget Office's cost estimates for each of the initial five years of the programs are required.

3. The Budget Office's assessment must be compared with those submitted to the committees by other agencies.

4. When the bills deal with revenues, the reports need only include statements dealing with the gains or losses for one year.

Reports issued by the Committees on Appropriations, on Rules, and on Standards of Official Conduct are exempt from these requirements.

Reports introduced during each Congress are numbered sequentially according to their House or Senate series. S. Rept. 95-3 represents the third Senate report submitted during the ninety-fifth Congress, whereas H. Rept. 95-3 is the third one submitted to that chamber during the same Congress. The subject matter of S. Rept. 95-3 will not necessarily be related to that of H. Rept. 95-3. They will, more than likely, have only one common characteristic—both were the third reports submitted to their respective bodies during the ninety-fifth Congress.

Besides being indexed in the manners described in this chapter, reports are also accessed through the *Monthly Catalog,* the *PRF,* and the *Congressional Information Service Index.*

Consult the discussion pertaining to the Serial Set (Chapter 5) for more information concerning the Congressional report series.

Congressional Record

The debates and proceedings of Congress are printed in the *Congressional Record.* This publication is issued daily while Congress is in session. Following the termination of a session, libraries usually discard the daily versions after the permanent hard bound copies of the *Record* are distributed.

The *Congressional Record* includes speeches and articles read on the floors of either house, voting records, and materials inserted upon requests from legislators. Though summaries of all bills are provided, Congressmen and Senators can also ask that the entire texts be printed.

Changes were made in the *Record,* effective March 1, 1978. Since then, a bullet (•) precedes and then follows materials not read on the floors. Previously, Congressmen were able to insert statements by merely leaving copies at the appropriate office, without having to read them on the floors, or even attend their chambers on the days in question. Prior to March 1, 1978, this added information was not distinguished from that actually read in Congress. A loophole, however, still exists—to avoid the bullets, Congressmen need only present the "beginnings" of their speeches, rather than the entire statements. Also, the Public Printer, upon requests by legislators, edits and revises speeches without indicating the changes.

Besides the proceedings of the House and the Senate, the *Congressional Record* also includes Extension of Remarks and Daily Digest sections. Information irrelevant to the day's proceedings are printed in the Extension of Remarks. Reprints of newspaper articles, telegrams, and excerpts from periodicals, among other sources, are included. However, this type of information is printed as part of the proceedings when it is relevant to the day's activities.

One of the most recent controversies involving the *Congressional Record* was the refusal of the Joint Committee on Printing to allow excerpts from writings by Kurt Vonnegut, Bernard Malamud, Langston Hughes and others to be printed in the Extension of Remarks. The Committee Chairman, the same Wayne Hayes who was associated with the Elizabeth Ray scandal, defended his Committee's decision by arguing that Congress cannot let its *Record* become a "pornographic document." He added, "You preserve the dignity of the Congress if you don't put all the four letter words in (the *Record*)."[1]

The Daily Digest section of the *Congressional Record* summarizes bills introduced, resolutions agreed upon, and committee hearings. It also gives a list of hearings scheduled for the following day.

Journals of the House and Senate

Following the termination of a Congressional session, the official proceedings of Congress are printed in the *Journals*. *Journals* are the only publications required by the Constitution—Article I, Section 5 states: "Each House shall keep a Journal of its Proceedings, and from time to time publish the same . . ." Legislative histories, voting records, summaries of petitions and papers, and presidential messages are included. Unlike the *Congressional Record, Journals* contain neither debates nor Extensions of Remarks. Separate volumes are published for each chamber.

Calendars

House and Senate agendas are printed on each chamber's respective *Calendar*. Bills reported from committee are placed on the appropriate *Calendars* in chronological order, according to the date reported. Congress, however, does not always consider bills in the order in which they were placed on their respective *Calendars*. *Calendars* are published each day Congress is in session.

Documents

Documents are reprints of Presidential messages to Congress (speeches, veto statements); statements to Congress by executive agencies; annual reports to Congress by patriotic organizations (Girl Scouts, Veterans of Foreign Wars), or materials which committees believe will be of public interest and value. Documents are numbered in the same fashion as reports. S. Doc. 95-3 represents the third document issued by the Senate during the ninety-fifth Congress, whereas H. Doc. 95-3 represents the third document issued by the House during the same Congress. Again, as with reports, the subject matter will, more than likely, be dissimilar.

"Congressional Documents," which refer to this particular group of publications, should not be confused with "government documents," or "documents" as used in a more general sense. The latter includes all types of government publications—Federal, State, local, and international, whereas "documents," as issued by Congress, is just one of many types of government publications.

Congressional documents are indexed in the *Monthly Catalog*, the *Publications Reference File*, and the *CIS*. Consult the discussion relating to the Serial Set in Chapter 5 for more information about the Congressional document series.

Senate Executive Documents   Presidential messages to the Senate which contain texts of proposed treaties and supplementary information supporting ratification are printed as Senate Executive documents. Besides being indexed in the *Congressional Index*, which is described below, they are also indexed in the *Monthly Catalog*, the *Publications Reference File*, and the *Congressional Information Service*.

Senate Executive Reports   Committee recommendations to the Senate on proposed treaties are printed as Senate Executive Reports. They are indexed in the *Monthly Catalog*, the *PRF*, the *CIS*, and the *Congressional Index*.

Compiling Legislative Histories:

Commercial, in addition to document, sources should be used when compiling legislative histories. The *Congressional Information Service Index*, a privately published reference tool considered in the next chapter, is the most comprehensive guide to legislative histories. The *Congressional Quarterly Almanac*, published annually since 1945, and the *Congressional Index*, a loose-leaf service issued weekly since 1937, are two references described in this chapter. Significant government documents used when compiling legislative histories are the *House* and *Senate Journals*, the *Congressional Record*, the *House Calendar*, and the *Digest of Public General Bills and Resolutions*.

Congressional Quarterly Almanac:

Suppose you are interested in locating bills about public housing that were either considered by Congress or enacted into law during the mid-1970's and you know of neither a specific bill, nor law number. The *Congressional Quarterly Almanac* is a good starting point. The index to the 1976 issue indicates that the public housing program is described on pages 343-351. The first two paragraphs on page 343 offer much information—Senate Bill 3295 became Public Law 94-375 (P.L. 94-375), the three hundred and seventy-fifth Public Law enacted by the ninety-fourth Congress. The *Almanac* outlines the provisions of the law, actions taken by the House and the Senate and their committees, various amendments to the original bill, and conference actions. Within this summary, appropriate committee reports are noted, previous legislation is mentioned and access to information that was published in earlier *Almanacs* is cited.

Other features of the *Almanac* include an analysis of Federal elections, evaluations of Supreme Court decisions, a list and index of lobbyists, Presidential messages to Congress, veto statements, results of Congressional roll call votes, and a list of public laws arranged in numerical order. (figure 3-1)

Figure 3-1

Congressional Quarterly Almanac, 1976.
Public Laws

PL94-375 (S 3295)—Extend certain housing programs under the National Housing Act. PROXMIRE (D Wis.)—4/12/76—Senate Banking, Housing and Urban Affairs reported April 12, 1976 (S Rept 94-749). Senate passed April 27. House passed, amended, May 26. Conference report filed in House June 22 (H Rept 94-1291). House recommitted conference report June 24. Conference report filed in House June 25 (H Rept 94-1304). House agreed to conference report June 30. Senate agreed to conference report July 20. President signed Aug. 3, 1976.

Reproduced with permission from *Congressional Quarterly Almanac,* published and copyrighted by Congressional Quarterly, Inc., 1414 22 Street NW, Washington, D.C. 20037

Researchers should be aware of two related sources. The *Congressional Quarterly Weekly Report,* issued since 1945, offers information similar to that in the *Congressional Quarterly Almanac. Congress and The Nation,* printed every four years, is a fine multiyear summary of legislative activities.

The *Congressional Quarterly Almanac,* which is written at the high school/undergraduate level, will often satisfy the information needs of laymen. More serious researchers should consult the sources below as well.

Congressional Index:

The *Congressional Index* is another fine source for locating bills which have been introduced or enacted into law. It is published in two volumes. The first depicts Senate activities; the second describes those of the House. A different set of binders is issued for each Congress. During the course of the two years, supplementary loose-leaf pages are filed each week.

Both the Senate and House volumes incorporate the following five sections:

1. A list of respective members, their biographical sketches and lists of committees on which they serve.

2. A list of hearings which do not relate to specific bills.

3. A list of bills and resolutions arranged consecutively by their numbers.

4. Status of bills.

5. Voting records.

The Senate volume contains four additional sections—indexes for both volumes and sections dealing with matters involving the Executive Branch.

1. A Subject Index.

2. An Index by Authors.

3. Reorganization Plans, Treaties, Nominations section.

4. An Enactments-Vetoes section.

The Subject Index appears at the beginning of volume one. It is arranged in three parts: the basic index, the Current Subject Index, and Headline Legislation. The Current Index is used for locating recent information that is inaccessible through the basic index, and Headline Legislation indexes very selectively bills which have received much media publicity. Researchers must sometimes search all three parts of the Subject Index to locate information. Legislation,

vetoes, treaties, reorganization plans, nominations, and voting records are indexed elsewhere. The Subject Index is limited to bills only.

S. 3295, the bill discussed when considering the *Congressional Quarterly
Almanac,* is indexed in the Current Subject Index and Headline Legislation.
(figure 3-2)

Figure 3-2

Congressional Index, 1975-76

Current Subject Index

lousing—continued
. **elderly and handicapped**
. . loans . . . H 13,139
. . sponsors . . . H 12,932
. **equity adjusted mortgages**
. . insurance . . . S 3692
. **federally related mortgage**
. . foreclosure . . . H 15,107
. **home ownership** . . . S 3159
. **homeowners** . . . H 12,625
. **in lieu of taxes** . . . H 11,649
. **inspection standards** . . . H 12,194
. **insured loans** . . . H 15,108
. **loans**
. . elderly and handicapped housing . .
. . . . H 12,978; 12,979; 13,614
. . rehabilitation . . . S 3158
. **low and middle income**
. . eligibility . . . H 12,782
. . rural areas . . . H 12,524
. **low and moderate income**
. . homestead programs . . . H 11,431
. **low income**
. . annual contribution . . . H Res 1214
. . annual contributions . . . S 3188; H 12,945
. . programs extension . . . S 3295

Headline Legislation

Higher education
. student loans . . . H 14,070
. . defaults . . . H 3801

Highways
. Highway Trust Fund
. . extension . . . H 8235

Housing
. direct loan program
. . limits . . . S 2529; H 13,724
. middle income . . . H 4485
. real estate settlement procedures
. . advance disclosures . . S 2327; H 10,283

Housing Authorization Act of 1976 . . . S 3295;
H 12,945

Imports
. tariffs
. . suspension of authority . . SJR 12;
. . . . H 1767

Reproduced with permission from *Congressional Index,* published and copyrighted by Commerce Clearing House, Inc., 4025 W. Peterson
Avenue, Chicago, Illinois 60646.

Underline the appropriate citation in each case.

After obtaining the bill number, consult the "Senate Bills" section, which
summarizes bills. The summary of S. 3295 appears as follows. (figure 3-3).

Figure 3-3

Congressional Index, 1975-76
Senate Bills

S 3290-3291—Private bill
S 3292—Social security
    By Pearson.
    To amend Title XIX of the Social Security Act
to repeal the provisions, relating to consent by
States to certain suits, which were included in
such Title by reason of the enactment of
Section 111 of Public Law 94-182. (To
Finance.)
S 3293—Atomic Energy Commission—funds
    By Haskell.
    To amend the Act entitled An Act to
authorize appropriations to the Atomic Energy
Commission in accordance with section 261 of
the Atomic Energy Act of 1954, as amended.
(To Atomic Energy.)

S 3294—Education expenses—college—tax
   deduction
  By Roth.
  To provide for tax deductions for college
education. (To Finance.)
S 3295—Housing—low income—programs
   extension
  By Proxmire.
  To extend the authorization for annual
contributions under the United States Housing
Act of 1937, to extend certain low-income
housing programs under the National Housing
Act. (To Calendar.)

Reproduced with permission from *Congressional Index,* published and copyrighted by Commerce Clearing House, Inc., 4025 W. Peterson Avenue, Chicago, Illinois 60646.

Refer to figure 3-3 when answering the following questions:

S. 3295 was introduced by Senator _____

Proxmire

Does the summary of S. 3295 in the *Congressional Almanac* give you more information about the bill than the abstract in figure 3-3?

Yes. The *Congressional Quarterly* notes the committee to which S.3295 was referred, and cites both report and law numbers, in addition to relevant dates.

Suppose you know that S. 3295 was introduced by Senator Proxmire, but you are uncertain of the bill number, consult the Index by Authors. (figure 3-4)

Figure 3-4

Congressional Index, 1975-76
Index by Authors

Proxmire
. animals—humane treatment...S 811
. antitrust—laws...S 1136
. armed forces—chemical warfare...S 1288
. . missing in action...S 474
. . Selective Service...S 1628
. authorizations—fiscal 1976 and 1977...
   S 1262
. . supplemental 1975...SJR 97
. banking—U.S. notes...S 3670
. bankruptcy—New York City ..S 2615
. banks—audit...S 2509
. . credit...S 2347
. . Federal Reserve Banks...SJR 134
. . Federal Reserve System...S 2050
. . foreign...S 958
. . foreign branches...S 2233
. . holding companies...S 890; 2721
. government contracts—defense...S 1537
   SJR 94
. government operations— agencies ...S 2234
. . audits...S 653
. . forms revision...S 2132
. . meetings...S 5

Metal and Nonmetallic Safety Board of
        Review . . . S 1774
. . travel expenses . . SCR 74
. Great Lakes-Saint Lawrence Seaway—
        winter navigation season . . . S 3584
. housing—closing costs . . . S 2596
. . low income . . . S 3295
. low rent projects . . . S 1589
. imports—tariffs . . SJR 12
income tax—returns . . . S 2342

Refer to figure 3-4 when answering the following:

S. _____ is another bill introduced by Senator Proxmire which deals with housing for the underprivileged.

S. 1589

After confirming that S. 3295 is a bill which interests you, search the Status of Senate bills section to learn how far the proposed legislation has progressed. This section is arranged in two parts, Status of Bills and Current Status of Bills. The Current Status of Bills for the 94th Congress is reproduced in figure 3-5.

Figure 3-5

Congressional Index, 1975-76
Current Status of Senate Bills

★ 3295
Reptd., no amend., S. Rept. 94-749 . . . .
. . . . 4/12/76
Passed S. with amend. [Roll-call] . . . .
. . . . 4/27/76
To H. Banking, Currency and
    Housing 4/28/76
H. Com. discharged 5/24/76
Passed H., with amend., in lieu of H.
    12945 [Voice] 5/26/76
S. appoints conferees 6/2/76
H. appoints conferees 6/7/76
Conf. Rept. submitted to H., H. Rept.
    94-1291 . . . . 6/22/76
Conf. Rept. recommitted by H. . . . 6/24/76
Conf. Rept. submitted to H., H. Rept.
    94-1304 . . . . 6/25/76
Conf. Rept. agreed to by H. 6/30/76
Conf. Rept. agreed to by S. 7/20/76
Approved [Public Law 94-375] 8/3/76

The star at the top of figure 3-5 indicates the bill has been enacted into law.

Refer to figure 3-5 when answering the following:

S. 3295 was first reported to the Senate without amendments on _____,

_____.

   April 12, 1976

It passed the Senate on April 27 (*with*/*without*) amendments.

   with

The bill was forwarded to the House Committee on _____

and _____ on April 28, 1976

   Banking, Currency, and Housing

The House approved S. 3295 on May 26, in lieu of House Bill_____.

   12945

The conference report submitted to the House on June 25 was H. Rept.

_____.

   94-1304

S. 3295 became Public Law _____ on _____ , _____

   94-375 on August 3, 1976

The Voting Records on Senate Bills section indicates the results of votes taken in the Senate. The tabulations, which are broken down by political parties, are arranged by dates. The finding list, located immediately before the voting records, indicates the pages of the *Index* where the votes appear.

Bills which have become law are listed in Enactments-Vetoes. This section of the *Congressional Index* incorporates a subject index to public laws, a list of Representatives and Senators and the laws they sponsored, and a list of Presidential vetoes by bill numbers.

The Senate volume's Reorganization Plans, Treaties, Nominations section includes information set forth in its title. All three types of data are listed in one alphabetical index located in this section.

House and Senate Journals:

Information is accessed from *House* and *Senate Journals* in two manners, by bill numbers and by subjects. To locate a concise legislative history of S. 3295, consult the History of Bills and Resolutions section of the 1976 *Senate Journal.* Both House and Senate bills discussed in the Senate that year are listed by chambers in numerical order. (figure 3-6)

Figure 3-6

Senate Journal, 1976
History of Bills and Resolutions

3295. A bill to extend the authorization for annual contributions under the U.S. Housing Act of
1937, to extend certain low-income-housing
programs under the National Housing Act,
and for other purposes—
read twice and placed on the calendar_____   410
submitted a report (Rept. 749) accompanied
  by a bill_____   410
considered _____ 459, 463
considered, amended, read the third time, and
  passed _____   469
Secretary authorized to make necessary technical and clerical corrections_____   469
passed the House with amendments_____   649
Senate disagrees to House amendments and
  asks conference_____   652
House agrees to conference report_____   893
conference report submitted_____   951
Senate agrees to conference report_____   956
examined and signed_____   976
presented _____   992
approved [Public Law 375]_____ _____ 1183

Refer to figure 3-6 when answering the following questions:

Reference to S. Rept. 749 can be found on page ____.

   410

Reference to the conference report agreed to by the House can be found on

page _____.

   893

Does figure 3-6 tell you the conference report number?

   No

The identical bill, S. 3295, appears in the Subject Index under "Housing,
Community Development." (figure 3-7)

Figure 3-7

Senate Journal, 1976
Subject Index

Housing—(See also Department of Housing and Urban   Page
      Development.)
   Aged—
     Gain from sale after 65—(See S. 3505.)
     Housing programs, increase amount author-
       ized—(See S. 3174.)

Tax credit, real property taxes on principal
residence—(See S. 3754.)
All Electric Homes in the United States, report___ 672
Block grant assistance, adverse economic condi-
tions—(See S. 2986.)
Coinsurance program, annual report_____ 225
Community development—(See S. 3295.)
  Block grants, draft of proposed legislation_____ 557
Condominiums, loans—(See S. 3842.)
Construction resources, more efficient use of—
  (See S. 865.)

Congressional Record:

Although the official proceedings of Congress are published in the *Journals,*
serious researchers will find it more advantageous to consult the *Congressional
Record.* The *Record* includes not only proceedings, but also debates which take
place in each chamber. Its index has two parts, the Index To The Proceedings
and the History of Bills and Resolutions. The former incorporates subjects and
names, whereas the latter lists bills and resolutions in numerical order and provides legislative histories for each. Indexes to the daily issues of the *Congressional Record* are issued every two weeks. The index to the permanent bound
edition is published annually. To obtain a complete legislative history of a bill
introduced during the initial session of a Congress, consult the History of Bills
and Resolutions in the *Record's* index to the second, as well as the first, session
because bills are carried over from the initial session into the following one of the
same Congress. If the bill is not listed in the second session's index, Congress
did not take further action on it.

Entries in the Index To The Proceedings are often subdivided into various
parts, depending upon the type of information considered. For instance, the 1976
cumulative index had seventeen subdivisions under Housing.

1. Addresses
2. Analyses
3. Articles and editorials
4. Bills and resolutions
5. Letters
6. Lists
7. Memorandums
8. Messages
9. Newsletters
10. Papers
11. Petitions
12. Press releases
13. Remarks in House
14. Remarks in Senate
15. Reports
16. Tables
17. Texts of (bills and their
    amendments)

S. 3295 appears in the Index To The Proceedings section. (figure 3-8)

Figure 3-8

Congressional Record, 1976
Index To The Proceedings

HOUSING
Addresses
  Alternative National Policy, Senator Humphrey,
    6637
  Energy Conservation, Senator G. Hart, 8641
  Financial Reform—Why, What and For Whom?
    Representative St Germain, 555
  Housing for Rural People, Clay L. Cochran, 15881
  National Association of Homebuilders, Senator
    Humphrey, 1483
  National Growth Policy and Habitat, Senator
    Humphrey, 11037

Bills and resolutions
Allocation formula: revise (see H.R. 13159)
Appropriations: authorize certain (see H.R. 12617)
Assistance payments: disregard certain (see H.R. 12457)
Loans: provide for low- and moderate-income housing construction (see H.R. 11503)
Low- and middle-income housing: prohibit discrimination against (see H.R. 12782)
Low- or moderate-income housing: prohibit requirement of, in certain areas (see H.R. 15707)
Low-cost: availability of reserve funds for (see H.R. 12865)
Low-income housing programs: extend certain (see S. 3295*)

In figure 3-8, underline the citation referencing S. 3295. The asterisk following the bill number indicates that the measure was acted upon. Consult the History of Bills and Resolutions to obtain more information about the measure. (figure 3-9)

Figure 3-9

Congressional Record, 1976
History of Bills and Resolutions

S. 3295—To amend and extend laws relating to housing and community development. Mr. Proxmire; Ordered placed on the calendar, 10427.—Reported (S. Rept. 94-749), 10427.—Debated 11252, 11336, 11344, 11351.—Amended and passed Senate, 11362.—Referred to Committee on Banking and Currency, 11683.—Committee discharged, 15517.—Amended and passed House (in lieu of H.R. 12945), title amended, 15520.—Senate disagreed to House amendments and asked for a conference. Conferees appointed, 16165.—House insisted on its amendments and agreed to a conference. Conferees appointed, 16801.—Conference report (H. Rept No. 94-1291) submitted in House, 19775.—House recommitted conference report, 20428.—Conference report (H. Rept. 94-1304) submitted in House and agreed to, 20603, 21632.—Conference report submitted in the Senate and agreed to, 22811.—Examined and signed, 23217, 23279.—Presented to the President, 23279.—Approved [Public Law 94-375], 25651.

Refer to figure 3-9 when answering the following:

The first congressional debate relating to S. 3295 begins on page _____ of the *Congressional Record.*

11,252

Underline the pertinent part of the illustration indicating the House passed S. 3295 in place of H.R. 12945.

Two conference reports were issued in relation to S. 3295,

H. Rept. ___ - _____ and H. Rept. ___ - _____.

H. Rept. 94-1291 and 94-1304

The *Daily Digests* to the *Record* are appended to each daily issue. However, they appear in a separate volume in the permanent bound *Record.* The bound *Digest* includes a self-contained index and a table, arranged by public law numbers, that outlines legislative histories. (figure 3-10)

Figure 3-10

Daily Digest to the *Congressional Record,* 1976

Title	Bill No.	Date Intro-duced	Committee		Date reported		Report No.		Page of passage in Congressional Record		Date of passage		Public Law	
			House	Senate	House	Senate	House	Senate	House	Senate	House	Senate	Date ap-proved	No.
To extend for 1 year the authority of the Secretary of Transportation to issue aviation war risk insurance.	H.R. 13308	Apr. 27	PWT	Com	May 12	....	94-1123	....	14291	22799	May 18	July 20	July 31	94-374
Extending certain housing programs under the National Housing Act.	S. 3295 (H.R. 12945)	Apr. 12	BC&H	BHUA	May 6	Apr. 12	94-1091	94-749	15520	11362	May 26	Apr. 27	Aug. 3	94-375
Extending to 90 days the period of notice required before a common carrier tariff may be changed.	S. 2054 (H.R. 13961)	July 8 1975	IFC	Com	June 30	May 23	94-1315	94-918	22864	13793	July 20	May 27	Aug. 4	94-376

This table is of limited value, since it excludes conference reports and citations to significant House and Senate debates.

On-Line Availability of The Congressional Record:

The *Congressional Record* is available on-line from two sources. The *Congressional Record Abstracts* covers 1976 to date and the *Federal Index* covers October 1976 to date.

House Calendar:

The *House Calendar's* most significant value is its Numerical Order of Bills and Resolutions. Bills and Resolutions, excluding Senate resolutions which the editors believe would be of no interest to the House, are listed in this section. A complete legislative history is given for each citation. Proposals which have passed either or both houses, and those currently pending on the *Calendars* are included. S. 3295 is cited as indicated in figure 3-11.

Figure 3-11
House Calendar, 1976
Numerical Order of Bills and Resolutions

S. 3295 (H.R. 12945).—Housing Amendments of 1976. Reported in Senate Apr. 12, 1976; Banking, Housing and Urban Affairs; Rept. 94-749. Passed Senate Apr. 27, 1976. In House, referred to Banking, Currency and Housing Apr. 28, 1976. Committee discharged. Passed House amended May 26, 1976. Senate asked for a conference June 2, 1976. House agreed to a conference June 7, 1976. Conference report filed in the House June 22, 1976; Rept. 94-1201. *House recommitted conference report June 24, 1976.* Conference report filed in the House June 25, 1976; Rept. 94-1304. House agreed to conference report June 30, 1976. Senate agreed to conference report July 20, 1976. Approved Aug. 3, 1976. Public Law 94-375.

Bills which are identical and those having reference to each other are noted in parentheses. H.R. 12945 is indicated in figure 3-11. It has already been shown that S. 3295 passed the House in lieu of H.R. 12945. (see figures 3-5 and 3-9)

The index to the *House Calendar* is published every Monday. It is arranged by agency names, names of programs, and selected subjects. Unlike the index to the *Congressional Record,* that of the *House Calendar* is cumulated by Congress. When consulting the final *Calendar* issued for the second session of a Congress, researchers are given complete legislative histories covering the entire Congress.

Another feature of the *House Calendar* is a list of Public Laws and corresponding bill numbers similar to that found in the *Congressional Index.* Also, a list of bills in conference is arranged chronologically according to the date the House or Senate asked that a conference be established. A list of bills reported from their conference committees immediately follows that section. It is arranged chronologically according to the date on which the second chamber agreed to the conference. (figure 3-12)

Figure 3-12

House Calendar, 1976
Bills Through Conference

Bill No. Date Con-fer-ence Asked Agreed to	Brief of title	Conferees		Report filed in—		Report agreed to in –	
		House	Senate	House	Senate	House	Senate
8. 3295 June 2 June 7	Housing Amendments of 1976.	Messrs. Reuss, Ashley, Mrs. Sullivan, Messrs. Moorhead of Pennsylvania, Stephens, St Germain, Gonzales, Mitchell of Maryland, Patterson of California, LaFalce, AuCoin, Brown of Michigan, Stanton, J. Wm., Rousselot, Wylie, and McKinney. (*House acts first.*)	Messrs. Proxmire, Sparkman, Williams, Cranston, Stevenson, Tower, Brooke, and Garn. (*Senate asks.*)	June 22 94-1291 (*Recommitted June 24*) June 25 94-1304	········	June 30 (*Approved Aug. 3, 1976; Public Law 94-375.*)	July 20

The *House Calendar* is far more valuable than the *Senate Calendar*. The latter merely represents its chamber's agenda on a particular day. Moreover, the *Senate Calendar* is neither cumulated nor indexed.

Digest of Public General Bills and Resolutions:

The *Digest of Public General Bills and Resolutions* offers the most detailed summaries of bills, resolutions, and public laws that are available. It is published during each session of a Congress in two cumulative issues. Monthly supplements complement each cumulation. Final editions are published annually following the conclusion of Congressional sessions. Since 1977, the *Digest* has been arranged in four parts—Action Taken During the Congress, Digests of Public General Bills and Resolutions, Indexes to Digested Bills and Resolutions, and Factual Descriptions of the bills and resolutions.

The four indexes to the *Digest* are arranged by subjects, sponsors and co-sponsors, identical bills, and short titles. A list of approximately one hundred and twenty-five subject headings immediately precedes the Subject Index. The Sponsors and Co-sponsors and Identical Bill Indexes are similar to others already illustrated in which bills are listed under the names of the legislators who introduced them and under comparable numbers that correspond to appropriate measures in the second house. The Short Title Index is useful when bills have informative titles. In each index, asterisks follow the bill numbers when the measures were acted upon by either or both houses, or became law.

The abstracts of public laws, bills and resolutions printed in this reference tool are invaluable. Measures which have been acted upon by either or both houses or have been enacted into law are summarized in Actions Taken During The Congress. That section is divided into two parts, a Public Law section and an Other Measures Receiving Action section. Figure 3-13 illustrates parts of the summary of Public Law 94-375.

Figure 3-13

Digest of Public General Bills and Resolutions, 1976
Public Laws

Public Law 94-375   Approved 8/3/76; S. 3295.

Housing Authorization Act - Increases the authorization of funds
for the following programs administered by the Secretary of the
Department of Housing and Urban Development (HUD): (1)
housing assistance, including public housing: (2) public housing
for Indians; (3) newly constructed, substantially rehabilitated, and
modernized low-income public housing projects: and (4) public
housing operating subsidies.
  Grants a ten percent preference in public housing and federally
assisted housing to single non-elderly persons (with priority to
elderly, handicapped or displaced persons).
  Increases mortgage limits, under the National Housing Act for
the Home Ownership Assistance Program, to $25,000 ($29,000
in high-cost areas), except that with respect to housing for families
of five or more persons, the limits would be $29,000 ($33,000 in
high-cost areas).

Following the summary of P.L. 94-375, which extends nearly three-quarters of a
page, a legislative history is outlined.

  Bills considered by Congress, but not enacted into law, are described in the
Other Measures Receiving Action section. For instance, Senator Kennedy's
Federal Program Information Act, S. 3281, which never got out of Committee
in the House is listed as follows: (figure 3-14)

Figure 3-14

Digest of Public General Bills and Resolutions, 1976
Other Measures Receiving Action

S. 3281   Mr. Kennedy, et al.; 4/8/76

Federal Program Information Act - Creates a Federal Program
Information Center, within the General Services Administration,
to establish and maintain a computerized program information
system which is capable of identifying all existing Federal domestic assistance programs. Requires that such identifications include
enough information to allow a prospective beneficiary to determine whether or not he qualifies for such program by utilizing the
system.
  Directs the President to publish an annual catalog of such
programs which includes all information in the Center's data base.
  Authorizes appropriations through fiscal year 1980 to carry out
the purposes of this Act.

5-13-76   Reported to Senate from the Committee on Govern-
            ment Operations with amendment, S. Rept. 94-841
6-11-76   Call of calendar in Senate
6-11-76   Measure considered in Senate
6-11-76   Measure passed Senate, amended
6-14-76   Referred to House Committee on Government Oper-
            ations

S. 3283   *See* Public Law 94-423

S. 3295   *See* Public Law 94-375

Note that bills which have become public law are listed in this section with cross references referring researchers to the Public Law segment. Both the Public Law section and the Other Measures Receiving Action section cumulate information for an entire Congress.

Unlike Action Taken During The Congress, the two remaining parts of the *Digest of Public General Bills and Resolutions,* Digests of Public General Bills and Resolutions and Factual Descriptions, cumulate only those bills and resolutions introduced during one Congressional session. The former provides very detailed abstracts of legislative proposals, whereas the latter, according to clause 5(d) of House Rule X, is required to provide summaries in one hundred words or less. The Factual Descriptions describe private bills that are excluded from the Digests of Public General Bills and Resolutions. Bills receiving action, plus those not acted upon, are included in both sections.

Locating Bills and Resolutions on Microfiche:

The Government Printing Office began distributing bills and resolutions on microfiche in 1979. The *Microfiche User's Guide For Congressional House and Senate Bills* is used to locate the measures on the fiche. It is published periodically while Congress is in session, with each issue cumulating information from the previous ones. Following the termination of a Congress, a two-year cumulative edition is prepared. The *User's Guide* is arranged in nine parts:

1. House bills (H.R.)
2. House resolutions (H. Res.)
3. House joint resolutions (H. J. Res.)
4. House concurrent resolutions (H. Con. Res.)
5. Senate bills (S)
6. Senate resolutions (S. Res.)
7. Senate joint resolutions (S. J. Res.)
8. Senate concurrent resolutions (S. Con. Res.)
9. Senate executive documents amendments.

The *finding aid* refers researchers to the appropriate frames on the relevant microfiche. For instance, figure 3-15 indicates that H.R. 379, introduced during the ninety-sixth Congress, first session, is located on frame A10 of fiche 21.

Figure 3-15

Final Cumulative Finding Aid, House and Senate Bills
(Microfiche Format) (Biennial) 96th Congress
First and Second Sessions

H.R. No.	Fiche No.	X-Y Coord.
379.	21	A10
380.	8	G14
381.	9	A2
382.	9	A4
383.	21	A13
384.	21	B2
385.	21	B8

Refer to figure 2-14 for an explanation of frames.

The reference tools cited in this chapter are excellent sources to use when tracing legislative histories. However, the *Congressional Information Service Index,* which is described in the next chapter, provides researchers with far more complete legislative histories than those seen above. The *CIS Index* is also the most comprehensive index to Congressional publications that do not relate to specific bills. This reference tool is described separately due to its special nature and importance.

Footnotes

[1]Martin Tolchin, "7 Writers' Words Barred by *Congressional Record,*" *New York Times,* May 11, 1976, p. 20.

BIBLIOGRAPHY

CIS Index To Publications of The United States Congress. Washington, D.C.: Congressional Information Service, Inc., 1970-monthly.

Calendar of Business—Senate of The United States. Washington, D.C.: GPO, ? - daily when Senate is in session.

Calendars of the United States House of Representatives and History of Legislation. Washington, D.C.: GPO, 1880(?)-daily when the House is in session.

Congress and The Nation: A Review of Government and Politics in The Postwar Years. Washington, D.C.: Congressional Quarterly, Inc., 1965-quadrennial. Volume 1 covers 1945-1964.

Congressional Index Service. Chicago: Commerce Clearing House, 1937-weekly while Congress is in session.

Congressional Quarterly Almanac. Washington, D.C.: Congressional Quarterly, Inc. 1948-annual. Published quarterly between 1945 and 1947.

Congressional Record. United States Congress. Washington, D.C.: GPO, 1873-daily while Congress is in session.

CQ Weekly Report. Washington, D.C.: Congressional Quarterly, Inc., 1945-weekly. Published under various titles between 1945 and 1950.

Digest of Public General Bills and Resolutions. Library of Congress. Congressional Research Service. Washington, D.C.: GPO, 1936-monthly.

GPO Sales Publications Reference File Microform. Superintendent of Documents. Washington, D.C.: GPO, 1977-bimonthly.

Journal of The House of Representatives of The United States. Washington, D.C.: GPO, 1789-annual.

Journal of The Senate of The United States of America. Washington, D.C.: GPO, 1789-annual.

Monthly Catalog of United States Government Publications. Superintendent of Documents. Washington, D.C.: GPO, 1895-monthly.

Superintendent of Documents Microfiche Users Guide For Congressional House and Senate Bills. Washington, D.C.: GPO, 1979-irregularly while Congress is in session.

US Congressional Committee Prints on Microfiche. Washington, D.C.: Congressional Information Service, Inc., 1980.

Legislative History Sources; Questions:

The Infant Formula Act of 1980 amended the Federal Food Drug and Cosmetic Act to insure the safety and nutrition of infant formulas. Compile a legislative history of that Act which includes the following:

A. The bill numbers for relevant House and Senate bills.

B. The name of the House Committee that considered the bill.

C. The name of the Senate Committee to which the bill was forwarded for consideration.

D. A list of relevant Congressional reports.

E. The dates on which the measure was approved by the House, the Senate, and the President.

F. The date on which the House agreed to the Senate amendment.

G. The public law number.

Legislative History Sources, Answers:

A. H.R. 5836, H.R. 5839, H.R. 6608, H.R. 6940 and S. 2490.

B. House Committee on Interstate and Foreign Commerce.

C. Senate Committee on Labor and Human Resources.

D. H. Rpt. 96-936 and S. Rpt. 96-916.

E. The measure was approved by the House on May 20, 1980, by the Senate on September 8, 1980, and by the President on September 26, 1980.

F. September 9, 1980.

G. P.L. 96-359.

CHAPTER 4

CONGRESSIONAL PUBLICATIONS, PART II: CIS/INDEX

The *CIS Index,* frequently referred to as the *CIS,* is the most comprehensive index to Congressional publications. It provides access to documents relating to bills, in addition to those dealing with all other issues of public importance that Congress has considered. Since 1970, the *CIS* has been distributed monthly in two separate volumes, the *Index To Congressional Publications and Public Laws* and the *Abstracts of Congressional Publications and Legislative Histories.* The *Abstract* volume is cumulated annually and the *Index* volume is cumulated quarterly and annually. To date, two multiyear cumulative indexes have been distributed, the *CIS Five-Year Cumulative Index, 1970-1974* and the *CIS Four-Year Cumulative Index, 1975-1978.*

This chapter considers the *six* sections of the *Index* volume:

The Index of Subjects and Names

The Index of Titles

The Index of Bill Numbers

The Index of Report Numbers

The Index of Document Numbers

The Index of Committee and Subcommittee Chairmen

The *Abstract* volume's two parts, the Abstracts of Congressional Publications and the Legislative Histories, are also described.

Index of Subjects and Names, Subject Approach:

The Index of Subjects and Names provides access to documents by subjects as well as names. The latter method is described below. For the sake of continuity, public housing is again used as a subject. The following entries are listed under "Public housing". (figure 4-1).

Figure 4-1

Cumulative Index, 1975-1978
Index of Subjects and Names
Subject Approach

Public housing
   DC Housing and Community Dev Dept
      programs, FY78 approp, 77 S181-54.18
   Discriminatory planning and zoning to
      exclude low income housing, prohibition,
      78 H521-34.6
   Elderly housing problems, Cleveland, Ohio,
      78 H141-9.4, 78 H141-9.5
   Emergency housing assistance programs,
      75 H243-9, 75 S243-6, 75 S243-7
   Energy crisis impact on public housing,
      75 S141-19.7
   Fed housing programs, extension and
      revision, 76 S241-40, 76 S243-8,
      76 PL94-375

First concurrent budget resolution, FY78,
    public recommendations, 77 H261-11.4
Housing and community dev programs
    overview, 78 S241-39.1
Housing and spec services for elderly,
    75 H401-15

Reproduced with permission from *CIS In-dex*, published and copyrighted by Congressional Information Service, Inc., 4520 East-West Highway, Washington, D.C. 20014.

After locating relevant entries in the index, note the *CIS* entry numbers and refer to the *Abstract* volume. Entry number 76 S241-40, indexed under "Federal housing programs extension and revision," will be discussed for illustrative purposes.

Abstract Volume:

The monthly *Abstract* volumes are arranged in three parts, each indicated by an H, J or S. They refer to House, Joint, and Senate publications. The entry numbers are listed numerically within each section. The annual cumulative *Abstract* volume has a fourth part, the Legislative Histories section, in which public laws are cited in numerical order. Comprehensive legislative histories are given for each.

The citation above, 76 S241-40, refers to entry 241-40 in the Senate section of the 1976 *Abstract* volume. Entries in either quarterly or multiyear cumulative indexes, both of which relate to more than one *Abstract* volume, are preceded by bold face numbers which indicate the appropriate monthly or annual *Abstract* issue to consult. "76" does not precede the S241-40 in the 1976 annual *Index* because researchers should assume that entries in one year's index refer to citations in that same year's *Abstract* volume. Portions from 76 S241-40 appear in figure 4-2.

Figure 4-2
CIS/Index
Abstract Volume, 1976

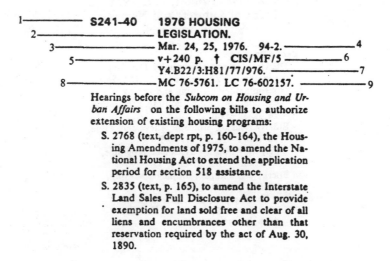

Hearings before the *Subcom on Housing and Urban Affairs* on the following bills to authorize extension of existing housing programs:

S. 2768 (text, dept rpt, p. 160-164), the Housing Amendments of 1975, to amend the National Housing Act to extend the application period for section 518 assistance.

S. 2835 (text, p. 165), to amend the Interstate Land Sales Full Disclosure Act to provide exemption for land sold free and clear of all liens and encumbrances other than that reservation required by the act of Aug. 30, 1890.

S. 3067 (text, p. 166), to authorize funds for comprehensive planning and management assistance under the Housing Act of 1954.

S. 3143 (text, dept rpt, p. 167-169), to amend the Housing Act of 1937 to make single individuals eligible for assistance.

S241-40.1: Mar. 24, 1976. p. 5-50.

Witness: RHINELANDER, John B., Under Sec of HUD; accompanied by Kliman, Albert J., Budget Officer.

Statement and Discussion: Review of HUD FY77 authorization needs; adequacy of current section 8 program and reasons for operational difficulties; analysis of and suggested amendments to H.R. 9852, to amend the National Housing Act.

S241-40.4: Mar. 25, 1976. p. 123-148.

Witnesses: KEANE, John, exec dir, Mass Union of Public Housing Tenants.
WEINER, Leon N., pres, Natl Housing Conf.

DOLBEARE, Cushing N., chairperson, Ad Hoc Low Income Housing Coalition.

Statements: Need to increase funding for public and low income housing modernization, operating subsidies, and construction; support for S. 3159 and suggestions for amendment. (p. 123-143)

Discussion: Appraisal of HUD operations and legislative position. (p. 143-148)

1. CIS entry number.
2. Title.
3. Dates of hearing.
4. Congress and session.
5. Pagination.
6. CIS price code.
7. Superintendent of Documents number.
8. *Monthly Catalog* entry number.
9. Library of Congress card number.

Refer to figure 4-2 when answering the following:

The title of this document is _____.

1976 Housing Legislation

It was issued during the _____ Congress, _____ session.

94th Congress, 2nd session

This document is a hearing held on March ____ and 25, 19 ____.

24, 1976

The Superintendent of Documents number is _____.

Y4.B22/3: H81/77/976

This document was entry number _____ in the 1976 *Monthly Catalog.*

76-5761

Is the document in question a depository or a non-depository one?

non-depository

CIS/MF/5, the CIS price code, which is indicated among the bibliographic information, is useful if you are interested in purchasing a microfiche copy of *1976 Housing Legislation* from the CIS. The microfiche program is described below.

CIS abstracts have numerous other features. Besides providing complete bibliographic information, they also summarize the documents. The names of witnesses who appeared before committee hearings, the organizations they represent—if any—and descriptions of their testimonies are included.

The abstracts are often subdivided with decimal points for more specific indexing. When using this type of entry number, refer from the decimal point to the whole number to obtain the bibliographic information and the SuDoc number. For instance, suppose the Index of Subjects and Names indicates that relevant information can be found under S241-40.4. The bibliographic information and the SuDoc number would then be located under S241-40, rather than 40.4.

Index of Subjects and Names, Name Approach:

The witnesses whose names appear in abstracts of hearings and the organizations they represent are indexed in the Index of Subjects and Names. If you wanted to know what John Keane said before Congress regarding public housing, you would search the index under his name. (figure 4-3)

Figure 4-3
Cumulative Index, 1975-1978
Index of Subjects and Names
Name Approach

Keane, John
  Fed housing programs, extension and
    revision, 76 S241-40.4
  HUD housing and community dev programs
    extension and revision, 78 S241-54.4
Keane, John T.
  Fed forest and range resources mgmt
    policies, 78 H161-25.13

Reproduced with permission from *CIS Index,* published and copyrighted by Congressional Information Service, Inc., 4520 East-West Highway, Washington, D.C. 20014.

This testimony is found in abstracts 76 S241-40.4 and 78 S241-54.4. Underline the relevant part of figure 4-2 which summarizes Keane's statement.

Figure 4-2 indicates that Keane represented the Massachusetts Union of Public Housing Tenants at the hearing. Suppose you were unaware of this but were interested in reading the Union's opinions. You would then search the Index of Subjects and Names under the name of the organization. (figure 4-4)

Figure 4-4

Cumulative Index, 1975-1978
Index of Subjects and Names
Organization Approach

Massachusetts Title XX Coalition
State federally assisted social services
programs eligibility tests flexibility,
76 H781–52.8

Massachusetts Trial Lawyers Association
Medical malpractice insurance availability,
75 S541–83.3

**Massachusetts Union of Public Housing
Tenants**
Fed housing programs, extension and
revision, 76 S241–40.4
HUD housing and community dev programs
extension and revision, 78 S241–54.4

Massachusetts Wildlife Federation
Offshore oil and gas leasing, Fed-State
coastal zone mgmt issues, 75 S441–71.6

Massachusetts Wood Producers' Association
Fed forest and range resources mgmt
policies, 78 H161–25.11

Massad, Alexander H.
Offshore oil and gas dev, 77 H961–15.18
Petroleum cos jt venture activities,
77 H521–7.4

Reproduced with permission from *CIS In-
dex*, published and copyrighted by Congressional
Information Service, Inc., 4520 East-West
Highway, Washington, D.C. 20014.

Index of Titles:

Documents are listed in the Index of Titles alphabetically according to
their titles, except when titles begin with numbers. In those cases, entries are
listed numerically and alphabetically. *1976 Housing Legislation,* the title of the
publication in figure 4-2, is listed as follows. (figure 4-5) Underline the relevant
citation.

Figure 4-5

Cumulative Index, 1975-1978
Index of Titles

1976 ERDA Authorization., 75 H701–21
1976 ERDA Authorization and Transition
Period: Fossil Fuels., 75 H701–20
1976 First Concurrent Resolution on the
Budget, Part 1., 75 S251–3
1976 First Concurrent Resolution on the
Budget, Part 2., 75 S251–4
1976 Housing Legislation., 76 S241–40
1976 Joint Economic Report., 76 J843–1
1976 Midyear Review of the Economy.,
76 J843–2
1976 NASA Authorization., 75 H701–35

1976 NASA Authorization, Vol. I.,
    75 H701–25
1976 NASA Authorization, Vol. II, Part 1.,
    75 H701–26
1976 NASA Authorization, Vol. II, Part 2.,
    75 H701–27
1976 NASA Authorization, Vol. II, Part 3.,
    75 H701–28
1976 NASA Authorization, Vol. II, Part 4.,
    75 H701–29
1976 NASA Authorization, Vol. III.,
    75 H701–30

Index of Bill Numbers:

The Index of Bill numbers provides access to all Congressional publications
issued in relation to a specific bill. The measure studied in Chapter 3, S. 3295, is
listed as follows. (figure 4-6)

Figure 4-6

Cumulative Index, 1975-1978
Index by Bill Numbers

(94) S. 3283	....	**77** PL94–423
(94) S. 3285	....	**77** S541–21
(94) S. 3287	....	**76** S441–87
(94) S. 3295	....	**76** H243–11
(94) S. 3295	....	**76** H243–13
(94) S. 3295	....	**76** S243–8
(94) S. 3295	....	**76** PL94–375
(94) S. 3296	....	**77** H501–23.1
(94) S. 3296	....	**77** S521–35
(94) S. 3297	....	**77** S521–35

This index shows researchers that three citations relate directly to S. 3295 and
that it was eventually enacted into Public Law 94-375.

Legislative Histories:

This section of the annual cumulative *Abstract* volume provides the most
detailed legislative histories of public laws found in any source. P.L. 94-375 appears in the 1976 *Abstracts* as follows. (figure 4-7)

Figure 4-7

CIS/Index
Abstract Volume, 1976
Legislative Histories

PL94–375 HOUSING AUTHORIZATION ACT OF 1976.
Aug. 3, 1976. 94-2. 13 p.
* CIS/MF/3 •Item 575.
LC 90 STAT. 1067.

"To amend and extend laws relating to housing and community development."

Extends authorizations, most through FY77, for Federal aid to housing programs under Housing Act of 1937, National Housing Act, Emergency Homeowners' Relief Act, National Flood Insurance Act of 1968, Housing and Community Development Act of 1974, and Housing and Urban Development Act of 1970. Provides new program authorizations for low-income and public housing; loans for elderly and handicapped; and homeownership, rehabilitation, and community assistance.

Also amends Flood Disaster Protection Act of 1973 pertaining to residential loans.

Legislative history: (S. 3295 and related bills):

1975 CIS/Annual:
House Report: H243-17 (No. 94-545, accompanying H.R. 9852).
Senate Report: S243-26 (No. 94-520, accompanying H.R. 9852).
1976 CIS/Annual:
Senate Hearings: S241-40.
House Reports: H243-4, H243-5 (No. 94-1091, Pts. 1 and 2, both accompanying H.R. 12945); H243-11 (No. 94-1291, Conference Report); H243-13 (No. 94-1304, Conference Report).
Senate Report: S243-8 (No. 94-749).

Congressional Record Vol. 121 (1975):
Oct. 20, H.R. 9852 considered and passed House.
Congressional Record Vol. 122 (1976):
Jan. 23, H.R. 9852 considered and passed Senate, amended.
Apr. 27, considered and passed Senate.
May 26, considered and passed House, amended, in lieu of H.R. 12945.
June 30, House agreed to conference report.
July 20, Senate agreed to conference report.
Weekly Compilation of Presidential Documents Vol. 12, No. 32 (1976):
Aug. 4, Presidential statement.

Reproduced with permission from *CIS Index*, published and copyrighted by Congressional Information Service, Inc., 4520 East-West Highway, Washington, D.C. 20014.

The Index of Subjects and Names, like the Index of Bill Numbers, refers researchers to the Legislative Histories section. "PL" citations are noted under subject headings, as well as under the popular names of the laws. Underline the reference in figure 4-1 that tells you Public Law 94-375 deals with public housing.

Figure 4-7 indicates that *CIS* legislative histories not only incorporate references to reports and the *Congressional Record,* but also bring attention to hearings and the *Weekly Compilation of Presidential Documents,* a periodical which compiles public documents and statements issued in print or made verbally by the President. Although neither committee prints, nor Congressional documents (used as a proper noun) were published in relation to P.L. 94-375, the Legislative Histories section will also list those publications when appropriate.

Close examination of figure 4-6 delineates an interesting point. The hearing illustrated in figure 4-2, *1976 Housing Legislation* (S241-40), is not included in the Index of Bill Numbers because it did not relate directly to S. 3295. S241-40 is still listed in the legislative history of Public Law 94-375 because the issues discussed are very similar to those addressed in the legislation.

Furthermore, the Legislative Histories section lists relevant citations even when the titles were distributed during previous Congresses. For instance, the history of P.L. 96-22, the Veterans Health Care Amendments of 1979, incorporates materials printed during the 92nd Congress in 1971. (figure 4-8)

Figure 4-8

CIS/Index

Abstract Volume, 1979

Legislative Histories

PL96–22   VETERANS HEALTH CARE AMENDMENTS OF 1979.
June 13, 1979.   96-1.   21 p.
• CIS/MF/3 •Item 575.
93 STAT. 47.

"To amend title 38, United States Code, to revise and improve certain health-care programs of the Veterans' Administration, to authorize the construction, alteration, and acquisition of certain medical facilities, and to expand certain benefits for disabled veterans; and for other purposes."

Includes the following sections: Health Services Programs, to provide readjustment counseling for Vietnam era veterans, alcohol and drug abuse treatment, preventive health care services for eligible veterans, outpatient dental benefits for disabled veterans and former prisoners of war, and hospital care to eligible Filipino veterans; Contract-Care Programs, to authorize medical services on a private fee basis to eligible disabled veterans; Construction, Alteration, Lease, and Acquisition of Medical Facilities, to require House and Senate Committees on Veterans' Affairs approval for construction and acquisition of major VA medical facilities; Benefits Payable to Persons Residing Outside the U.S., to revise benefits eligibility of veterans residing outside the U.S., and provide for a VA study of such benefits.

Legislative history: (S. 7 and related bills):

1971 CIS/Annual:
House Report: H763-6 (No. 92-323, accompanying H.R. 9265).

1972 CIS/Annual:
Senate Hearings: S761-1; S761-4.
House Report: S763-7 (No. 92-1084, accompanying S. 2108).

1973 CIS/Annual:
Senate Committee Print: S762-10.
Senate Reports: S763-3 (No. 93-56, pt. 1, accompanying S. 284); S763-4 (No. 93-56, pt. 2, accompanying S. 284).

1974 CIS/Annual:
House Hearings: H761-7.

1976 CIS/Annual:
Senate Reports: S763-8 (No. 94-1206, pt. 1, accompanying S. 2908); S763-9 (No. 94-1206, pt. 2, accompanying S. 2908).

1977 CIS/Annual:
House Hearings: H761-1; H761-6.
Senate Hearings: S761-2; S761-3; S761-12.
House Reports: H763-1 (No. 95-109, accompanying H.R. 5025); H763-2 (No. 95-110, accompanying H.R. 5027); H763-3 (No. 95-111, accompanying H.R. 5029).
Senate Report: S763-5 (No. 95-390, accompanying H.R. 5027).

1978 CIS/Annual:
House Hearings: S761-5.
Senate Report: S763-1 (No. 95-825, accompanying H.R. 5029).

1979 CIS/Annual:
House Hearings: H761-6; H761-23.
Senate Hearings: S761-5; S761-12.
House Reports: H763-2 (No. 96-138, accompanying H.R. 3892); H763-4 (No. 96-140, accompanying H.R. 1608); H763-6 (No. 96-223, Conference Report).
Senate Reports: S763-2 (No. 96-100); S763-5 (No. 96-195, Conference Report).

Congressional Record Vol. 125 (1979):
May 16, considered and passed Senate.
May 21, H.R. 1608 considered and passed House; proceedings vacated and S. 7, amended, passed in lieu.
May 30, House agreed to conference report.
June 4, Senate agreed to conference report.

Weekly Compilation of Presidential Documents Vol. 15, No. 24 (1979):
June 14, Presidential statement.

Indexes of Report and Document Numbers:

The Indexes of Report and Document Numbers list reports and documents in numerical order and provide corresponding *CIS* entry numbers. Remember, House and Senate documents, like reports, are numbered in consecutive order by Congress. For instance, Report 749, issued by the Senate during the 94th Congress, is cited as S. Rept. 94-749. Figure 4-9 below illustrates how reports are listed in the Index of Report Numbers and in the *Abstract* volume.

Figure 4-9

Cumulative Index, 1975-1978
Index of Report Numbers

CIS/Index
Abstract Volume, 1976

S. Rpt. 94-734	....	76 S443–5
S. Rpt. 94-735	....	76 S443–6
S. Rpt. 94-736	....	76 S443–7
S. Rpt. 94-737	....	76 S443–8
S. Rpt. 94-738	....	76 S443–9
S. Rpt. 94-739	....	76 S263–15
S. Rpt. 94-740	....	76 S383–9
S. Rpt. 94-741	....	76 S643–4
S. Rpt. 94-742	....	76 S183–7
S. Rpt. 94-743	....	76 S543–8
S. Rpt. 94-744	....	76 S543–9
S. Rpt. 94-745	....	76 S443–86
S. Rpt. 94-746	....	76 S383–10
S. Rpt. 94-747	....	76 S163–11
S. Rpt. 94-748	....	76 S403–3
S. Rpt. 94-749	....	76 S243–8

S243–8   HOUSING AMENDMENTS
OF 1976.
Apr. 12, 1976. 94-2.
ii+30 p. † CIS/MF/3
•Item 1008-A.
S. Rpt. 94-749.
MC 76-4358.

Recommends passage of S. 3295, to amend and to provide for continuation of Federal aid to certain housing programs under the Housing Act of 1937 and the National Housing Act. Includes provisions for low-income and public housing, new construction, rehabilitation loans, housing for the elderly and the handicapped, and homeownership and community assistance.

Reproduced with permission from *CIS Index*, published and copyrighted by Congressional Information Service, Inc., 4520 East-West Highway, Washington, D.C. 20014.

Index of Committee and Subcommittee Chairmen:

Senators and Representatives who chair committees and subcommittees are noted alphabetically in two separate lists. The relevant committees and/or subcommittees are listed under their names. (figure 4-10)

Figure 4-10
CIS/Index
Index Volume, 1979
Index of Committee and Subcommittee Chairmen

BAYH, Birch (D-Ind)
Intelligence, Select, S420
Constitution, S520
Transportation Appropriations, S180

BENTSEN, Lloyd M. (D-Tex)
Economic, J840
Economic Growth and Stabilization,
    J840
Private Pension Plans and Employee
    Fringe Benefits, S360
Transportation, S320

BIDEN, Joseph R., Jr. (D-Del)
Criminal Justice, S520
European Affairs, S380
Intelligence and the Rights
    of Americans, S420

Reproduced with permission from *CIS Index,* published and copyrighted by Congressional Information Service, Inc., 4520 East-West Highway, Washington, D.C. 20014.

Following the committee/subcommittee names, appropriate *CIS* entry numbers are given. For instance, figure 4-10 tells us that Lloyd Bentsen chaired both the Joint Economic Committee and that Committee's Subcommittee on Economic Growth and Stabilization in 1979. All publications issued by the Joint Economic Committee and its subcommittees are abstracted in the J840's.

CIS Microfiche Library of United States Congressional Publications:

All titles indexed and abstracted in the *CIS Index* are reproduced as part of the *CIS Microfiche Library of United States Congressional Publications.* These fiche are sold either on a subscription or on a demand basis. For those who purchase titles through the "Documents on Demand" service, the CIS price code referred to in the explanation following figure 4-2 designates the cost of the materials. Researchers must contact CIS at (301) 654-1550 or write:

> 4520 East-West Highway
> Suite 800
> Washington, D.C. 20014

to understand what the code represents.

On-Line Availability of CIS:

The *CIS Index* is available on-line from the Lockheed and the Systems Development Corporations. Both vendors cover the index from its beginning in 1970 to date.

Further Information:

Consult *CIS Index User Handbook For Librarians and Researchers Using Congressional Publications.* This is available from the publisher for a nominal fee. The Congressional Information Service also publishes a two page flier, *CIS Index Search Guide,* that explains how this reference tool is used. Single copies are available gratis. Multiple copies are sold at $3.00 per one hundred.

BIBLIOGRAPHY

CIS Five-Year Cumulative Index, 1970-1974. Washington, D.C.: Congressional Information Service, Inc., 1975. 2 vols.

CIS Four-Year Cumulative Index, 1975-1978. Washington, D.C.: Congressional Information Service, Inc., 1979. 3 vols.

CIS Index Search Guide. Washington, D.C.: Congressional Information Service, Inc., 1978.

CIS Index To Publications of The United States Congress. Washington, D.C.: Congressional Information Service, Inc., 1970-monthly.

CIS Index User Handbook For Librarians and Researchers Using Congressional Publications. Washington, D.C.: Congressional Information Service, Inc., 1977.

CIS Microfiche Library of United States Congressional Publications. Washington, D.C.: Congressional Information Service, Inc., 1970-monthly.

Congressional Record. United States Congress. Washington, D.C.: GPO, 1873-daily while Congress is in session.

Weekly Compilation of Presidential Documents. National Archives and Records Service. Office of The Federal Register, Washington, D.C.: GPO, 1965-weekly.

Congressional Information Service, Questions:

1. Using the 1977 *CIS*, locate the legislative history of an act authorizing permanent resident status for Vietnamese refugees.

2. Col. Charles A. Beckwith, commander of the rescue mission which attempted to free the American hostages in Iran, along with three additional Pentagon and military personnel, presented testimony before the House Appropriations Committee describing the mission.

    A. When was this testimony presented?

    B. What is the title and SuDoc number of this hearing?

    C. What pages of the hearing include the relevant information?

3. Using the 1980 *CIS*, compile a bibliography of hearings relating to the nutritional content of infant formula. Include the title, the date, and the SuDoc number of each hearing.

Congressional Information Service, Answers:

1. The legislative history of P.L. 95-145 appears on page 1132 of the 1977 *Abstract* volume.

    2. A. April 28 and June 2, 1980.

        B. *Defense Department Appropriations for 1981, Part 4,* Y4.Ap6/1:D36/5/981/pt.4.

        C. Pages 605-675.

    3. *Infant Formula,* November 1, 1979. Y4.In8/4:96-79.

    Nutritional Quality of Infant Formula, February 28 and March 6, 1980. Y4.In8/4:96-132.

CONGRESSIONAL PUBLICATIONS, PART III:
ADDITIONAL GUIDES TO REPORTS AND DOCUMENTS
(SERIAL SET), HEARINGS, AND COMMITTEE PRINTS

Four significant sources of Congressional publications not discussed in chapters three and four are described in this one. They are listed in order of their significance.

CIS US Serial Set Index

Numerical List and Schedule of Volumes

Index of Congressional Committee Hearings (Not Confidential In Character)

CIS U.S. Congressional Committee Hearings Index

CIS US Congressional Committee Prints Index

Special emphasis is placed upon the Serial Set because it is probably the single most important collection of United States government publications. The series, which began publication in 1817, is still published today, but its significance is in its historical value. A detailed explanation of the kinds of materials found in the Serial Set and its development follows. The *CIS US Serial Set Index* is the most comprehensive guide to the series. The *Numerical List and Schedule of Volumes,* an important bibliographic tool issued by the Superintendent of Documents, is a second source of which researchers using the Serial Set should be aware. The *Index of Congressional Committee Hearings (Not Confidential In Character),* which provides access to Congressional hearings published between the late 1860's and 1978 and available in the Senate Library, is still an important source. However, it will soon be superseded by the new Congressional Information Service publication, the *CIS U.S. Congressional Committee Hearings Index,* to be issued in eight parts between 1981 and 1985. The *CIS US Committee Prints Index* is the most comprehensive guide to committee prints. This reference tool is listed fourth in order of importance because most researchers have traditionally consulted the Serial Set and hearings far more often than committee prints. Prior to the 1980 publication of the *Prints Index,* access to these documents was quite poor.

What Is The Serial Set?

In its current format, the Serial Set consists of House and Senate reports and documents. Reports are statements issued by Congressional committees to Congress summarizing proceedings of hearings and occasionally offering recommendations for legislation. Sometimes, significant bills are analyzed section by section. Three types of publications comprise the Congressional document series:

1. Executive communications to Congress, such as Presidential messages or reports prepared by or for the executive departments.

2. Annual reports issued by patriotic organizations, such as the Veterans of Foreign Wars, the Daughters of The American Revolution and the Girl Scouts.

3. Other publications considered by Congress to be in the public interest, such as histories of Congress and its committees, and House and Senate rule manuals.

More detailed definitions are given in Chapter 3.

Reports and documents are first published as separate titles while Congress is in session. Besides being indexed in the *CIS Index,* both are also indexed in the *Monthly Catalog* and the *Publications Reference File.* Moreover, reports are also accessed through most of the reference tools considered in Chapter 3. Following the termination of a Congressional session, reports and documents are compiled and reissued in bound Serial Set volumes.

Historical Development of the Serial Set:

On December 8, 1813, a motion was introduced into the House by Representative Pickering calling for the regular printing of Congressional documents. It stated:

> . . . henceforward, all Messages and communications from the President of the United States; all letters and reports from the several departments of the Government; all motions and resolutions offered for the consideration of the House; all reports of committees of the House; and all other papers which, in the usual course of proceeding, or by special order of the House, shall be printed in octavo fold, and separately from the Journals—shall have their pages numbered in one continued series of numbers, commencing and terminating with each session.[1]

The first Serial Set volume was published by the fifteenth Congress in 1817. In 1831, Congress contracted with Gales and Seaton, a private publisher, for the compilation and publication of a retrospective series covering the first through the fourteenth Congresses. This series, entitled the *American State Papers,* was printed under Congressional guidance between 1832 and 1861. Its thirty-eight volumes were published in ten subject categories:

1. Foreign Relations
2. Indian Affairs
3. Finance
4. Commerce and Navigation
5. Military Affairs
6. Naval Affairs
7. Post Office
8. Public Lands
9. Claims
10. Miscellaneous Documents

Depending upon subject categories, the various volumes, which deal with information published between 1789 and 1838, somewhat overlap the Serial Set.

The *American State Papers* are numbered from 01 through 038 to distinguish them from the first thirty-eight volumes of the Serial Set, which are numbered 1 through 38. The *National State Papers,* a series currently being published by Michael Glazer, is an attempt to provide access to additional publications issued by the first fourteen Congresses which had been omitted from the *American State Papers.*

Although selection policies have never been consistent, Congress has generally included materials in the Serial Set when they meet any of the following criteria:

1. Legislators and their staffs require information in carrying forth their duties.

2. Congress has a desire to create permanent records of its activities for use by those in and outside government.

3. Congress sometimes attempts to influence public opinion through publication of information.

While the numbering of Serial Set volumes has been, for the most part, consistent, the organization of the volumes and the kinds of materials they include have varied over time. The series has been numbered sequentially since its inception. To date, nearly 13,400 volumes have been published.

The following chart summarizes the Serial Set's organization since 1817.

Time Period	House of Representatives	Senate
1817-mid 1819	*Journals* Documents (included reports)	*Journals* Documents (included reports)
mid 1819-mid 1848	*Journals* Reports Documents	*Journals* Documents (included reports)
mid 1848-mid 1894	*Journals* Reports Executive Documents[a] Miscellaneous Documents[a]	*Journals* Reports Executive Documents[a] Miscellaneous Documents[a]
mid 1894-1952	*Journals*[b] Reports[c] Documents	*Journals*[b] Reports[c] Documents
1953-present	Reports Documents	Reports Documents

[a]Executive documents are those publications that originated in the Executive Branch, whereas miscellaneous documents included those materials that originated from sources other than the Executive Branch. In mid-1894, Congress dropped the distinction between Executive and miscellaneous documents.

[b]Between 1895 and 1938, distribution of *Journals* was limited to three libraries in each state or territory chosen by the Superintendent of Documents.

[c]Between 1905 and 1938, reports on private bills, and simple and concurrent resolutions were excluded from Serial Set volumes.

1913 was a significant year in the development of the Serial Set. Since that time, Congress has excluded volumes containing materials which originated in executive agencies from wide distribution in Serial Set editions. This was done because the same materials were being distributed by the Government Printing Office to its depository libraries in editions published by the issuing agencies. However, for the sake of tradition, special Serial Set volumes containing these Executive publications are prepared for five Washington libraries—the House and Senate Libraries, the Library of Congress, the Public Documents Library, and the National Archives Library. Because these special volumes maintain the Serial Set's consecutive numerical order, those distributed to GPO depository libraries have gaps in their numbering sequences. For instance, volume 13,216 was the last one distributed to depository libraries covering publications of the ninety-fifth Congress, whereas volume 13,220 was the first one compiled for the ninety-sixth Congress which was made available widely. Numbers 13,217-1 through 13,219-3 were distributed only to the five research centers cited above.

Congressional Publications Excluded From The Serial Set:

Researchers should not only be aware of what the Serial Set includes, but also of what it excludes. Besides limiting the inclusion of many titles originating in executive agencies since 1913, three types of Congressional publications have generally been omitted: bills and resolutions, hearings, and committee prints. Bills and resolutions were included only during the earlier years, and even then, it was done irregularly. Hearings and committee prints have usually been by-passed; Congress recognizes them as committee publications. When considering Congressional publications for inclusion in the Serial Set, the House and Senate have, with few exceptions, incorporated materials issued by their full chambers, or reports issued by committees to their full chambers.

Copies of bills introduced between the first Congress in 1789 and the seventy-second in 1933 are available from the Library of Congress on microfilm. The Library has also filmed those introduced during the ninety-second Congress (1971-72). Bills introduced between 1959 and 1980, the eighty-sixth through the ninety-sixth Congresses, are also available as part of the *CIS Congressional Bills, Resolutions and Laws on Microfiche*. Availabilities of retrospective hearings and committee prints are described below.

CIS US Serial Set Index:

The *CIS US Serial Set Index* was published in twelve parts by the Congressional Information Service between 1975 and 1979. The time periods covered by each part are as follows:

Part I	1st - 34th Congresses (1789-1857)
Part II	35th - 45th Congresses (1857-1879)
Part III	46th - 50th Congresses (1879-1889)
Part IV	51st - 54th Congresses (1889-1897)
Part V	55th - 57th Congresses (1897-1903)
Part VI	58th - 60th Congresses (1903-1909)
Part VII	61st - 63rd Congresses (1909-1915)
Part VIII	64th - 68th Congresses (1915-1925)
Part IX	69th - 73rd Congresses (1925-1934)
Part X	74th - 79th Congresses (1935-1946)
Part XI	80th - 85th Congresses (1947-1958)
Part XII	86th Congress - 91st Congress, 1st Session (1959-1969)

Reports and documents issued since 1970 are indexed in the *CIS Index*.

Each part of the *Serial Set Index* consists of three volumes. The Index of Subjects and Keywords appears in the first two. The third includes three supplementary finding aids.

  Private Relief and Related Actions—Index of Names of Individuals and
     Organizations
  Numerical List of Reports and Documents
  Schedule of Serial Volumes

Index of Subjects and Keywords:

The Index of Subjects and Keywords is based upon keywords taken from titles. Although the editors have made the terms within each part consistent, those in volumes dealing with different time periods may differ, reflecting changes in language over the years. Ample cross-references are included.

If you were looking for information concerning financial aspects of public housing during the late 1940's, you would consult appropriate subject headings in the Index of Subjects and Keywords. Materials included under "Public Housing Administration" are reproduced in figure 5-1.

Figure 5-1

CIS US Serial Set Index, Part XI
Index of Subjects and Keywords

1. PUBLIC HOUSING ADMINISTRATION
    Financial records and procedures of Federal Public Housing
    Authority *S.rp. 665 (80-1) 11117* ——————————3.
2. ——————————————————————————————————4.
    Investigation of Public Housing Authority at San Diego and Los
    Angeles
    H.rp. 2351 (80-2) 11213
    Proposed supplemental appropriation for Public Housing
    Administration for annual contributions, 1954
    H.doc. 321 (83-2) 11776
    Report on audit of Federal Public Housing Authority, 1946
    H.doc. 342 (81-1) 11322

Reproduced with permission from *CIS US
Serial Set Index,* published and copyrighted by
Congressional Information Service, Inc., 4520
East-West Highway, Washington, D.C. 20014.

1. Title   3. Serial Set volume number.
2. Report number.   4. Congress and session.

Refer to figure 5-1 when answering the following questions:

A senate report which includes relevant information is entitled _____

_____

_____.

*Financial Records and Procedures of
Federal Public Housing Authority*

This citation is Senate Report _____-_____.

80-665

The Report is reprinted in Serial Set volume number _____ .

11,117

Report on Audit of Federal Public Housing Authority, 1946, was printed as

House Document _____-_____ and appeared in Serial Set volume

_____.

81-342, 11,322

Private Relief and Related Actions—Index of Names of Individuals and Organizations:

This alphabetical index includes the names of individuals and organizations that are affected by private legislation. When searching the *CIS US Serial Set Index* for a report about a bill designed to assist Lewis H. Rich, consult his name in the Index. (figure 5-1)

Figure 5-2

CIS US Serial Set Index, Part XI
Private Relief and Related Actions

Rice, William B.
  H.rp. 2313 (83-2) 11742
  S.rp. 487 (84-1) 11818
  H.rp. 139 (84-1) 11825
Rich, Lewis H.
  S.rp. 671 (80-1) 11117
  H.rp. 761 (80-1) 11121
Richa, Elias Y.
  S.rp. 2342 (83-2) 11732
  H.rp. 2130 (83-2) 11741

Reproduced with permission from *CIS US Serial Set Index,* published and copyrighted by Congressional Information Service, Inc., 4520 East-West Highway, Washington, D.C. 20014.

Refer to figure 5-2 when answering the following questions:

Senate Report _____-_____ deals with Lewis H. Rich.

80-671

It appeared in Serial Set volume _____.

11,117

House Report _____-_____, which appears in Serial Set volume

_____ also deals with Rich.

80-761, 11,121

Numerical List of Reports and Documents:

The *CIS US Serial Set Index's* Numerical List of Reports and Documents cites in numerical order all reports and documents issued during a Congressional session in the following sequence:

> Senate reports
> House reports
> Senate documents
> House documents.

Senate reports 80-665 and 671, which were considered above, appear in the Numerical List as seen in figure 5-3.

Figure 5-3

CIS US Serial Set Index, Part XI
Numerical List of Reports and Documents

80th Congress, 1st Session (1947)
Senate Reports

No.	Vol.	Serial
665. Financial records and procedures of Federal Public Housing Authority	4	11117
666. Include under civil service retirement system personnel of national farm loan associations	4	11117
667. Conveyance to Delaware of portion of Pea Patch Island	4	11117
668. District court of Arkansas to hear claims arising out of deaths of Norman R. Pedron and Carl F. Morris	4	11117
669. Incorporating Franco-American War Veterans	4	11117
670. Incorporating Catholic War Veterans of United States of America	4	11117
671. Relief of Lewis H. Rich	4	11117
672. Relief of J. Rutledge Alford	4	11117

The volume number "4" printed to the left of the Serial Set indication in figure 5-3 is irrelevant to library users. This indicates that volume 11,117 was the fourth issued in the Senate report series during the Eightieth Congress, first session. When report and document numbers are known, use this finding aid to locate Serial Set volume numbers, rather than the Index of Subjects and Keywords or the Private Relief and Related Actions section.

Schedule of Serial Volumes:

The Schedule of Serial Volumes lists Serial Set volumes in numerical order, indicating publications included in each volume. When a volume consists of five or fewer titles, each is cited. Otherwise, only the relevant numerical sequences are given. The entry for volume 11,117, the one discussed above, is reproduced in figure 5-4.

Figure 5-4

CIS US Serial Set Index, Part XI
Schedule of Serial Volumes

80th Congress, 1st Session
Jan. 3, 1947-Dec. 19, 1947

Serial	Vol.	JOURNALS
11112	-	Senate Journal, 80th Congress, 1st session
11113	-	House Journal, 80th Congress, 1st session
		SENATE REPORTS
11114	1	Miscellaneous Senate Reports: 1-160
11115	2	Miscellaneous Senate Reports: 161-370
11116	3	Miscellaneous Senate Report: 371-570
11117	4	Miscellaneous Senate Reports: 571-809

Reproduced with permission from *CIS US Serial Set Index,* published and copyrighted by Congressional Information Service, Inc., 4520 East-West Highway, Washington, D.C. 20014.

CIS US Serial Set on Microfiche:

All reports and documents indexed in the *CIS US Serial Set Index* are available on microfiche from the Congressional Information Service. Citations are arranged in numerical order by Serial Set volume numbers and are subdivided by report and document numbers. This fiche collection, the *CIS US Serial Set on Microfiche,* is comparable to the complete Serial Set located in the five libraries mentioned above. Reprints of executive documents unavailable for general distribution since 1913 are included among the fiche.

Numerical List and Schedule of Volumes:

The *Numerical List and Schedule of Volumes,* compiled annually under the direction of the Superintendent of Documents since 1933-34, is an important reference tool which facilitates use of the Serial Set. It is arranged in two parts, the Numerical Lists and the Schedule of Volumes. This source is used to ascertain Serial Set volume numbers by researchers who already have report and/or document numbers. The *Numerical List and Schedule of Volumes* is of special value for locating publications issued since 1970 because the indexes to reports and documents considered in chapters 3 and 4 fail to give Serial Set volume numbers. For instance, figures 3-1, 5, 6, 9, 10, and 11, and 4-7 and 9 all cite Senate report 94-749. Knowing the report number, consult the Numerical Lists section to discover the Serial Set volume. (figure 5-5)

Figure 5-5

Numerical Lists and Schedules of Volumes,
94th Congress, 2nd session
Numerical Lists

747.	Grain inspection reform act of 1976	1–3; 13130–3
748.	Disapprove regulations proposed by Administrator of General Services under sec. 104, Presidential recordings and materials preservation act	1–3; 13130–3
749.	Housing amendments of 1976	1–3; 13130–3
750.	Waive sec. 303(a), Congressional Budget act with respect to consideration of conference report on H.R. 8325	1–3; 13130–3
751.	Reorganization of National Credit Union Administration	1–3; 13130–3
752.	GAO audits of Internal Revenue Service and Bureau of Alcohol, Tobacco and Firearms	1–3; 13130–3

Refer to figure 5-5 when answering the following question:

Senate Report 94-749 is located in serial volume _____ .

13,130-3

The "1-3," which appears in figure 5-5 at the left of the serial volume number and in figure 5-6 along the left hand column, is irrelevant to researchers. The code indicates that volume 13,130-3 was the third one issued as part of the series of Senate miscellaneous reports on public bills during this Congressional session. The initial group of serial volumes for a given session are reserved for these reports.

The identical serial volume number is also listed in the Schedule of Volumes section. (figure 5-6)

Figure 5-6

Numerical List and Schedule of Volumes,
94th Congress, 2nd Session
Schedule of Volumes

SENATE REPORTS

			Serial no.
Vol.	1–1.	Nos. 589–590, 592–596, 598–605, 617–632, 634, 637–677: **Miscellaneous reports on public bills. I**	13130–1
Vol.	1–2.	Nos. 678–689, 691–716: **Miscellaneous reports on public bills. II**	13130–2
Vol.	1–3.	Nos. 717–729, 731–754, 756–769: **Miscellaneous reports on public bills. III**	13130–3
Vol.	1–4.	Nos. 770–778, 780–781, 789–825, 828–836: **Miscellaneous reports on public bills. IV**	13130–4
Vol.	1–5.	Nos. 837–879: **Miscellaneous reports on public bills. V**	13130–5

Additionally, the Schedule of Volumes indicates the volumes containing executive reports which are unavailable for general distribution. (figure 5-7)

Figure 5-7
Numerical Lists and Schedule of Volumes,
94th Congress, 2nd Session
Schedule of Volumes—statement of volumes
unavailable for general distribution

> Note.—The documents listed below originated in executive departments and agencies. They were or will be furnished to depository libraries and international exchanges at the time of printing in the format used by the departments and agencies. They will not be furnished as Congressional documents nor in the volumes as indicated hereby.

Vol.	9.	No. 334: Economic report of the President, Jan. 1976	13153
Vol.	10–1.	No. 343: Budget, fiscal 1977	13154–1
Vol.	10–2.	No. 344: Appendix to budget, fiscal 1977	13154–2
Vol.	11.	No. 345: Annual report of American Historical Association, 1974	13155
Vol.	12.	Nos. 346, 348, 408, 415, 541, 612: Annual reports of Department of Housing and Urban Development, 1974, National Advisory Council on International Monetary and Financial Policies, Department of Housing and Urban Development, National Science Foundation, Aeronautics and Space Activities, Department of Transportation, 1975	13156

Further Information About The Serial Set:

Two significant sources provide detailed information about the development and current status of the Serial Set. The *CIS US Serial Set Index, 1789-1969: User Handbook* is a brief, but very informative pamphlet. It describes the Serial Set's history in detail and illustrates how the *Serial Set Index* is used. Sample pages from the *Index* are reproduced. Another fine reference is Laurence F. Schmeckebier's *Government Publications and Their Use.* This source emphasizes the history of the Serial Set.

Index of Congressional Committee Hearings
(Not Confidential In Character):

The *Index of Congressional Committee Hearings (Not Confidential In Character)* was first printed in 1935. That edition indexed all hearings in the Senate Library published prior to 1935. A second volume, the *Cumulative Index of Congressional Committee Hearings (Not Confidential In Character): From Seventy-Fourth Congress (January 3, 1935) Through Eighty-Fifth Congress (January 3, 1959) In The United States Senate Library,* appeared in 1959. Six supplements to these documents have since been issued.

Quadrennial Supplement To Cumulative Index of Congressional Committee Hearings covers 1959-1962.[2]

Second Quadrennial Supplement covers 1963-1966.[3]

Third Quadrennial Supplement covers 1967-1970.[4]

Fourth Quadrennial Supplement covers 1971-1974.[5]

Fifth Supplement covers 1975-1976.[6]

Sixth Supplement covers 1977-1978.[7]

In each edition, hearings are listed by subjects, committees and bill numbers.

The hearings published prior to 1969 are available in the Congressional Information Service's *U.S. Congressional Committee Hearings on Microfiche.* The fiche for those materials dated prior to 1939 are of particular importance because the Government Printing Office did not distribute hearings as depository items until then.

Subject Index:

The Subject Index is based upon keywords from the titles of hearings. To locate hearings pertaining to a subject or an agency consult this index. Relevant information pertaining to the Federal Public Housing Authority, the agency about which you are seeking information, is reproduced in figure 5-8.

Figure 5-8

Index of Congressional Committee Hearings,
January 3, 1935-January 3, 1959
Subject Index

Subject and Committee	Date	Bill or Resolution	Congress	Senate Library	
				Volume	Tab No.
Federal Public Housing Authority.					
H. To Investigate Disposition of Surplus Property.	Nov.-Dec. 1946	H. Res. 385	79th	H. 1116	1
Federal reclamation. (*See* Reclamation.)					
Federal Register Act:					
Amend.					
H. Judiciary.	Feb. 21, 1936	H.R. 10932, 11337	74th	H. 765	
Federal regulatory commissions:					
Effect on small business.					
H. Select Small Business:					
Pt. 1 (FTC)	July 18-27, 1956				
Pt. 2 (FPC)	July 28, 1955	H. Res. 114	84th	H. 1568	
Pts. 3-5 (FCC), (CAB), (SEC)	Mar. 26-July 20, 1956				

Refer to figure 5-8 when answering the following questions:

The first citation lists relevant hearings held by the ___(House/Senate)___

Select Committee To _____

_____

House, Investigate Disposition of
Surplus Property

These hearings took place during _____ and

_____, _____
(year)

November and December, 1946

They were held in relation to House Resolution _____

introduced during the _____ Congress.

 385, 79th

Volume H 1116, Tab no. 1, indicated under "Federal Public Housing Authority" at the far right in figure 5-8, is the Senate Library's classification number for this hearing. The collection of *US Congressional Committee Hearings on Microfiche* is accessed through this number.

Committee Indexes:

The second section of the *Index of Congressional Committee Hearings* lists hearings by committee names. Those held by Senate, House, and joint, select and special committees are cited in three separate lists. Each one is arranged alphabetically by names of committees, and within each committee, publications are arranged alphabetically by keywords from titles. The identical hearing seen in figure 5-8 is listed under "Hearings before House Select Committee to Investigate Disposition of Surplus Property." (figure 5-9)

Figure 5-9

Index of Congressional Committee Hearings,
January 3, 1935-January 3, 1959
Hearings before House Select Committee on —

Subject and Committee	Date	Bill or Resolution	Congress	Senate Library	
				Volume	Tab No.
Hearings before House Select Committee to Investigate—					
SURPLUS PROPERTY, DISPOSITION OF					
Surplus property: Disposition, investigation:					
Pt. 1	July 12–Sept. 6, 1946	H. Res. 385	79th	H. 1114	1
Pts. 3, 4	Sept. 23–Nov. 19, 1946	do	79th	H. 1115	1
Pts. 4, 5	November–December, 1946	do	79th	H. 1116	1

Refer to figure 5-9 when answering the following questions:

The hearings described in figure 5-8 were parts _____ and _____ in its

series.

 4 and 5

Part 1 was held between _____ and _____, _____ and is
                                                         (year)

available on microfiche H. _____, section _____.

 July 12 and September 6, 1946
 H. 1114, section 1

Parts 3 and 4 were held between _____ and

_____ , _____ and are available on
(year)
microfiche _____, section _____.

       September 23 and November 19, 1946
       H. 1115, section 1

According to figure 5-9, is part 2 of this series available in the Senate Library?

       No

The final question illustrates a significant point. As comprehensive as the Senate Library is, it does not include a complete set of all hearings. This is especially true for those held prior to 1935. To compensate for this, CIS published a *Supplement* to the original volume. This reference tool is described below.

Index By Bill Numbers:

The Index by Bill Numbers lists bills and resolutions in numerical order by Congresses and indicates the Senate Library's classification numbers for hearings pertaining to the proposed legislation. The hearings discussed above, which relate to House Resolution 385 introduced in the seventy-ninth Congress, are illustrated as seen in figure 5-10.

Figure 5-10

Index of Congressional Committee Hearings,
January 3, 1935-January 3, 1959
Index by Bill Numbers

Bill or Resolution	Senate Library	
	Volume	Tab No.
79th Cong.		
H. Res.		
75............	H. 1120	7
88............	{H. 1084	....
	{H. 1107	3
98............	H. 1108	4
154...........	{H. 1088	2
	{H. 1123	1
155...........	H. 1108	1
	{H. 1068	....
	{H. 1079	....
192...........	{H. 1121	1
	{H. 1122	1
195...........	{H. 1062	1
	{H. 1074	1
215...........	H. 1056	9
236...........	{H. 1099	2
	{H. 1120	2
272...........	H. 1111	4
325...........	H. 1117	9
353...........	}H. 1086	10
356...........		
	{H. 1114	1
385...........	{H. 1115	1
	{H. 1116	1
406...........	H. 1092	1
485...........	H. 1091	1
645...........	H. 1107	5

**Supplement To The Index of Congressional
Committee Hearings Prior To 1935:**

The *Supplement To The Index of Congressional Committee Hearings Prior To 1935* indexes hearings omitted from the basic *Index.* Access is by subjects, committee names, and bill numbers. Entry numbers in this volume differ from those in the bibliography described above. An alphanumeric code designates names of committees, Congresses, and specific hearings held by the committees during the indicated Congresses. For instance, "SD 57-C" represents the third hearing held by the Senate Committee on the District of Columbia during the fifty-seventh Congress. Most titles indexed are available in the collection of committee hearings on microfiche. The supplementary fiche follow in alphanumeric sequence the numbered ones noted in the *Indexes of Congressional Committee Hearings.* An Addendum to the *Supplement* lists the selected hearings which were unavailable for filming, informing researchers of the existence of the information.

CIS U.S. Congressional Committee Hearings Index:

The *Indexes to Congressional Committee Hearings (Not Confidential In Character)* will soon be superseded by a new series published by the Congressional Information Service, the *CIS U.S. Congressional Committee Hearings Index.* This new index will provide access to the identical publications cited in the earlier indexes, plus additional hearings located in selected research libraries throughout the nation. All materials included in the *Committee Hearings Index* will be available from CIS on microfiche. The *Hearings Index* will be issued in reverse chronological order in eight parts:

Part I	Earliest Hearings through 63rd Congress, early 1800's-1914.
Part II	64th - 68th Congresses, December 1915-March 1925.
Part III	69th - 73rd Congresses, December 1925-1934.
Part IV	74th - 79th Congresses, 1935-1946.
Part V	80th - 82nd Congresses, 1947-1952.
Part VI	83rd - 85th Congresses, 1953-1958.
Part VII	86th - 88th Congresses, 1959-1964.
Part VIII	89th - 91st Congress, 1st session, 1965-1969.

To date, Part VIII is the only one to have been issued. The series will be completed in 1985.

Each part of the *Committee Hearings Index* will have six indexes:

1. Index by Subjects and Organizations.

2. Index by Personal Names.

3. Index by Titles.

4. Index by Bill Numbers.

5. Index by Superintendent of Documents Classification Numbers.

6. Index by Report and Document Numbers.

The Reference Bibliography section of each part cites bibliographic information. Both the indexes and the Reference Bibliography are described below.

Index by Subjects and Organizations, Subject Approach:

In addition to subject headings which reflect contents of hearings, the Index by Subjects and Organizations also includes special terms, such as glossaries and bibliographies, and official and popular names of laws and bills. To locate information relating to public housing, consult appropriate subject headings in the Index by Subjects and Organizations. (figure 5-11)

Figure 5-11

CIS U.S. Congressional Committee Hearings Index, Part VIII
Index by Subjects and Organizations
Subject Approach

Public housing
    Elderly, comprehensive care through integration of existing public
      and private programs, Atlanta, Ga
      (90) S1983-1-B
    Elderly, comprehensive care through integration of existing public
      and private programs, Syracuse, N.Y.
      (90) S1983-1-A
    Elderly Mexican-Amers, Fed community services coordination and
      delivery
      (90) S1983-2-D
    Elderly Mexican-Amers, Fed community services coordination and
      delivery by local agencies, El Paso, Tex
      (90) S1983-2-B
    Elderly Mexican-Amers, Fed community·services coordination and
      delivery by local agencies, Los Angeles, Calif
      (90) S1983-2-A
    Elderly Mexican-Amers, Fed community services coordination and
      delivery by local agencies, San Antonio, Tex
      (90) S1983-2-C
    Fed aid to school dists with public housing
      (91) S1975-6
1 ————Housing assistance and urban renewal programs, authorization
2 ———— *(89) H2048-4-A; (89) H2048-4-B*

Reproduced with permission from *CIS US Congressional Committee Hearings Index,* published and copyrighted by Congressional Information Service, Inc., 4520 East-West Highway, Washington, D.C. 20014.

1. Content notations.
2. Reference Bibliography number.

Content notations describe the kind of information the hearings contain, and reference bibliography numbers are used to locate bibliographic information in the Reference Bibliography section.

Reference Bibliography Section:

Entry number "(89) H2048-4-A," which appears under "Housing assistance and urban renewal programs, authorization" in figure 5-11, is reproduced below for illustrative purposes. (figure 5-12)

Figure 5-12
CIS U.S. Congressional Hearings Index, Part VIII
Reference Bibliography

(89) H2048-4-A

1. ————— HOUSING AND URBAN DEVELOPMENT
   ACT OF 1965. Part 1
2. ————— Mar. 25, 26, 29-31, 1965. 89-1. v+580 p. —————— 4.
   ————— Y4.B22/1:H81/40/pt.1.   └————————————————3.
5. —————

Considers H.R. 5840 and related H.R. 6501, to authorize rent
supplements for elderly and handicapped, to extend FHA mortgage insurance, and to authorize grants for low rent public housing and urban renewal.

Committee: House Committee on Banking and Currency

Subcommittee: House Subcommittee on Housing

Subject descriptors: Rent supplements; Urban development;
Public housing; Open space land programs; Urban
beautification; Mortgages; Property insurance; Federal aid to
housing; Housing and Urban Development Act

Bills: (89) H.R. 5840; (89) H.R. 6501; [(89) H.R. 5841;
(89) H.R. 6284; (89) H.R. 6399; (89) H.R. 6623;
(89) H.R. 6740; (89) H.R. 6826]

Witnesses:
Bertsch, Howard, Administrator, FmHA, USDA, p. 300.
Carstenson, Blue A., dir, Sr Members Council, Natl Farmers
Union, p. 376.
Cavanagh, Jerome P., mayor, Detroit, Mich, p. 517.
Edelman, John W., pres, Natl Council of Sr Citizens, p. 365.
Keith, Nathaniel S., pres, Natl Housing Conf, p. 319.
Padula, Arthur H., builder, Newark, N.J., p. 405.
Robbins, Ira S., pres, Natl Assn of Housing & Redev
Officials, p. 425.

Reproduced with permission from *CIS US
Congressional Committee Hearings Index*, published and copyrighted by Congressional Information Service, Inc., 4520 East-West Highway,
Washington, D.C. 20014.

1. Title.
2. Dates of hearing.
3. Congress and session.

4. Pagination.
5. Superintendent of Documents number.

Refer to figure 5-12 when answering the following:

The title of this hearing is ————————————————————

————————————————— .

*Housing and Urban Development Act of 1965,
Part 1*

It was held in March 1965 before the House Committee on

————————— and ————————— , Subcommittee on

————————— .

Banking and Currency, Subcommittee on Housing.

The SuDoc number for this document is _____ .

Y4.B22/1:H81/40/Pt. 1

The "subject descriptors" in figure 5-12 indicate alternate subject headings under which the identical hearing is indexed, permitting researchers to locate related materials under the additional terms. The "Bills" section of figure 5-12 lists relevant bills relating to the hearing. Under "Witnesses" in the same illustration, the names of witnesses, their affiliations, and the pages on which their testimonies begin are noted.

Index by Personal Names:

The Index by Personal Names cites the names of witnesses who had testified before Congressional hearings, the names of personal authors whose work had been inserted into hearings, and the names of individuals who are considered as subjects. Suppose you were attempting to locate testimony presented by John W. Edelman, President of the National Council of Senior Citizens, regarding housing assistance, you would consult his name in the Index by Personal Names. (figure 5-13)

Figure 5-13

CIS U.S. Congressional Committee Hearings Index, Part VIII
Index by Personal Names

Edelman, John W.
Aged, future problems examination
(90) S1895-1
Antipoverty programs impact on elderly
(89) S1672-3-A.
(89) S1739-1
Credit finance charges disclosure; govt
emergency power to regulate credit
(90) H2300-1-B
DC minimum wage increase and coverage
expansion
(89) H2245-2.
(89) S1682-4
Health care services and costs for the
elderly, review
(90) S1800-4

Housing assistance and urban renewal
programs, authorization
(89) H2048-4-A
Older Amers Act programs expansion
(90) H2285-2.
(90) S1819-2

In figure 5-13, underline the entry that refers you back to figure 5-12.

Figure 5-12 tells you that Edelman's testimony begins on page

_____.

365

Index by Subjects and Organizations, Organization Approach:

The Index by Subjects and Organizations not only lists subject headings, but also cites names of organizations as affiliations of witnesses, as subjects, and as authors of materials which had been inserted into hearings. Organization entries are also included under names of Congressional committees and their subcommittees. If you were interested in studying the position taken by the National Council of Senior Citizens on housing assistance, but did not know Edelman represented the group at a hearing, consult the Index by Subjects and Organizations. (figure 5-14)

Figure 5-14
CIS U.S. Congressional Committee Hearings Index, Part VIII
Index by Subjects and Organizations
Organization approach

National Council of Senior Citizens
Age discrimination in employment, prohibition
(90) S1793-4
Aged, future problems examination
(90) S1895-1
Antipoverty programs impact on elderly
(89) S1672-3-A;   (89) S1739-1

Hearing loss among the aged; hearing aid industry alleged
improprieties
(90) S1895-2
Housing assistance and urban renewal programs, authorization
(89) H2048-4-A
Manpower employment programs review and additional manpower
programs funding
(91) S2096-1
Medicare Alert, elderly poor assistance needs and programs
(89) S1739-4

Underline the relevant entry which refers to Edelman's statement.

Supplementary Indexes:

The *CIS U.S. Congressional Committee Hearings Index* has four additional indexes which supplement those for subjects and organizations, and personal names:

1. Index by Titles.

2. Index by Bill Numbers.

3. Index by Superintendent of Documents Classification Numbers.

4. Index by Report and Document Numbers.

Hearings are arranged alphabetically by titles in the Index by Titles. The document seen in figure 5-12 appears in this index as follows: (figure 5-15)

Figure 5-15

CIS U.S. Congressional Committee Hearings Index, Part VIII
Index by Titles

Housing and Urban Development Act of 1965.
Part 1
(89) H2048-4-A
Housing and Urban Development Act of 1965.
Part 2
(89) H2048-4-B
Housing and Urban Development
Legislation—1969
(91) H2449-3
Housing and Urban Development Legislation
and Urban Insurance. Part 1
(90) H2337-3-A
Housing and Urban Development Legislation
and Urban Insurance. Part 2
(90) H2337-3-B

Reproduced with permission from *CIS US Congressional Committee Hearings Index*, published and copyrighted by Congressional Information Service, Inc., 4520 East-West Highway, Washington, D.C. 20014.

The Index by Bill Numbers is arranged by Congress, and within each Congress numerically by bill numbers, first by House bills and then by Senate bills. H.R. 5840, among other related bills, refers to the document reproduced in figure 5-12. (figure 5-16)

Figure 5-16

CIS U.S. Congressional Committee Hearings Index, Part VIII
Index by Bill Numbers

(89) H.R. 5811	(89) H2154-3
(89) H.R. 5812	(89) H2154-3
(89) H.R. 5813	(89) H2154-3
(89) H.R. 5840	(89) H2048-4-A
(89) H.R. 5840	(89) H2048-4-B
(89) H.R. 5840	(89) H2148-6
(89) H.R. 5841	(89) H2048-4-A
(89) H.R. 5858	(89) H2239-0-I
(89) H.R. 5863	(89) H2150-4
(89) H.R. 5869	(89) H2124-1
(89) H.R. 5876	(89) H2129-4

Reproduced with permission from *CIS US Congressional Committee Hearings Index*, published and copyrighted by Congressional Information Service, Inc., 4520 East-West Highway, Washington, D.C. 20014.

Refer to figure 5-16 when answering the following question:

Reference Bibliography citations to two additional hearings other than that seen in figure 5-12 pertain to H.R. 5840. Their Reference Bibliography numbers are _____ and _____.

(89) H2048-4-B and (89) H2148-6

The Index by Superintendent of Documents Numbers is arranged in alphanumeric sequence according to SuDoc numbers. (figure 5-17)

Figure 5-17

CIS U.S. Congressional Committee Hearings Index, Part VIII
Index by Superintendent of Documents Numbers

	(91) H2506-1
Y4.B22/1:G81	Proposed World Bank Loan to NIBID of Greece
	(90) H2313-6
Y4.B22/1:H81/40/pt.1	Housing and Urban Development Act of 1965. Part 1
	(89) H2048-4-A
Y4.B22/1:H81/40/pt.2	Housing and Urban Development Act of 1965. Part 2
	(89) H2048-4-B
Y4.B22/1:H81/45	To Amend and Extend Laws Relating to Housing and Urban Development
	(90) H2278-1
Y4.B22/1:H81/46/pt.1	Housing and Urban Development Legislation and Urban Insurance. Part 1
	(90) H2337-3-A

The *CIS U.S. Congressional Committee Hearings Index*, like the *Congressional Committee Hearings (Not Confidential In Character)*, is based for the most part upon holdings in the Senate Library. That Library sometimes binds hearings and their related reports in the same volumes. The Index by Report and Document Numbers lists by Congresses and then by chambers reports and documents which had been bound with hearings. (figure 5-18) Furthermore, during earlier Congresses hearings were sometimes published as reports and/or documents. The Indexes by Report and Documents Numbers covering those time periods will include the pertinent citations.

Figure 5-18

CIS U.S. Congressional Committee Hearings Index, Part VIII
Index by Report and Document Numbers

H. Rpt. 89-2	(89) H2102-1
H. Rpt. 89-37	(89) H2059-1
H. Rpt. 89-51	(89) H2089-1
H. Rpt. 89-131	(89) S1687-B-H
H. Rpt. 89-143	(89) H2072-1
H. Rpt. 89-185	(89) H2108-0
H. Rpt. 89-205	(89) H2110-0

Reproduced with permission from *CIS US
Congressional Committee Hearings Index*, published and copyrighted by Congressional Information Service, Inc., 4520 East-West Highway,
Washington, D.C. 20014.

Further Sources of Congressional Hearings:

*The Checklist of Hearings Before Congressional Committees Through The
Sixty-Seventh Congress* was published in nine parts. Parts one through seven
deal with House Standing Committees; parts eight and nine cover those of the
Senate. The concluding section of part nine incorporates hearings held by joint
special and select committees. It is arranged alphabetically by committees and
within each committee, by Congress. Titles, dates held, dates of publication and
when appropriate, *National Union Catalog* symbols indicating libraries where
the information can be consulted, are provided. This reference tool is not
indexed.

Four additional guides may also be useful. The *Index To Congressional
Committee Hearings In the Library of The House of Representatives Prior to
January 1, 1951* and the *Supplemental Index To Congressional Committee
Hearings January 3, 1949 To January 3, 1955, 81st, 82nd, and 83rd Congresses In
The Library of The United States House of Representatives* are comparable to
the volumes of Senate Library holdings discussed above. *Printed Hearings of the
House of Representatives Found Among Its Committee Records in the National Archives of the United States, 1824-1958* and *Hearings in the Records of
the U.S. Senate and Joint Committees of Congress* are limited to material
located in the National Archives. Both sources are arranged by Congress, then
subdivided by committees, but neither is indexed.

CIS US Congressional Committee Prints Index:

The *CIS US Congressional Committee Prints Index* is the most comprehensive guide to committee prints. Prints are publications the purpose of which is to
serve as background information for Representatives or Senators. These titles
are sometimes draft editions of materials eventually issued as reports or
documents. The various kinds of information available in committee prints include monographic studies, results of investigative activities, analyses of bills,
comparisons of bills to existing law, bibliographies, and directories.

The *Index* includes not only items indicated as being committee prints, but
also "print-like" publications. These consist of materials which fall into neither
the hearings, reports, nor documents series. CIS considers them "print-like"
through a process of elimination, and consequently includes them with titles
specifically labeled as committee prints.

The fifteen thousand publications listed in the *Committee Prints Index* are
available on microfiche in the collection of *US Congressional Committee Prints
on Microfiche*. The materials were reproduced from copies held in the House and

Senate Libraries, the Library of Congress, the National Archives, the Public Documents Library, the Detroit Public Library and House and Senate committee offices. Until the CIS began indexing, abstracting and filming committee prints in its *CIS Index* in 1970 and until the GPO began distributing prints regularly to its depository libraries in the mid-1970's, these publications were relatively inaccessible. The *Congressional Committee Prints Index* and its corresponding fiche collection make prints published between the 1830's and 1969 widely available for the first time.

The *CIS US Congressional Committee Prints Index* was published in five volumes. The Index by Subjects and Names comprises the first two volumes and the Reference Bibliography, which provides full bibliographic data, encompasses volumes three and four. The Index by Titles, the Index by Congress and Committees, the Index by Bill Numbers and the Index by Superintendent of Documents Classification Numbers are included in volume five. These features, plus the Jurisdictional Histories of Standing Committees Represented in the Collection, an Appendix to the fifth volume, are described below.

Index by Subjects and Names:

Information is accessed in the Index by Subjects and Names by subjects, as well as names of authors, issuing committees and subcommittees, and official and popular names of bills and laws. Special subject terms cited include "Bibliographies," "Glossaries," "Statistical data," and "Legislative histories." Ample cross references are cited throughout.

To locate information pertaining to the historical background of Federal involvement in public housing through the 1940's, search the Index of Subjects and Names under relevant headings. Selected entries listed under "Public housing" are reproduced in figure 5-19.

Figure 5-19

CIS US Congressional Committee Prints Index
Index by Subjects and Names

Public housing
    Aged (senior citizens), housing for. Report on
        (87/2/62) S1208
    Aged and aging, studies of: Summary of federal legislation relating to
        older persons
        (84/2/56) S3510
    District of Columbia, defense housing and community facilities for.
        Hearings on H.R. 6483
        (77/2/42) S3559
    District of Columbia public relief, report of investigation of
        (75/3/38) H4977 ——————————————————————3.
  1. ——Federal housing programs. Chronology and brief summary of
        congressional and executive action affecting housing from 1892 to
        Oct. 25, 1949, and description of present programs
  2. —— *(81/2/50) S0353*

1. Title.   3. Reference Bibliography Number.
2. Congress, session, and date.

Refer to figure 5-19 when answering the following questions:

Is a relevant citation listed?

>Yes

This document was issued during the _____ Congress,

_____ session, in _____.

>81st Congress, 2nd session in 1950

This citation is entry number _____ in the Senate/House section of the Reference Bibliography.

>0353, Senate

Refer from the Index by Subjects and Names to the Reference Bibliography to locate more information about this document.

Reference Bibliography:

The Reference Bibliography section provides complete bibliographic information. It is separated into two parts, one for House publications and the other for those issued by the Senate. Citations within each section are preceded by "H" or "S," then listed in numerical sequence. This alphanumeric designation is used for accessing prints in the microfiche collection. Complete titles, subtitles, personal authors, issuing committees and subcommittees, dates, paginations, congresses and sessions, and Superintendent of Documents classification numbers are indicated. All subject headings under which the publications are indexed are also listed. This enables researchers to locate related sources under entries other than those already searched.

The committee print considered in figure 5-19 appears in the Reference Bibliography as seen below. (Figure 5-20)

Figure 5-20
CIS US Congressional Committee Prints Index
Reference Bibliography

1.—— **S0353** Federal housing programs. A chronology and brief summary of
congressional and executive action affecting housing from——2.
1892 to Oct. 25, 1949, and a description of present federal
housing programs [identical to S1740]   .
3.——————— *vi+61 p. Feb. 24, 1950. (81/2/50) Y4.B22/3:H81/24.* ———4.

5.——————— Senate Committee on Banking and Currency;
Senate Subcommittee on Housing and Rents

Federal aid to housing; Public housing; Veterans housing;
Federal Home Loan Bank Board; Federal Housing ————6.
Administration; Public Housing Administration; Housing
and Home Finance Agency; U.S. statutes

1. Reference Bibliography number.
2. Title.
3. Pagination and date.

4. Congress, session, date, and Superintendent of Documents number.
5. Committee and subcommittee.
6. Subject headings.

Refer to figure 5-20 when answering the following:

The primary title of this document is _____

_____.

   Federal Housing Programs

It was published on _____ , _____.

   February 24, 1950

Its SuDoc number is _____ .

   Y4.B22/3:H81/24

It was published by the Senate Subcommittee on _____ and

_____ , which is part of the Senate Committee on

_____ and _____ .

   Housing and Rents, Banking and
   Currency

This print has _____ introductory pages which are followed by _____

pages of text.

   6, 61

The identical document, plus related ones, can be located in the Index by Subjects and Names under many subject headings.

Selected ones include "Federal aid to _____," and "Veterans

_____."

   housing, housing

Index by Titles:

Use this Index, rather than the one for Subjects and Names when titles of prints are known. The print in figure 5-20 is listed in the Index by Titles as seen in figure 5-21.

Figure 5-21

CIS US Congressional Committee Prints Index
Index by Titles

Federal Home Loan Bank Board and Federal Savings and Loan
  Insurance Corporation. A study of relationships. Staff report
  (84/2/56)   S0158
Federal housing programs. A chronology and brief summary of
  congressional and executive action affecting housing from 1892 to
  Oct. 25, 1949, and a description of present federal housing programs
  (81/2/50)   S0353,   S1740
Federal housing programs. Chronology and description
  (80/2/48)   S1741
Federal income tax treatment of capital gains and losses. Supplement
  to statement by Secretary of Treasury on Tax Revision Act of 1951,
  H.R. 4473, before the Committee on Finance on June 28, 1951.
  Prepared by the Tax Advisory Staff of the Secretary, Treasury
  Department
  (82/1/51)   S1489

Index by Congress and Committees:

The Index by Congress and Committees lists committee prints in
chronological order by Congress. Within each Congress, the titles are separated
by committees. *Federal Housing Programs,* the citation analyzed above, appears
in this Index as seen in figure 5-22.

Figure 5-22

CIS US Congressional Committee Prints Index
Index by Congress and Committees

81st CONGRESS, 1949-1951

Senate Committee on Banking and Currency
  Conference on section 608. Report upon section 608, title VI,
  National Housing Act
  (81/2/50)   S1666
Cooperative housing in Europe
  (81/2/50)   S2227
Federal housing programs. A chronology and brief summary of
  congressional and executive action affecting housing from 1892 to
  Oct. 25, 1949, and a description of present federal housing
  programs
  (81/2/50)   S0353,   S1740
Housing Act of 1949, what it is and how it works
  (81/1/49)   S2226

Index By Superintendent of Document Numbers:

Documents are listed in alphanumeric sequence according to their Superintendent of Documents classification numbers. Reference Bibliography notations follow each SuDoc number. Approximately half of the titles included in the *Committee Prints Index* have Superintendent of Document numbers.

Index By Bill Numbers:

Committee prints relate frequently to specific bills. The Index by Bill Numbers lists bills by Congresses and then indicates Reference Bibliography citations to relevant committee prints. (figure 5-23)

Figure 5-23

CIS US Congressional Committee Prints Index
Index by Bill Numbers

81st CONGRESS, 1949-1951 Senate	
(81) S. Con. Res. 107	H7875
(81) S.J. Res. 11	H4881
(81) S.J. Res. 135	H4721
(81) S. Res. 243	S3360
(81) S. 75	H3954
(81) S. 266	H7662
(81) S. 372	H7557
(81) S. 526	S4218
(81) S. 578	H7603

Reproduced with permission from *CIS US Congressional Committee Prints Index,* published and copyrighted by Congressional Information Service, Inc. 4520 East-West Highway, Washington, D.C. 20014.

Jurisdictional Histories:

Histories and responsibilities of committees whose publications are included in the *Committee Prints Index* are given in the Jurisdictional Histories section. Entries are arranged alphabetically by names of committees. The information provided includes dates of formation, reorganization, and dissolution; names of subcommittees and predecessor committees, and charges which the committees are required to meet. This section contributes toward an understanding of functional interrelationships among committees. After locating names of committees which oversee various issues, researchers can search the Index by Subjects and Names under the committee names to locate pertinent references.

**Further Information About Committee Prints
and the CIS US Congressional Committee Prints Index:**

The "Introduction" to the *Prints Index* includes a detailed history of committee prints, plus illustrations from the Reference Bibliography, the indexes, and the Jurisdictional Histories section. *An Introduction To Congressional Commmittee Prints and The CIS US Congressional Committee Prints Index From The Earliest Publications Through 1969,* a brief pamphlet available from CIS, is a reprint of the above.

Chapter 5 Footnotes

[1] *The Debates and Proceedings In The Congress of The United States With An Appendix Containing Important State Papers and Public Documents and All The Laws of A Public Nature With Copious Index.* 13th Cong., 1st sess. (December 8, 1813), p. 784.

[2] *Quadrennial Supplement To Cumulative Index of Congressional Committee Hearings (Not Confidential In Character) From Eighty-Sixth Congress (January 7, 1959) Through Eighty-Seventh Congress (January 3, 1963) Together With Selected Committee Prints In The United States Senate Library.* Comp. and indexed by Mary F. Sterrett (Washington, D.C.: GPO, 1963).

[3] *Cumulative Index of Congressional Committee Hearings (Not Confidential In Character): Second Quadrennial Supplement From Eighty-Eighth Congress (January 3, 1963) Through Eighty-Ninth Congress (January 3, 1967) Together With Selected Committee Prints In The United States Senate Library.* Comp. under direction of Francis R. Valeo, Secretary of The Senate (Washington, D.C.: GPO, 1967).

[4] *Cumulative Index of Congressional Committee Hearings (Not Confidential In Character): Third Quadrennial Supplement From Ninetieth Congress (January 10, 1967), Through Ninety-First Congress (January 2, 1971) Together With Selected Committee Prints In The United States Senate Library.* Comp. under direction of Francis R. Valeo, Secretary of The Senate (Washington, D.C.: GPO, 1971).

[5] *Cumulative Index of Congressional Committee Hearings (Not Confidential In Character): Fourth Quadrennial Supplement From Ninety-Second Congress (January 21, 1971) Through Ninety-Third Congress (December 20, 1974) In The United States Senate Library.* Comp. under direction of Francis R. Valeo, Secretary of The Senate (Washington, D.C.: GPO, 1976).

[6] *Cumulative Index of Congressional Committee Hearings (Not Confidential In Character): Fifth Supplement Ninety-Fourth Congress (January 14, 1975 Through October 1, 1976) In The United States Senate Library.* Comp. under direction of Francis R. Valeo (Washington, D.C.: GPO, ?).

[7] *Cumulative Index of Congressional Committee Hearings (Not Confidential In Character): Sixth Supplement Ninety-Fifth Congress (January 4, 1977 Through October 15, 1978) In The United States Senate Library.* Comp. under direction of William F. Hildenbrand, Secretary of The Senate (Washington, D.C.: GPO, ?).

BIBLIOGRAPHY

American State Papers. Documents, Legislative and Executive of the Congress of the United States. Ed. under authority of Congress. Washington, D.C.: Gales and Seaton, 1832-1861. 38 vols.

Checklist of Hearings Before Congressional Committees Through The Sixty-Seventh Congress. Comp. by Harold O. Thomen. Reference Department. General Reference and Bibliography Division. Washington, D.C.: Library of Congress, 1957-1959.

CIS Congressional Bills, Resolutions and Laws on Microfiche. Washington, D.C.: Congressional Information Service, Inc., ?.

CIS Index To Publications of The United States Congress. Washington, D.C.: Congressional Information Service, Inc., 1970-monthly.

CIS U.S. Congressional Committee Hearings Index. Washington, D.C.: Congressional Information Service, Inc., 1981-1985? 8 parts.

CIS US Congressional Committee Prints Index From the Earliest Publications Through 1969. Washington, D.C.: Congressional Information Service, Inc., 1980. 5 vols.

CIS US Serial Set Index. Washington, D.C.: Congressional Information Service, Inc., 1975-1979. 12 parts.

CIS US Serial Set Index, 1789-1969. Users Handbook. Washington, D.C.: Congressional Information Service, Inc., 1980.

CIS U.S. Serial Set on Microfiche. Washington, D.C.: Congressional Information Service, Inc., 1975-1979.

Cumulative Index of Congressional Committee Hearings (Not Confidential In Character): Fifth Supplement Ninety-Fourth Congress (January 14, 1975 Through October 1, 1976) In The United States Senate Library. Comp. under direction of Francis R. Valeo. Washington, D.C.: GPO, ?.

Cumulative Index of Congressional Committee Hearings (Not Confidential In Character): Fourth Quadrennial Supplement From Ninety-Second Congress (January 21, 1971) Through Ninety-Third Congress (December 20, 1974) In The United States Senate Library. Comp. under direction of Francis R. Valeo. Washington, D.C.: GPO, 1976.

Cumulative Index of Congressional Committee Hearings (Not Confidential In Character) From Seventy-Fourth Congress (January 3, 1935) Through Eighty-Fifth Congress (January 3, 1959) In The United States Senate Library. Indexed and comp. under direction of Felton M. Johnston. Washington, D.C.: GPO, 1959.

Cumulative Index of Congressional Committee Hearings (Not Confidential In Character): Second Quadrennial Supplement From Eighty-Eighth Congress (January 3, 1963) Through Eighty-Ninth Congress (January 3, 1967) Together With Selected Committee Prints In The United States Senate Library. Comp. under direction of Francis R. Valeo. Washington, D.C.: GPO, 1967.

Cumulative Index of Congressional Committee Hearings (Not Confidential In Character): Sixth Supplement Ninety-Fifth Congress (January 4, 1977 Through October 15, 1978) In The United States Senate Library. Comp. under direction of William F. Hildenbrand. Washington, D.C.: GPO, ?

Cumulative Index of Congressional Committee Hearings (Not Confidential In Character): Third Quadrennial Supplement From Ninetieth Congress (January 10, 1967) Through Ninety-First Congress (January 2, 1971) Together With Selected Committee Prints In The United States Senate Library. Comp. under direction of Francis R. Valeo. Washington, D.C.: GPO, 1971.

Government Publications and Their Use. Laurence F. Schmeckebier and Roy B. Eastin. 2d rev. ed. Washington, D.C.: Brookings Institution, 1969.

GPO Sales Publications Reference File Microform. Superintendent of Documents. Washington, D.C.: GPO, 1977-bimonthly.

Hearings in the Records of The U.S. Senate and Joint Committees of Congress. Comp. by Charles E. South and James C. Brown. Special List No. 32. Washington, D.C.: National Archives and Records Service, 1972.

Index of Congressional Committee Hearings (Not Confidential In Character) Prior to January 3, 1935 In The United States Senate Library. Rev. by James D. Preston et al. Washington, D.C.: GPO, 1935. Reprinted: Westport, Connecticut: Greenwood Publishing Company, 1971.

Index To Congressional Committee Hearings In The Library of The House of Representatives Prior to January 1, 1951. Comp. by Russell Saville. Washington, D.C.: GPO, 1954.

An Introduction To Congressional Committee Prints and The CIS US Congressional Committee Prints Index From The Earliest Publications Through 1969. Washington, D.C.: Congressional Information Service, Inc., 1981.

Monthly Catalog of United States Government Publications. Superintendent of Documents. Washington, D.C.: GPO, 1895-monthly. Title varies.

The National State Papers of The United States: Part II, Texts of Documents (1789-1817). Ed. by Martin P. Claussen. Wilmington, Delaware: Michael Glazier, 1980- .

National Union Catalog Pre-1956 Imprints. Comp. and ed. with the cooperation of the Library of Congress and the National Union Catalog Subcommittee of the Resources Committee of the Resources and Technical Services Division American Library Association. Chicago: Mansell, 1968-1981. 685 vols. plus supplements.

Numerical List and Schedule of Volumes. Superintendent of Documents. Washington, D.C.: GPO, 1934-annual.

Printed Hearings of The House of Representatives Found Among Its Committee Records In The National Archives of The United States, 1824-1958. Comp. by Buford Rowland et al. Special List No. 35. Washington, D.C.: National Archives and Records Service, 1974.

Quadrennial Supplement To Cumulative Index of Congressional Committee Hearings (Not Confidential In Character) From Eighty-Sixth Congress (January 7, 1959) Through Eighty-Seventh Congress (January 3, 1963) Together With Selected Committee Prints In The United States Senate Library. Comp. and indexed by Mary F. Sterrett. Washington, D.C.: GPO, 1963.

Supplemental Index To Congressional Committee Hearings January 3, 1949 To January 3, 1955, 81st, 82d, and 83d Congresses In The Library of The United States House of Representatives. Comp. by John A. Cooper. Washington, D.C.: GPO, 1956.

Supplement To The Index of Congressional Committee Hearings Prior To January 3, 1935 Consisting of Hearings Not Catalogued By The U.S. Senate Library With Subject Index From The Twenty-Fifth Congress, 1839 Through The Seventy-Third Congress, 1934. Comp. by Harold O. Thomen. Westport, Connecticut: Greenwood Press, 1973.

U.S. Congressional Committee Hearings on Microfiche. Washington, D.C.: Congressional Information Service, Inc., 1977- .

U.S. Congressional Committee Prints on Microfiche. Washington, D.C.: Congressional Information Service, Inc., 1980.

CIS U.S. Serial Set Index, Questions:

1. A three part study pertaining to the creation of the Federal Trade Commission was published during the 63rd Congress.

    A. Which part of the *Serial Set Index* would you consult to locate the citation to this study?

    B. Under what subject heading is the study listed?

    C. This study was published during the _____ session.

    D. The information is cited as House __(Report/Document)__ 63-533.

    E. The study was reprinted in Serial Set volume _____.

    F. Without going to the study, do you suspect that it will include a section-by-section analysis of the appropriate bill(s)?

    G. H. Rept. 63-533 is cited on page _____ of the *Serial Set Index's Finding Lists Section.*

Numerical List and Schedule of Volumes, Questions:

2. In which Serial Set volume was House Document 96-148, *National Health Plan,* reprinted?

Index of Congressional Committee Hearings
(Not Confidential in Character), Questions:

3. Hearings were held in 1921 concerning problems of prostitution in the District of Columbia.

    A. The citation is listed in the *Index of Congressional Committee Hearings (Not Confidential in Character)* Prior to _____, page

    _____.

    B. The hearing was held during the _____ Congress, _____ session.

    C. The committee holding these hearings was the _____

    _____ .

    D. _____ is the related bill number.

    E. The hearing is bound in volume _____, part _____.

    F. Part 2 of this *Index* is an alphabetical list of hearings before Senate Committees arranged alphabetically by Committees. On what page does the citation to the hearing in question appear?

G. On what page of the "Index of Senate Hearings by Bill Number" does S. 1616 (67th Congress) appear?

CIS U.S. Congressional Committee Hearings Index, Part VIII, Questions:

4. Locate a Congressional hearing which describes the events surrounding the Gulf of Tonkin incident.

   A. The Reference Bibliography number is _____ .

   B. The title of the hearing is _____

   _____ .

   C. Its SuDoc number is _____.

   D. The only witness to appear at this hearing was _____ ,

   whose testimony begins on page _____.

   E. His name is listed in the Index by Personal Names on pages _____ through _____.

5. A Congressional hearing pertaining to S. 1003 (90th Congress) is cited at Reference Bibliography number _____.

CIS U.S. Congressional Committee Prints Index, Questions:

6. You are attempting to locate information which describes applications of the Apollo program.

   A. What is the Reference Bibliography number of a relevant citation?

   B. The complete title of this committee print is _____

   _____ . _____

   _____ .

   C. Its SuDoc number is _____ .

   D. What Committee and Subcommittee published this document?

   E. On what page of the Index by Titles is this document cited?

CIS U.S. Serial Set Index, Answers:

1. A. Part VII.
   B. Federal Trade Commission.
   C. 2nd session.

    D. House Report 63-533.

    E. 6559

    F. Yes. Reports very often indicate Congressional intent in section-by-section analysis of key bills.

    G. Page 1035.

Numerical List and Schedule of Volumes, Answers:

  2. 13270.

**Index of Congressional Committee Hearings
(Not Confidential in Character), Answers:**

  3. A. 1935, page 399.

    B. 67th Congress, 1st session.

    C. Senate Committee on the District of Columbia.

    D. S. 1616.

    E. Volume 177, part 1. It is important to distinguish Senate volumes from those of the House. Volume 177 is part of the Senate series because the hearing was held by a Senate Committee. Volume 177, part 1, in the House series would include a different hearing. Differentiating between Senate and House volumes is essential when attempting to retrieve microfiche copies of the information. Remember, hearings cited in the *Index of Congressional Committee Hearings (Not Confidential in Character)* have been issued on microfiche by the Congressional Information Service. They are accessed through Senate Library volume numbers.

    F. 572.

    G. 931.

**CIS U.S. Congressional Committee Hearings Index,
Part VIII, Answers:**

  4. A. (90) S1859-9

    B. *Gulf of Tonkin, The 1964 Incident.*

    C. Y4.F76/2:T61

    D. Robert S. McNamara, page 3.

    E. 505 through 506.

  5.(90) S1807-2.

CIS U.S. Committee Prints Index, Answers:

  6. A. H1450.

    B. *Apollo and Apollo Applications. Staff Study on Research and Development Schedules and Progress.*

    C. Y4.Sci2:90-2/M.

    D. House Committee on Science and Astronautics, Subcommittee on NASA Oversight.

    E. Page 15.

CHAPTER 6

INDEXES AND GUIDES TO LEGISLATION
AND REGULATIONS

There are many ways of retrieving Federal laws and regulations. Chapters 3 and 4 described Congressional publications and methods of accessing them. Emphasis was given to the compilation of legislative histories from the introduction of bills through their enactment into laws. This chapter considers basic methods of locating laws and regulations. Regulations are administrative documents issued by executive and independent agencies which have the effect of law. Because it is difficult, if not impossible, for Congress to draft legislation that deals with minute details of all issues, it delegates authority to executive and independent agencies to establish regulations in their appropriate areas.

Five sources which reprint laws will be examined in this chapter:

The *Statutes at Large* (Stat.)

The *United States Code Congressional and Administrative News*

The *United States Code (USC)*

The *United States Code Annotated (USCA)*

The *United States Code Service (USCS)*

Afterwards, two primary sources for regulations, the *Federal Register* and the *Code of Federal Regulations,* will be examined. Two secondary sources, the *Calendar of Federal Regulations* and the *Federal Regulatory Directory* will also be discussed.

Statutes at Large:

The *Statutes at Large* is the official compilation of Federal laws. Volumes 1-17 were published irregularly by a commercial firm between 1789 and 1873. With Volume 18, the State Department assumed responsibility for publication. Between 1873 and 1936, Volumes 18-49 were issued irregularly, some biennially by Congress, while others covered more than one Congress. Since 1937 (Volume 50-current), the *Statutes at Large* has been published annually, by the State Department through 1950 and by the Office of the Federal Register, a division of the General Services Administration, beginning in 1951.

Public laws comprise the largest part of the *Statutes at Large*. Following their enactment, they are first printed as slip laws. Acts are reprinted in consecutive numerical order in the *Statutes at Large* at the termination of a Congressional session. Figure 6-1 illustrates portions of Public Law 94-375, the legislation studied in chapters 3 and 4. Private laws, reorganization plans, concurrent resolutions approved by both houses of Congress and Presidential proclamations are also reprinted in the *Statutes*.

Figure 6-1
Statutes at Large, Volume 90, 1976
Public Law 94-375

PUBLIC LAW 94-375—AUG. 3, 1976   90 STAT. 1067

Public Law 94-375
94th Congress

An Act

To amend and extend laws relating to housing and community development.

Be it enacted by the Senate and House of Representatives of the United States of America in Congress assembled,

SHORT TITLE

SECTION 1. This Act may be cited as the "Housing Authorization Act of 1976".

AMENDMENTS TO THE UNITED STATES HOUSING ACT OF 1937

SEC. 2. (a) Section 5(c) of the United States Housing Act of 1937 is amended—
    (1) by striking out the first sentence and inserting in lieu thereof the following new sentence: "The Secretary is authorized to enter into contracts for annual contributions aggregating not more than $1,524,000,000 per annum, which limit shall be increased by $965,000,000 on July 1, 1974, by $662,300,000 on July 1, 1975, and by $850,000,000 on October 1, 1976, except that the additional authority to enter into contracts for annual contributions provided on or after July 1, 1975, shall be effective only in such amounts as may be approved in appropriation Acts."; and
    (2) by inserting immediately after "on July 1, 1975," in the fourth sentence thereof the following: "and by not less than $17,000,000 per annum on October 1, 1976,".
(b)(1) Effective on October 1, 1976, the second and third sentences of section 5(c) of such Act are amended to read as follows: "Of the

Aug. 3, 1976
[S. 3295]

Housing
Authorization Act
of 1976.

12 USC 1701
note.

Low-income
housing projects,
contracts for
annual
contributions.
42 USC 1437c.

LEGISLATIVE HISTORY:

HOUSE REPORTS: No. 94-545 accompanying H.R. 9852 and No. 94-1091 and No. 94-1091, pt. II, accompanying H.R. 12945 (Comm. on Banking, Currency and Housing) and Nos. 94-1291 and 94-1304 (Comm. of Conference).
SENATE REPORTS: No. 94-520 accompanying H.R. 9852 and No. 94-749 (Comm. on Banking, Housing and Urban Affairs).
CONGRESSIONAL RECORD:
    Vol. 121 (1975): Oct. 20, H.R. 9852 considered and passed House.
    Vol. 122 (1976): Jan. 23, H.R. 9852 considered and passed Senate, amended.
        Apr. 27, considered and passed Senate.
        May 26, considered and passed House, amended, in lieu of H.R. 12945.
        June 30, House agreed to conference report.
        July 20, Senate agreed to conference report.
WEEKLY COMPILATION OF PRESIDENTIAL DOCUMENTS:
    Vol. 12, No. 32 (1976): Aug. 4, Presidential statement.

The marginal notes in figure 6-1 describe briefly the topics considered and refer researchers to the *United States Code,* a subject codification of Federal law. The *Code* is separated into titles which encompass broad subjects. These are subdivided by sections and paragraphs. 42 USC 1437c refers to Title 42, section 1437, paragraph c. The *U.S. Code* is described in more detail below. The legislative histories of public laws have been printed in the *Statutes* since 1963 (Volume 77).[1]

Public laws were not always printed in the *Statutes at Large* in this format. Unlike the present system which numbers public and private laws separately, prior to 1957 both were numbered in the same sequence and were assigned chapter numbers. Through 1935, both kinds of legislation were numbered by session, rather than Congress.

Private laws were defined in chapter 3 as legislation which applies only to specific individuals, rather than to the general public. Figure 6-2 is an example of a private law.

Figure 6-2
Statutes at Large, Volume 90, 1976
Private Laws

Private Law 94–28   90 STAT. 2967
94th Congress

An Act

For the relief of Yong Won Lee.   Feb. 13, 1976
                                                            [H.R. 8907]

Be it enacted by the Senate and House of Representatives of the United States of America in Congress assembled, That, in the administration of the Immigration and Nationality Act, Yong Won Lee may be classified as a child within the meaning of section 101(b)(1)(F) of the Act, upon approval of a petition filed in his behalf by Mr. and Mrs. Melvin Haas, citizens of the United States, pursuant to section 204 of the Act: *Provided,* That the natural parents or brothers or sisters of the beneficiary shall not, by virtue of such relationship, be accorded any right, privilege, or status under the Immigration and Nationality Act.

Yong Won Lee.

8 USC 1101.

8 USC 1154.

SEC. 2. Section 204(c) of the Immigration and Nationality Act, relating to the number of petitions which may be approved, shall be inapplicable in this case.

Approved February 13, 1976.

Refer to figure 6-2 when answering the following questions:

An Act for the relief of Yong Won Lee was the _____ private law enacted by the 94th Congress.

28th

The legislation was approved on _____ , _____

February 13, 1976

It was introduced into the House of Representatives as bill number H.R. _____ .

8907

Three types of information are printed in the *Statutes* following private legislation. Concurrent resolutions, which are described in chapter 3, are listed in chronological order according to the dates on which they were approved. Citations include titles, numbers, dates approved and marginal notations. Reorganization plans, which are also listed in chronological order, are submitted to Congress by the President and automatically become effective after sixty days, unless either house passes resolutions of disapproval. Proclamations, which are arranged in numerical order, are one of two types of Presidential edicts, the other being executive orders. Both are described below.

Indexes:

The *Statutes at Large* has two primary indexes, the Subject Index and the Individual Index. Both are based upon sessions, rather than Congresses, and refer users to page numbers.

Broad subject headings and popular names of legislation are used in the Subject Index. PL 94-375, the Housing Authorization Act of 1976, is indexed as seen in figure 6-3.

Figure 6-3

Statutes at Large, Volume 90, 1976
Subject Index

Subject Approach

Housing:
Air Force, Department of, family
housing—
Appropriation for.................................... 995
Construction and acquisition, au-
thorization.................................... 1359
Army, Department of, family hous-
ing—
Appropriation.................................... 995
Construction and acquisition, au-
thorization.................................... 1359
Coast Guard personnel, leases.............. 2077
Defects, expenditures for correc-
tion.................................... 1072
Flood insurance.................................... 1075
Indian homes and communities,
water and waste disposal facili-
ties, construction.................................... 1407
Low-income housing assistance............ 1067
Military Construction Appropriation
Act, 1977.................................... 993
Military Construction Authorization
Act, 1977.................................... 1349

Popular Name Approach

Housing and Urban Development Act,
Department of, amendments 1077
Housing and Urban Development Act
of 1965, appropriation for effecting
provisions.................................... 1096
Housing and Urban Development Act
of 1968, appropriation for effecting
provisions.................................... 1097
Housing and Urban Development Act
of 1970:
Amendments....................... 1077, 1078, 1162
Appropriation for effecting provi-
sions.................................... 1098
Housing Authorization Act of 1976........ 1067
"How Our Laws Are Made", publica-
tion as House document..................... 3029
Howard University, D.C., appropri-
ation for.................................... 611, 1431

In both parts of figure 6-3, underline relevant citations referring you to that legislation, 90 Stat. 1067 or Volume 90, page 1067.

The Individual Index lists names of individuals who are affected by private legislation. Yong Won Lee's name, referred to in private law 94-28 (figure 6-2), is seen as follows. (figure 6-4)

Figure 6-4
Statutes at Large, Volume 90, 1976
Individual Index

Webb, James E.	693
West, Sol, III	2996
Whalen, Louise G.	2974
Williams, Paul W.	2974
Winkler, Dr. Gernot M. R.	2979
Wolski, Helen and sons, Michael and Steven	3011
Won, Hyo-Yun	2976
Wurzel, Rafael S.	2987

Y

Yassine, Afaf and children Najla, Walid, Mona, and Maher	3001
Yong Won Lee	2967
Young, Leonor	2990

U.S. Code Congressional and Administrative News:

The *United States Code Congressional and Administrative News,* a commercial publication, reprints public laws, congressional reports, reorganization plans, proclamations and executive orders. Unlike the *Statutes at Large,* private laws and concurrent resolutions are omitted. Although the *Statutes* is recognized as the official source for citing Federal legislation, the *Congressional and Administrative News* uses *Statutes at Large* page numbers as well. *Congressional and Administrative News* has been published since 1941, semimonthly while Congress is in session and monthly when it is adjourned. Cumulative editions are issued annually. Once Congressional sessions terminate, this reference tool is distributed sooner than the *Statutes at Large.*

Public Law Section:

Information provided in the headings of laws in the *Congressional and Administrative News* is almost identical to that given in the *Statutes.* The public law numbers, bill numbers, popular names of the acts or their short titles, dates they became effective and marginal notes are cited. (figure 6-5)

Figure 6-5
U.S. Code Congressional and Administrative News, 1976
Public Laws

PUBLIC LAW 94–375 [S. 3295];   Aug. 3, 1976

HOUSING AUTHORIZATION ACT OF 1976

For Legislative History of Act, see p. 1885

An Act to amend and extend laws relating to housing and community development.

*Be it enacted by the Senate and House of Representatives of the
United States of America in Congress assembled,*

SHORT TITLE

SECTION 1. This Act may be cited as the "Housing Authorization
Act of 1976".

AMENDMENTS TO THE UNITED STATES HOUSING ACT OF 1937

SEC. 2. (a) Section 5(c) of the United States Housing Act of 1937
is amended—
    (1) by striking out the first sentence and inserting in lieu
thereof the following new sentence: "The Secretary is authorized
to enter into contracts for annual contributions aggregating not
more than $1,524,000,000 per annum, which limit shall be increased
by $965,000,000 on July 1, 1974, by $662,300,000 on July 1, 1975,
and by $850,000,000 on October 1, 1976, except that the additional
authority to enter into contracts for annual contributions provided on or after July 1, 1975, shall be effective only in such
amounts as may be approved in appropriation Acts."; and
    (2) by inserting immediately after "on July 1, 1975," in the
fourth sentence thereof the following: "and by not less than
$17,000,000 per annum on October 1, 1976,".

Right margin notes:

Housing
Authorization
Act of 1976.

12 USC 1701
note.

Low-income
housing proj-
ects, contracts
for annual
contributions.

42 USC 1437c.

Reproduced with permission from *U.S. Code
Congressional and Administrative News,* published and copyrighted by West Publishing Company, 50 W. Kellogg Blvd., P.O. Box 3526, St.
Paul, MN 55165.

Legislative History Section:

The Legislative History section of this reference tool is an added feature not
seen in the *Statutes at Large.* Depending upon circumstances, the editors reprint
either full texts or excerpts from Congressional reports. Figure 6-5 indicates that
the history of PL 94-375 is found on page 1885. (figure 6-6). Portions of Senate
Report 94-749 and House Report 94-1304 are reprinted for the case in point.

Figure 6-6
Congressional and Administrative News, 1976
Legislative Histories

HOUSING AUTHORIZATION ACT OF 1976

P.L. 94–375, see page 90 Stat. 1067

Senate Report (Banking, Housing and Urban Affairs Committee)
No. 94–749, Apr. 12, 1976 [To accompany S. 3295]

House Report (Banking, Currency and Housing Committee)
No. 94–1091, May 6, 18, 1976 [To accompany H.R. 12945]

House Conference Report No. 94–1291, June 22, 1976
[To accompany S. 3295]

House Conference Report No. 94–1304, June 25, 1976
[To accompany S. 3295]

Cong. Record Vol. 122 (1976)

DATES OF CONSIDERATION AND PASSAGE

Senate April 27, July 20, 1976

House May 26, June 24, 30, 1976

The Senate bill was passed in lieu of the House bill. The Senate
Report and the second House Conference
Report are set out.

SENATE REPORT NO. 94–749

[page 1]

The Committee on Banking, Housing and Urban Affairs, having
considered the same, reports favorably a Committee bill (S. 3295)
to extend the authorization for annual contributions under the United
States Housing Act of 1937, to extend certain housing programs
under the National Housing Act, and for other purposes, and recommends that the bill do pass.

INTRODUCTION

The primary purpose of this bill is to provide for the continuation
of a number of current housing programs, either by extending the
dates on which they expire or by increasing their funding authorizations, usually through September 30, 1977. The bill contains no sig-

This convenient feature facilitates legislative research.

Proclamations, Executive Orders and Reorganization Plans:

Presidential proclamations, executive orders and reorganization plans are
arranged within their numerical sequences. *Federal Register* citations, discussed
below, are indicated for each.

Indexes and Tables:

Information is located in the *U.S. Code Congressional and Administrative
News* through thirteen access points.

A Subject Index

Ten tables

The Housing Authorization Act of 1976 is listed in the Subject Index as follows.
(figure 6-7)

Figure 6-7

Congressional and Administrative News, 1976
Subject Index

HOUSING
Coast Guard, leases, 90 Stat. 2077
    Legislative history, 4708
Department of Housing and Urban Development—Independent Agencies Appropriation Act, 1977, 90 Stat. 1095
Housing Authorization Act of 1976, 90 Stat. 1067
    Legislative history, 1885
Military Construction Appropriation Act, 1977, 90 Stat. 993
Veterans Housing Amendments Act of 1976, 90 Stat. 720
    Legislative history, 1344

HOUSING AND URBAN DEVELOPMENT, DEPARTMENT OF
Appropriations, Second Supplemental Appropriations Act of 1976, 90 Stat. 603

Table one lists public laws and refers researchers to appropriate page numbers. Table two, *U.S. Code* and *U.S. Code Annotated* Classifications, lists public laws and the various titles and sections of the *U.S. Code* and the *U.S. Code Annotated,* into which the legislation has been codified. (figure 6-8). The *Code Annotated,* discussed below, is a second codification of Federal law.

Figure 6-8

Congressional and Administrative News, 1976
U.S. Code and *U.S. Code Annotated* Classifications, Table 2

90 Stat. at Large and 1976 Cong.News			U.S.Code and U.S.C.A.	
Pub.Law	Sec.	Page	Title	Sec.
94-375	1	1067	12	1701 note
	2(a)(1), (2)	1067	42	1437c(c)
	2(b)(1)	1067	42	1437c(c)
	2(b)(1)	1067	42	1437c note
	2(b)(2)	1067	42	1437c note
	2(b)(2)	1067	42	1437c(c)
	2(c)	1068	42	1437g(c)
	2(d)	1068	42	1437f(c)(4)
	2(e)	1068	42	1437f(f)(4) to (6)
	2(f)	1068	42	1437a(2) (C), (D)
	2(g)	1068	42	1437f(e)(1)

Figure 6-8 indicates that section 2(a)(1), (2) of Public Law 94-375 appears on page 1067 of the *Statutes at Large* (or the *Congressional and Administrative*

News) and section 1437c(c) of Title 42 in both the *U.S. Code* and the *Code Annotated*. Underline the appropriate part of the illustration that provides this information.

Refer to figure 6-8 when answering the following questions:

Section 2(g) of Public Law 94-375 appears on page _____ in both the

U.S. Code Congressional and Administrative News and the _____.

page 1068, *Statutes at Large*

2(g) is codified into section _____ of Title _____ of the *U.S. Code* and the *Code Annotated*.

section 1437f(e)(1), Title 42

Section 1 of PL 94-375 is referred to in a note in the *U.S. Code* and the *Code*

Annotated, Title _____ , section _____
      12   1701

Table three lists the titles and sections of the *U.S. Code* and the *Code Annotated* which have been amended or repealed because of legislation enacted during the period covered. For instance, figure 6-9 shows that title 12, section 249 was affected by 90 Stat. 1258.

Figure 6-9

Congressional and Administrative News, 1976
U.S. Code and *U.S. Code Annotated* Sections Amended, Repealed, New, Etc.

Table 3

U.S.Code and U.S.C.A.		90 Stat. at Large and 1976 Cong.News
Title	Sec.	Page
11 (Cont'd)		
	404	317
	405	317
	406	319
	407	320
	408	320
	409	321
	410	321
	411	322
	412	322
	413	322
	414	323
	415	323
	416	324
	417	324
	418	325
12	249	1258
	548 note	197, 198

Reproduced with permission from *U.S. Code Congressional and Administrative News,* published and copyrighted by West Publishing Company, 50 W. Kellogg Blvd., P.O. Box 3526, St. Paul, MN 55165.

Brief legislative histories of public laws are provided in table four. (figure 6-10)

Figure 6-10

Congressional and Administrative News, 1976
Legislative History, Table 4

Public Law		90 Stat. Page	Bill No.	Report No. 94—		Comm. Reporting		Cong.Rec.Vol.122 (1976) Dates of Consideration and Passage	
No.94—	Date App.			House	Senate	House	Senate	House	Senate
375	Aug. 3	1067	S. 3295	1091 1291 1304	749	B, CH Conf Conf Conf (H.R. 12945)	B, HUA	May 26, June 24, 30	Apr. 27, July 20

Reproduced with permission from *U.S. Code Congressional and Administrative News,* published and copyrighted by West Publishing Company, 50 W. Kellogg Blvd., P.O. Box 3526, St. Paul, MN 55165.

Table five lists bills and joint resolutions which have been enacted into law. Table six is blank. Proclamations and executive orders are listed by number in tables seven and eight. Table nine, Major Bills Enacted, provides brief legislative histories, but unlike the fourth table, is arranged by popular titles instead of law numbers. The popular names or short titles of public laws are listed alphabetically in table ten. (figure 6-11)

Figure 6-11

Congressional and Administrative News, 1976
Popular Name Acts, Table 10

Housing and Community Development Act of 1974, Amendment 1067
Housing and Urban Development Act of 1970, Amendment 1067, 1125
Housing Authorization Act of 1976 1067
Immigration and Nationality Act, Amendment 1255, 2243, 2534, 2703
Immigration and Nationality Act Amendments of 1976 2703
Independent Agencies Appropriations Act, 1977 963
Independent Safety Board Act of 1974, Amendment 2080
Indian Claims Commission Act, Amendment 1990

Reproduced with permission from *U.S. Code Congressional and Administrative News,* published and copyrighted by West Publishing Company, 50 W. Kellogg Blvd., P.O. Box 3526, St. Paul, MN 55165.

The United States Code (USC):

The *United States Code* is a subject compilation of Federal law. It includes legislation of general and permanent value currently in effect. Private, superseded and repealed laws, plus selected revenue measures, are excluded.

The Code is arranged into the following titles.

1. General Provisions.
2. The Congress.
3. The President.
4. Flag and Seal, Seat of Government, and the States.
5. Government Organization and Employees.
6. Surety Bonds.
7. Agriculture.
8. Aliens and Nationality.
9. Arbitration.
10. Armed Forces.
11. Bankruptcy.
12. Banks and Banking.
13. Census.
14. Coast Guard.
15. Commerce and Trade.
16. Conservation.
17. Copyrights.
18. Crimes and Criminal Procedure.
19. Customs Duties.
20. Education.
21. Food and Drugs.
22. Foreign Relations and Intercourse.
23. Highways.
24. Hospitals and Asylums.
25. Indians.
26. Internal Revenue Code.
27. Intoxicating Liquors.
28. Judiciary and Judicial Procedure.
29. Labor.
30. Mineral Lands and Mining.
31. Money and Finance.
32. National Guard.
33. Navigation and Navigable Waters.
34. No longer published.
35. Patents.
36. Patriotic Societies and Observances.
37. Pay and Allowances of the Uniformed Services.
38. Veterans' Benefits.
39. Postal Service.
40. Public Buildings, Property, and Works.
41. Public Contracts.
42. The Public Health and Welfare.
43. Public Lands.
44. Public Printing and Documents.
45. Railroads.
46. Shipping.
47. Telegraphs, Telephones, and Radiotelegraphs.
48. Territories and Insular Possessions
49. Transportation.
50. War and National Defense; and Appendix.

In reality there are forty-nine, not fifty titles. Title 34 was incorporated into Title 10 in 1956. The *Code* has been published every six years since 1926. Annual supplements are issued during the invervening years.

The text of the *USC* sometimes differs from that of the *Statutes at Large*. In codifying public laws, the compilers of the *Code* delete all which is repetitious or not of permanent value. Moreover, the compilers will sometimes summarize the statutes instead of printing them in their entireties. When the *Statutes at Large* conflicts with the *Code,* the former receives precedence, unless the specific title has been re-enacted into positive law. Re-enactment occurs when the title is introduced before Congress as a bill and is then approved as a public law. This is necessary because the *USC's* text differs from that which Congress approved in the original legislation. Since 1947 when the House Judiciary Committee created its Office of The Law Revision Counsel, over twenty titles have been re-enacted. The goal is to re-enact all forty-nine titles. The introductory sections of *USC* volumes list all titles. Those re-enacted are indicated with asterisks.

General Index:

Usually, the best way to begin research using the *United States Code* is to consult the General Index. Entries are arranged under both subject headings and agency names. Ample cross-references are provided. When searching for information pertaining to "Public Housing Agencies," researchers are told to consult "Lower Income Housing." Relevant citations are illustrated in figure 6-12.

Figure 6-12

U.S. Code
General Index

LOWER INCOME HOUSING—Continued
Public housing agencies,
    Annual contributions,
        Contract with, provision for assistance
        payments to owners of existing dwell-
        ing units, 42 § 1437f
        Operation of low-income housing pro-
        jects, 42 § 1437g
    As mortgagee of multifamily housing proj-
    ect, contract provisions, 12 § 1715z-9
    Board of directors or similar governing
    body, tenants serving as, 42 § 1437

Title 42—The Public Health and Welfare Law:

According to figure 6-12, relevant information is found in various subdivisions of section 1437 of Title 42. Excerpts are illustrated below. (figure 6-13)

Figure 6-13

U.S. Code, Title 42

Page 895   TITLE 42—THE PUBLIC HEALTH AND WELFARE   § 1437a

§ 1437. Declaration of policy

It is the policy of the United States to promote the general welfare of the Nation by employing its funds and credit, as provided in this chapter, to assist the several States and their political subdivisions to remedy the unsafe and unsanitary housing conditions and the acute shortage of decent, safe, and sanitary dwellings for families of low income and, consistent with the objectives of this chapter, to vest in local public housing agencies the maximum amount of responsibility in the administration of their housing programs. No person should be barred from serving on the board of directors or similar governing body of a local public housing agency because of his tenancy in a low-income housing project.

(Sept. 1, 1937, ch. 896, § 2, as added Aug. 22, 1974, Pub. L. 93-383, title II, § 201(a), 88 Stat. 653.)

PRIOR PROVISIONS

A prior section 2 of act Sept. 1, 1937, ch. 896, 50 Stat. 888, relating to definitions, was classified to section 1402 of this title prior to the revision of act Sept. 1, 1937 by Pub. L. 93-383.

Prior similar provisions were contained in section 1 of act Sept. 1, 1937, ch. 896, 50 Stat. 888, which was classified to section 1401 of this title prior to the revision of such act by Pub. L. 93-383.

EFFECTIVE DATE

Section 201(b) of Pub. L. 93-383 provided that: "The provisions of subsection (a) of this section [enacting sections 1437 to 1437j of this title] shall be effective on such date or dates as the Secretary of Housing and Urban Development shall prescribe, but not later than eighteen months after the date of the enactment of this Act [Aug. 22, 1974]; except that (1) all of the provisions of section 3(1) of the United States Housing Act of 1937, as amended by subsection (a) of this section [section 1437a(1) of this title], shall become effective on the same date, (2) all of the provisions of sections 5 and 9(c) of such Act as so amended [sections 1437c and 1437g(c) of this title] shall become effective on the same date, and (3) section 8 of such Act [section 1437f of this title] as so amended shall be effective not later than January 1, 1975."

Section 3(1) of the United States Housing Act of 1937, as amended, referred to hereinabove effective Sept. 26, 1975, see Effective Date note set out under section 1437a of this title.

SHORT TITLE

Section 1 of act Sept. 1, 1937, ch. 896, as added by section 201(a) of Pub. L. 93-383 provided that: "This Act [which enacted this chapter and provision set out as a note under this section] may be cited as the 'United States Housing Act of 1937'."

LIMITATION ON WITHHOLDING OR CONDITIONING OF ASSISTANCE

Assistance provided for in Housing and Community Development Act of 1974 [42 U.S.C. 5301 et seq.], National Housing Act [12 U.S.C. 1701 et seq.], United States Housing Act of 1937 [42 U.S.C. 1437 et seq.], Housing Act of 1949 [see Short Title note under section 1441 of this title], Demonstration Cities and Metropolitan Development Act of 1966 [see Short Title note under section 3301 of this title], and Housing and Urban Development Acts of 1965, 1968, 1969, and 1970 not to be withheld or made subject to conditions by reason of tax-exempt status of obligations issued or to be issued for financing of assistance, except as otherwise provided by law, see section 817 of Pub. L. 93-383, set out as a note under section 5301 of this title.

§ 1437a. Definitions

When used in this chapter—

(1) The term, "low-income housing" means decent, safe, and sanitary dwellings within the financial reach of families of low income, and embraces all necessary appurtenances thereto. Except as otherwise provided in this section, income limits for occupancy and rents shall be fixed by the public housing agency and approved by the Secretary. The rental for any dwelling units shall not exceed one-fourth of the family's income as defined by the Secretary. Notwithstanding the preceding sentence, the rental for any dwelling unit shall not be less than the higher of (A) 5 per centum of the gross income of the family occupying the dwelling unit, and (B) if the family is receiving payments for welfare assistance from a public agency and a part of such payments, adjusted in accordance with the family's actual housing costs, is specifically designated by such agency to meet the family's housing costs, the portion of such payments which is so designated. At least 20 per centum of the dwelling units in any project placed under annual contributions contracts in any fiscal year beginning after the effective date of this section shall be occupied by very low-income families. In defining the income of any family for the purpose of this chapter, the Secretary shall consider income from all sources of each member of the family residing in the household, except that there shall be excluded—

(A) the income of any family member (other than the head of the household or his spouse) who is under eighteen years of age or is a full-time student;
(B) the first $300 of the income of a secondary wage earner who is the spouse of the head of the household;
(C) an amount equal to $300 for each member of the family residing in the household (other than the head of the household or his spouse) who is under eighteen years of age or who is eighteen years of age or older and is disabled or handicapped or a full-time student;
(D) nonrecurring income, as determined by the Secretary;
(E) 5 per centum of the family's gross income (10 per centum in the case of elderly families);
(F) such extraordinary medical or other expenses as the Secretary approves for exclusion; and

(G) an amount equal to the sums received by the head of the household or his spouse from, or under the direction of, any public or private nonprofit child placing agency for the care and maintenance of one or more persons who are under eighteen years of age and were placed in the household by such agency.

(2) The term "low-income families" means families of low income who cannot afford to pay enough to cause private enterprise in their locality or metropolitan area to build an adequate supply of decent, safe, and sanitary dwellings for their use. The term "very low-income families" means families whose incomes do not exceed 50 per centum of the median family income for the area, as determined by the Secretary with adjustments for smaller and larger families. The term "families" includes families consisting of a single person in the case of (A) a person who is at least sixty-two years of age or is under a disability as defined in section 423 of this title or in section 2691 of this title, or is handicapped, (B) a displaced person, (C) the remaining member of a tenant family and (D) other single persons in circumstances described in regulations of the Secretary: *Provided,* That in no event shall more than 10 percent of the units under the jurisdiction of any public housing agency be occupied by single persons under this clause (D): *Provided further,* That in determining priority for admission to housing under this chapter the Secretary shall give preference to those single persons who are elderly, handicapped, or displaced before those eligible under this clause (D); and the term "elderly families" means families whose heads (or their spouses), or whose sole members, are persons described in clause (A). A person shall be considered handicapped if such person is determined, pursuant to regulations issued by the Secretary, to have an impairment which (i) is expected to be of long-continued and indefinite duration, (ii) substantially impedes his ability to live independently, and (iii) is of such a nature that such ability could be improved by more suitable housing conditions. The term "displaced person" means a person displaced by governmental action, or a person whose dwelling has been extensively damaged or destroyed as a result of a disaster declared or otherwise formally recognized pursuant to Federal disaster relief laws. Notwithstanding the preceding provisions of this paragraph, the term "elderly families" includes two or more elderly, disabled, or handicapped individuals living together, or one or more such individuals living with another person who is determined under regulations of the Secretary to be a person essential to their care or well being.

(3) The term "development" means any or all undertakings necessary for planning, land acquisition, demolition, construction, or equipment, in connection with a low-income housing project. The term "development cost" comprises the cost incurred by a public housing agency in such undertakings and their necessary financing (including the payment of carrying charges), and in otherwise carrying out the development of such project. Construction activity in connection with a low-income housing project may be confined to the reconstruction, remodeling, or repair of existing buildings.

(4) The term "operation" means any or all undertakings appropriate for management, operation, services, maintenance, security (including the cost of security personnel), or financing in connection with a low-income housing project. The term also means the financing of tenant programs and services for families residing in low-income housing projects, particularly

where there is maximum feasible participation of the tenants in the development and operation of such tenant programs and services. As used in this paragraph, the term "tenant programs and services" includes the development and maintenance of tenant organizations which participate in the management of low-income housing projects; the training of tenants to manage and operate such projects and the utilization of their services in project management and operation; counseling on household management, housekeeping, budgeting, money management, child care, and similar matters; advice as to resources for job training and placement education, welfare, health, and other community services; services which are directly related to meeting tenant needs and providing a wholesome living environment; and referral to appropriate agencies when necessary for the provision of such services. To the maximum extent available and appropriate, existing public and private agencies in the community shall be used for the provisions of such services.

(5) The term "acquisition cost" means the amount prudently required to be expended by a public housing agency in acquiring a low-income housing project.

(6) The term "public housing agency" means any State, county, municipality, or other governmental entity or public body (or agency or instrumentality thereof) which is authorized to engage in or assist in the development or operation of low-income housing.

(7) The term "state" includes the several States, the District of Columbia, the Commonwealth of Puerto Rico, the territories and possessions of the United States, the Trust Territory of the Pacific Islands, and Indian tribes, bands, groups, and Nations, including Alaska Indians, Aleuts, and Eskimos, of the United States.

(8) The term "Secretary" means the Secretary of Housing and Urban Development.

(9) The term "low-income housing project" or "project" means (A) any low-income housing developed, acquired, or assisted by a public housing agency under this chapter, and (B) the improvement of any such housing.

(Sept. 1, 1937, ch. 896, § 3, as added Aug. 22, 1974, Pub. L. 93-383, title II, § 201(a), 88 Stat. 654, and amended Aug. 3, 1976, Pub. L. 94-375, § 2(f), 90 Stat. 1068.)

REFERENCES IN TEXT

For effective date of this section, referred to in par. (1), see Effective Date note below.

PRIOR PROVISIONS

A prior section 3 of act Sept. 1, 1937, ch. 896, 50 Stat. 889, as amended, which established the United States Housing Authority, was classified to section 1403 of this title prior to the revision of act Sept. 1, 1937 by Pub. L. 93-383.

Prior similar provisions were contained in section 2 of act Sept. 1, 1937, ch. 896, 50 Stat. 888, which was classified to section 1402 of this title prior to the revision of such act by Pub. L. 93-383.

AMENDMENTS

1976—Par. (2). Pub. L. 94-375 struck out "and" preceding (C), added cl. (D), and two provisos relating to the percentage of units to be occupied by single persons and the priority to be given to single persons who are elderly, handicapped, or displaced, following cl. (D).

EFFECTIVE DATE

Section effective on such date or dates as the Secretary of Housing and Urban Development shall prescribe, but not later than eighteen months after Aug. 22, 1974, except that all of the provisions of par. (1) shall become effective on the same date, see section

Note that the text is supplemented with references to public laws and *Statutes at Large* citations. The "Amendments" notation in figure 6-13 explains how PL 94-375 amended section 1437a. Underline the appropriate changes in that section.

Popular Name Index:

A Popular Name Index also aids researchers in locating information. Public law numbers, *Statutes* citations and *USC* references are given. The Housing Authorization Act of 1976, PL 94-375, is cited as follows. (figure 6-14)

Figure 6-14
U.S. Code
Popular Name Index

Housing Authorization Act of 1976
Pub. L. 94-375, Aug. 3, 1976, 90 Stat. 1067-1079 (Title 5, § 5315; Title 12, §§ 1464, 1701 note, 1701j-2, 1701q, 1706e, 1713, 1715e, 1715k, 1715l, 1715v, 1715y, 1715z, 1715z-1, 1715z-2, 1715z-3, 1715z-6, 1715z-7, 1715z-9, 1715z-10, 1723, 1723a, 1723e, 1735, 2708, 2709, 2710; Title 40, § 461; Title 42, §§ 1382 note, 1437a, 1437c, 1437f, 1437g, 1452, 1480, 1490, 1490a, 3535, 4056, 4106, 4127, 4521, 5303, 5305, 5307, 5316)

Housing Deficiency Act
Mar. 4, 1939, ch. 6, 53 Stat. 511

Hump Law
Pub. L. 86-155, Aug. 11, 1959, 73 Stat. 333
(Title 10, § 5701 note, § 6387)

Underline the relevant parts of figure 6-14 which show that this law has been codified into the indicated titles and sections seen in that illustration.

12 USC 1701

40 USC 461

42 USC 1437a

Tables:

Nine tables supplement the General and Popular Name Indexes. Table one, Revised Titles, lists sections of titles which have been revised, providing references from the former sections to the present ones. Title 44, the Public Printing and Documents law, is used for illustrative purposes. After the legislation was re-enacted in 1968, the definition of government publications, which had previously been in section 81a, was placed in section 1901. (figure 6-15)

Figure 6-15
U.S. Code
Revised Titles, Table 1

Title 44 Former Sections	Title 44 New Sections
79	1707
80	1713
81	1712
81a	1901
81b	1902
81c	1914
82	1905
83	1904
84	1910
84a	1912
85	1903, 1906
85a	1913
86	1909
87	1907

Table two lists sections of the *Revised Statutes of The United States* and provides corresponding *U.S. Code* citations. The *Revised Statutes* is the codification of Federal law enacted between 1789 and 1873, some of which is still in effect. Table three cites all public laws currently in effect and the corresponding sections of the *USC* into which the measures have been codified. (figure 6-16)

Figure 6-16
U.S. Code
Statutes at Large, Table 3

94th Cong. 90 Stat.	Pub. L.	Section	Page	Title	U.S.C. Section
Aug. 3	94-375	1	1067	12	1701 nt
		2(a)	1067	42	1437c
		2(b)	1067	42	1437c, 1437c nts
		2(c)	1067	42	1437g
		2(d), (e)	1067	42	1437f
		2(f)	1068	42	1437a
		2(g)	1068	42	1437f
		2(h)	1068	42	1382 nt
		3(a)-(c)	1068, 1069	12	1715z
		3(d)	1069	12	1715l
		3(e), (f)	1069	12	1715z
		4	1070	12	1715z-1
		5	1070	12	1715z-6
		6	1070	12	1715z-9
		7	1071	12	1715z-10
		8(a)	1071	12	1713, 1715e, 1715k, 1715l, 1715v, 1715y
		8(b)(1)	1071	12	1713
		8(b)(2)	1071	12	1713e
		8(b)(3)	1072	12	1715k
		8(b)(4), (5)	1072	12	1715l
		8(b)(6)	1072	12	1715v
		8(b)(7)	1072	12	1715y
		9, 10	1072, 1073	12	1735
		11	1074	12	1701q

Tables four and five of the *Code* refer to the laws of the District of Columbia. The first chart correlates that city's laws to *USC* citations and the second correlates *USC* references to the *District of Columbia Code*. Executive orders, proclamations and reorganization plans are listed in the sixth, seventh and eighth tables. Orders and proclamations are arranged in numerical order; reorganization plans are listed by year and plan numbers.

Internal References, the ninth table, was first used in the 1976 edition of the *Code*. This list tells researchers where in the *Code* specific sections are cited. For instance, figure 6-17 indicates that 42 USC 1437f is cited in sections 1437c and j of the same title, as well as in 12 USC 1715l, 26 USC 1250 and 40 App. USC 207 (Appendix to Title 40).

Figure 6-17
U.S. Code
Internal References, Table 9

1437d............ Section 1437f of this title; title 12 section 24.

1437f .... Sections 1437c, 1437j of this title; title 12 section 1715l; title 26 section 1250; title 40 App. section 207.

1439 .... Sections 1437c, 1437f of this title.

1440............ Title 12 sections 371, 1464.

1441... .... Title 12 section 1701t.

```
1441a............ Section 1441b of this title, title
                 12 section 1723e; title 40 sec
                 tion 461.
1441b.. ......... Title 12 section 1723e; title 40
                 section 461.
1441c ........... Title 12 section 1723e; title 40
                 section 461.
```

United States Code Annotated (USCA) and United States Code Service (USCS):

The *United States Code Annotated* and the *United States Code Service* are two annotated versions of the *United States Code.* Besides stating the law, both sources refer researchers to further references and interpretations. The *Code Annotated* includes the identical titles, sections and text as the *U.S. Code,* plus additional information. Following each section, citations to *Corpus Juris Secundum (CJS),* a legal encyclopedia, and West's *Key Number Digests,* a comprehensive compilation of digested or summarized case law are given. References to and abstracts of local, state and Federal cases which have interpreted each section of the *Code* are also noted. Revenue bills excluded from the *USC* are printed in the *Code Annotated's* appendix to Title 26.

The *United States Code Service* uses the identical title and section approach as the *USC,* but the *USCS* text is based upon that of the *Statutes at Large.* Annotations provide references to a limited number of cases, the *CFR* and law review articles.

Federal Register

The *Federal Register,* issued Monday through Friday since 1936 except on official holidays, and the *Code of Federal Regulations,* first published in 1937 and then annually since 1949, are two basic sources for Federal administrative or regulatory law. The latter is described below. The *Register* includes four kinds of materials: Presidential documents, rules, proposed rules and notices.

Presidential Documents:

Presidential documents are usually printed in the first section of the *Register.* There are three types, namely orders, proclamations and reorganization plans. The differences between orders and proclamations have never been defined clearly. Orders, which are usually directed to agencies, are generally based upon powers which Congress has delegated to the President. However, the absence of such delegated authority has not prevented Presidents from issuing orders. In such cases, the Constitution and "applicable statutes" are cited as the basis for actions. Proclamations usually deal with ceremonial matters, such as periods of special observance or more substantial issues relating to foreign trade. The Thanksgiving Day Proclamations issued annually by most Presidents since 1863 are among the most famous. There are some exceptions to the rule, President Lincoln's Emancipation Proclamation being one of the most extraordinary examples.

Although orders and proclamations are numbered consecutively, it is uncertain how many have been issued. They were neither published nor numbered systematically until the *Federal Register* began publication in 1936. The Department of State began numbering them in 1907. Though selected ones were numbered retrospectively, older documents were omitted from the list. Furthermore, between 1907 and 1935, materials were not always forwarded by the Executive to the State Department.

Rules and Regulations:

The Rules and Regulations section of the *Register* generally follows that of Presidential documents. The following types of information are included.

Final regulations

Interim rules with requests for comments

Finalized interim rules

Temporary regulations

Policy statements

Interpretations of existing rules

Corrections

Deferrals of effective dates.

Since April 1977, a standard format, which includes headings and preambles, has been required for the publication of all regulations. Headings indicate the agencies' names, the titles and parts of the *Code of Federal Regulations* affected by the rules and the subjects under consideration. Agencies can also include their file numbers for the rules, but are not required to do so. A typical six part heading is illustrated in figure 6-18.

Figure 6-18

Federal Register, March 25, 1981
Heading and Preamble of final rules

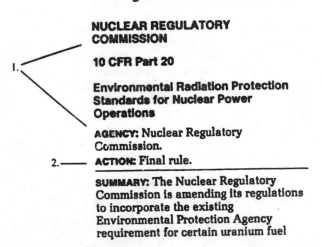

1. Agencies' names.

2. Actions. Natures of the documents in question are indicated in the Action section. The regulation in figure 6-18 is a final rule.

3. —— cycle licensees to comply with the EPA's "Environmental Radiation Protection Standards for Nuclear Power Operations". These standards require certain uranium fuel cycle facilities to be operated such that releases of radioactive materials and resulting radiation doses to the public are below specified limits. The amendments also require licensees to submit reports to NRC when those standards have been or may be exceeded.

EFFECTIVE DATES: The effective dates for the existing requirement to comply with EPA's 40 CFR Part 190 are already

4. —— specified in 40 CFR 190.12: December 1, 1979 for most operations; December 1, 1980 for uranium mills; and January 1, 1983 for discharges of krypton-85 and iodine-129. The effective date for these amendments to 10 CFR Part 20 is June 23, 1981.

FOR FURTHER INFORMATION CONTACT: Mr. John W. N. Hickey, Office of

5. —— Standards Development, U.S. Nuclear Regulatory Commission, Washington, D.C. 20555 (phone: (301) 443-5966).

SUPPLEMENTARY INFORMATION: The

6. —— Nuclear Regulatory Commission (NRC) is amending its regulations in 10 CFR Part 20, "Standards for Protection

3. Summaries. Regulations are summarized in laymen's terms. Abstracts usually answer the why's, what's and intended effects of the actions.

4. Effective dates.

5. Further information. Names, telephone numbers and addresses of officials responsible for implementing the regulations are provided.

6. Supplementary information. Regulatory histories of the issues, plus other background information necessary to comprehend them, are described in non-technical terms. Legal authorities under which the regulations are being implemented and lists of other rules and relevant studies are given. The differences between the final and the proposed rules are also explained.

Proposed Regulations:

Proposed regulations are generally printed in the third section of the *Register*. They are statements by regulatory agencies designed to inform the public of the intent to issue regulations. Prior to the finalizing of rules, the public must be given advance notice, enabling interested parties to comment either at hearings or in writing. Proposed rules, like final, interim and temporary ones, must have headings and preambles. The preambles to these documents differ slightly from those of final regulations. Names, addresses and phone numbers of individuals who will accept written comments, and the dates, times and places of public hearings must be given.

Besides proposed regulations, this section also includes:

Petitions or requests for rule-making activities

Advance notices of intended rule-making

Notices of extensions of periods for public comment

Semi-Annual Agendas of Significant Regulations (figure 6-19).

According to President Carter's Executive Order 12044, effective March 23, 1978, agencies are required to publish *Semi-Annual Agendas of Significant Regulations* which list significant regulations under review or development, explain the need for them and state their legal basis. Updated status of rules listed on previous *Agendas* must also be provided in forthcoming ones. In all cases, names and phone numbers of relevant individuals are given. The Order also required agencies to list the publication schedules of their *Agendas* for each fiscal year in the *Federal Register* issued on the first Monday of every October. President Reagan's Executive Order 12291 effective February 17, 1981, superseded number 12044. The more recent Order requires that *Agendas* be published in April and October, but because it fails to specify that they be printed in the *Federal Register,* agencies can now issue them in any format.

Figure 6-19

Federal Register, September 5, 1980
Semiannual Agenda of Significant Regulations

**3. H–13–80. Rent Supplement Program—
Definition of Eligible Tenant**

Description. Would change the definitions of tenant eligibility and adjusted income in the Section 101, Rent Supplement Program to that of the Section 8 program.

Need. To implement Section 203 of the Housing and Community Development Amendments of 1979.

Authority. Section 101(g), Housing and Urban Development Act of 1965, Pub. L. 89–117, 79 Stat. 451, 12 U.S.C. 1701s.

Regulatory Analysis. No.

Contact. James T. Tahash, 202–426–8730.

Status. Interim rule in preparation.

Regulatory analyses referred to in figure 6-19 are statements which analyze alternative methods for achieving the same goals and their cost effectiveness. Agencies prepare these documents when significant regulations are proposed. Significant rules are defined as those which have an annual effect of one hundred million dollars or more on the economy or cause major cost increases to consumers, industry, government or geographic regions.

Notices:

The Notices section of the *Register* follows the Proposed Rules section. Various types of notices include:

The availability of environmental impact statements and intentions to prepare such documents

Grant application deadlines

Agencies' decisions and rulings

Delegations of authority

Filing of petitions and applications

Lists of Sunshine Act meetings.

The Sunshine Act mandates that most agency meetings be open to the public and that the *Federal Register* print the appropriate times, places and subjects of such meetings, plus names and phone numbers of relevant officials.

Information in the *Federal Register* is not always printed in the sequence described above. Significant documents are sometimes given separate title pages and are printed as appendices to the *Register*. These appendices are noted as Parts II, III or IV, whichever the case calls for. This practice enables agencies wishing to distribute reprinted copies of their major regulations to do so more easily.

Code of Federal Regulations (CFR):

Final and interim regulations that originally appear in the *Federal Register* are codified into the *CFR* just as legislation is codified into the *U.S. Code*. The *Code of Federal Regulations* is divided into fifty titles which reflect broad subject headings. These title numbers and topics are not comparable to those in the *USC*. For instance, Title 20 in the *U.S. Code* deals with education, whereas the most significant regulations on the subject are found in Title 34 of the *CFR*. Each year titles one through sixteen are updated as of January 1, titles seventeen through twenty-seven as of April 1, titles twenty-eight through forty-one as of July 1, and titles forty-two through fifty as of October 1.

CFR titles are subdivided into chapters, parts, sections and paragraphs. Regulations pertaining to agencies or their subordinate units are codified into chapters identified by Roman numerals. Capital letters are used to divide chapters into parts that contain rules relating to a specific function. Parts are identified by Arabic numerals. Sections, which are subdivisions of parts, usually contain simple presentations of single propositions. They are signified with Arabic numerals following periods. That is, 25.1 represents part twenty-five, section one. Paragraphs are subdivisions of sections and are referred to by lower case letters. For example, a typical *Code of Federal Regulations* citation—Title twenty, part seventy-one, section five, paragraph a—is written as 20 *CFR* 71.5(a).

Locating Information in the Federal Register:

Federal Register Index:

The *Federal Register Index* is published monthly. Each successive index cumulates information listed in the previous issues. For example, the December *Index* provides access to materials published since January. The 1979 *Annual Index* is arranged in four sections where Presidential and agency entries, Privacy Act Publications, Freedom of Information Indexes Guide, and *Federal Register* Pages and Dates are cited. The Privacy and Freedom of Information Acts are discussed in chapter 11.

Continuing your research in public housing, locate the revised 1979 regulations governing the modernization of PHA (Public Housing Agencies) owned projects. Consult the Presidential and agencies' entries section of the 1979 *Index*. Through 1981, information pertaining to executive agencies was listed following that relating to Presidential documents. However, as of 1982, citations relating to the Executive Office are filed in their alphabetic sequence under

"Presidential Documents." Most entries are indexed under the agencies' names, but broad subject headings are included very selectively. Citations are separated according to rules, proposed rules and notices. Portions of entries indexed under "Housing and Urban Development Department are reproduced below. (figure 6-20)

Figure 6-20

Federal Register Index, 1979

HOUSING AND URBAN DEVELOPMENT DEPARTMENT

See also Community Planning and Development, Office of Assistant Secretary.
Environmental Quality Office, Housing and Urban Development Department.
Federal Disaster Assistance Administration.
Federal Housing Commissioner—Office of Assistant Secretary for Housing.

* — RULES

Housing assistance program (Section 8) for disposition of HUD-owned projects; interim rule, 70362
Indian housing program, 64204
Modernization program-PHA-owned projects, 64196
Public housing development; interim rule and inquiry, 46996
Public housing development; interim rule and inquiry; extension of time, 64405

PROPOSED RULES

Cost-effective energy conservation standards; transmittal to Congress, 21669
Disaster assistance community disaster loans; transmittal to Congress, 43290
Low income housing:
Congressional regulatory review; waiver requests, 17721
Individual metering utilities; PHA-owned projects, project management utilities; extension of time, 22472
Modernization program; PHA-owned projects, 25142

*"Rules" refers to final ones.

The following questions refer to figure 6-20:

The proposed rule for the modernization of low income PHA owned projects began on page _____ .

25142

The final rule was printed on page _____ .

64196

Consult the *Federal Register* Pages and Dates section of the *Index* to determine when pages 25142 and 64196 were printed. (figure 6-21)

Figure 6-21
Federal Register Index, 1979
Federal Register Pages and Dates

Pages	Date	Pages	Date
21757–22024	Apr. 12	63077–63508	Nov. 2
22025–22432	13	63509–64058	5
22433–22696	16	64059–64396	6
22697–23064	17	64397–64780	7
23065–23198	18	64781–65024	8
23199–23510	19	65025–65378	9
23511–23810	20	65379–65580	13
23811–24032	23	65581–65728	14
24033–24262	24	65729–65958	15
24263–24540	25		
24541–24824	26		
24825–25190	27		
25191–25392	30		

Refer to figure 6-21 when answering the following:

Page 25142 appeared in the _____ issue of the *Federal Register* and

page 64196 was in the _____ issue.

April 27, November 6

Excerpts from the final rule are reprinted in figure 6-22.

Figure 6-22
Federal Register, November 6, 1979

**PART 868—MODERNIZATION
PROGRAM—PHA-OWNED PROJECTS**

Sec.
868.1 Purpose and scope.
868.2 Definitions.
868.3 Priority work items.
868.4 Eligibility requirements for an allocation of modernization funds.
868.5 Resident participation--rental project.
868.6 Homebuyer participation—homeownership project.
868.7 Procedures for obtaining approval of a modernization program.
868.8 Modernization project.
868.9 Contracting requirements.
868.10 Labor provisions.
868.11 Requests for modernization funds.
868.12 Monitoring and evaluation.
868.13 Revisions of the modernization program budget.

868.14 Revisions of the modernization work programs.
868.15 Completion of modernization programs.
868.16 Effect on purchase price and amortization period.

Authority: United States Housing Act of 1937 (42 U.S.C. 1437 et seq.), sec. 7(d). Department of HUD Act (42 U.S.C. 3535(d)).

§ 868.1 Purpose and scope.

The purpose of this Part is to prescribe requirements and procedures for Modernization by Public Housing Agencies (PHAs)—including Indian Housing Authorities (IHAs)—of PHA-owned low-income public housing projects, including conveyed Lanham

Refer to figure 6-22 when answering the following questions:

This rule amends _____ CRF _____ (Title _____, part _____).

24 *CFR* 868, (Title 24, part 868)

The purpose and scope of the regulation is stated in 868.1 or part 868,

_____ 1.

section

The authority or legal basis for this rule is the United States Housing Act of

_____ and the Department of _____ Act.

1937, HUD

The legislation has been codified into the *U.S. Code,* Title _____ section

_____ and Title 42, section _____, paragraph _____ .

Title 42, section 1437 and
Title 42, section 3535, paragraph d

Locating Information In The Code of Federal Regulations:

It was shown above that the regulation seen in figure 6-22 amended 24 *CFR* 868. These amendments were incorporated into the *Code of Federal Regulations,* effective April 1, 1980. (figure 6-23)

Figure 6-23
24 CFR 868, April 1, 1980

PART 868—MODERNIZATION PRO-
GRAM—PHA-OWNED PROJECTS

Sec.
868.1 Purpose and scope.
868.2 Definitions.

868.3 Priority work items.

868.4 Eligibility requirements for an allocation of modernization funds.

868.5 Resident participation—rental project.

868.6 Homebuyer participation—homeownership project.

868.7 Procedures for obtaining approval of a modernization program.

868.8 Modernization project.

868.9 Contracting requirements.

868.10 Labor provisions.

868.11 Requests for modernization funds.

868.12 Monitoring and evaluation.

868.13 Revisions of the modernization program budget.

868.14 Revisions of the modernization work programs.

868.15 Completion of modernization programs.

868.16 Effect on purchase price and amortization period.

AUTHORITY: United States Housing Act of 1937 (42 U.S.C. 1437 et seq.), sec. 7(d), Department of HUD Act (42 U.S.C. 3535(d)).

SOURCE: 44 FR 64198, Nov. 6, 1979, unless otherwise noted.

§ 868.1 Purpose and scope.

The purpose of this Part is to prescribe requirements and procedures for Modernization by Public Housing Agencies (PHAs)—including Indian Housing Authorities (IHAs)—of PHA-owned low-income public housing projects, including conveyed Lanham and Public Works Administration (PWA)

The information in the *Code* is identical to that in the *Federal Register* with one exception. The source note in figure 6-23 explains that the rules were printed in the *Federal Register,* Volume 44, page 64198 on November 6, 1979. Note that the *Register's* 1979 *Index*, figure 6-20, indicates that the appropriate information begins on page 64196, rather than 64198. The *Federal Register* considers preambles to regulations, which in this case, appeared on pages 64196 and 64197. The *CFR* reprints only the text of the rules, which in this illustration, began on page 64198.

CFR Index and Finding Aids:

The *CFR Index and Finding Aids* is updated semi-annually. It consists of six parts.

CFR Index.

List of Agency-Prepared Indexes Appearing in Individual *CFR* volumes.

Table I, Parallel Table of Statutory Authorities and Rules.

Table III, Acts Requiring Publication In The *Federal Register.*

List of *CFR* Titles, Chapters, Subchapters and Parts.

Alphabetical List of Agencies Appearing In The *CFR.*

Table II, Presidential Documents Included or Cited In Currently Effective Rules, is no longer published.

CFR Index:

The *CFR Index* is a comprehensive one that incorporates agency names, plus far more subject headings than the *Federal Register Index*. 24 *CFR* 868 is indexed under both Housing and Urban Development Department, and Public Housing. (figure 6-24)

Figure 6-24

CFR Index and Finding Aids, July 1, 1980
CFR Index

Housing and Urban Development Department
See also Federal Housing Commissioner
    Government National Mortgage
    Association
    Interstate Land Sales Registration
    Office
    New Community Development
    Corporation
Administrative claims, 24 CFR 17

Public Housing Agency-owned projects
    Demolition of buildings or disposition
    of real property, 24 CFR 870
    Lease and grievance procedures, 24
    CFR 866
    Modernization program, 24 CFR 868

Public housing
See also Low and moderate income
    housing
    Rent subsidies
Evictions from certain subsidized and
    HUD-owned housing projects, 24
    CFR 450

Public housing agency-owned projects
    Demolition of buildings or disposition
    of real property, 24 CFR 870
    Modernization program, 24 CFR 868
    Personnel policies and compensation,
    24 CFR 867
    Project management, 24 CFR 865
    Rents, 24 CFR 861

Underline the relevant entries in figure 6-24.

Agency-Prepared Indexes:

Although not required to do so, selected agencies prepare indexes to their regulations. These indexes may or may not be similar to that prepared by the Office of the Federal Register. The second part of the *CFR Index and Finding Aids* is a List of Agency-Prepared Indexes Appearing In Individual *CFR* Volumes.

Tables:

Table I, Parallel Table of Authorities and Rules, is arranged in three parts which relate to *USC, Statutes at Large* and Presidential document citations. This table cites regulations and corresponding legislation or Executive edicts which relate to the rules. Figure 6-25 indicates where regulations relating to the various paragraphs of 42 *USC* 1437, seen above, have been placed in the *Code of Federal Regulations.*

Figure 6-25

CFR Index and Finding Aids, July 1, 1980
Parallel Table of Authorities and Rules, Table 1

42 U.S.C.—Continued	CFR
1436c	24 Part 805
1437 et seq	24 Parts 805, 860, 865, 868, 880-883

```
1437.............................. 24 Parts 811,
              841, 880-881, 888-889, 899
1437 note................................. 24 Parts 805,
              861, 866-867, 890
1437a..................... 24 Parts 811-812, 880-883
1437c................................ 24 Parts 803,
       805, 811, 866, 880-883, 886, 888-889
1437d................................ 24 Parts 861-867
1437e................................. 24 Part 803
1437f.................................. 24 Parts 811,
              880-883, 886
1437f note............................... 24 Part 805
1437g.................................. 24 Part 890
```

Figure 6-26 illustrates that rules relating to 90 Stat 1068, *Statutes at Large,* Volume 90, page 1068, have been incorporated into 20 *CFR* 416. 90 Stat 1068 is part of Public Law 94-375, the legislation considered above.

Figure 6-26

CFR Index and Finding Aids, July 1, 1980
Parallel Table of Authorities and Rules, Table 1

90 Stat.—Continued	CFR
1013	15 Parts 920, 923, 930, 932-933
1068	20 Part 416
1083—1092	43 Part 3400
1127	10 Parts 210-212, 214-215, 303-309
1188	36 Part 903
1211	43 Part 419
1241	12 Part 281
	29 Part 2203
	45 Parts 614, 702

Executive Orders 12044 and 12291, discussed above, are illustrated in figure 6-27.

Figure 6-27

CFR Index and Finding Aids, January 1, 1982
Parallel Table of Authorities and Rules, Table 1
Executive Orders

Executive Orders—Continued	CFR
12038	10 Parts 205, 213, 221
	14 Part 213
12044	10 Part 465
	14 Part 399
	18 Part 740
	24 Part 10
12046	47 Parts 201, 202, 211-215
12287	10 Parts 205, 211, 212, 220
12291	44 Part 1
12294	31 Part 535

Information that had appeared in the former Table II, Presidential Documents Included or Cited In Currently Effective Rules, is now indexed in the Presidential document section of Table I.

Table III, Acts Requiring Publication In The *Federal Register*, lists statutes that require specific information to be included in the *Register*. The list, arranged in chronological order according to dates enacted, provides *U.S. Code* and *Statutes at Large* citations. Public law numbers are also given for legislation ratified since 1973.

List of CFR Titles, Chapters, Subchapters, and Parts:

The List of *CFR* Titles, Chapters, Subchapters and Parts follows Table III. This conveniently outlines the entire *CFR*. Title 24, section 868, is illustrated as follows. (figure 6-28)

Figure 6-28
CFR Index and Finding Aids, July 1, 1980
List of CFR Titles, Chapters, Subchapters, and Parts

Chapter VIII—Low Income Housing, Department of Housing and Urban Development (Parts 800—899)

Part
860 Income limits with respect to, admission to, and occupancy of, low-incom housing owned by public housing agencies or leased by public housin agencies from private owners.
861 PHA-owned projects—rents.
865 PHA-owned projects—project management.
866 Lease and grievance procedures.
867 PHA-owned projects—personnel policies and compensation.
868 Modernization program—PHA-owned projects.

The last section of the *CFR Index and Finding Aids* is an alphabetical List of Agencies Appearing In The *CFR*. Titles, subtitles when appropriate, and chapters are indicated beside the agency name.

Supplementary Finding Aids to The Federal Register/Code of Federal Regulations System:

List of CFR Sections Affected (LSA):

The *List of CFR Sections Affected,* published monthly, is used for locating new rules and amendments which have affected existing ones. Time periods covered by the *List of Sections Affected* vary in each issue depending upon when the *CFR* titles were last revised. For example, the March 1981 issue of the *LSA* considers changes incorporated into titles one through sixteen between January and March of that year. Amendments prior to those dates would have already been printed in the revised *Code of Federal Regulations* effective January 1, 1981. That same March 1981 issue covers titles seventeen through twenty-seven from April 1, 1980 through March 1981, twenty-eight through forty-one from July 1, 1980 through March 1981, and forty-two through fifty from October 1, 1980 through March 1981. The dates covered for the various titles are indicated on the *LSA* covers.

Part one of the *LSA* is a checklist of current *CFR* volumes in print and their prices. The following section is arranged by *CFR* titles and their subdivisions. Researchers are referred to *Federal Register* page numbers if the titles and sections they are studying have been revised. For example, the March 1981 *LSA* indicates that the same Title 24, part 868, seen above, was revised by an interim rule printed on page 30350 in the 1980 *Register*. (figure 6-29)

Figure 6-29

LSA, March 1981
List of *CFR* Sections Affected

Chapter VIII—Low-Income Housing, Department of Housing and Urban Development

	Page
865.470—865.482 Undesignated center heading and sections added; interim	59505
865.501—865.504 (Subpart E) Added; interim	41936
865.503 (d) corrected	46380
868.17 Added; interim	30350
869 Added; interim rule	52372
880.201 Corrected	22923
880.208 (b)(1), (2), and (3) revised	62797

The Table of *Federal Register* Issue Pages and Dates, the final section of the *LSA*, converts *Federal Register* page numbers into dates just as the comparable table in the *Register's Index* does. (figure 6-21) Page 30350 was in the May 7 issue.

Regulatory changes which will be reflected in the *CFR Index's* Parallel Table of Authorities and Rules are indicated in the *LSA* table having the same name. *U.S. Code, Statutes at Large*, public law and Presidential document citations are provided with a corresponding list of *CFR* titles and parts affected. Figure 6-30 shows that 42 *USC* 1437 was cited as an authority for changes in 24 *CFR* 200. Underline the relevant part of the illustration.

Figure 6-30

LSA, March 1981
Parallel Table of Authorities and Rules

42 U.S.C.—Continued	CFR
1320b–2	45 Part 95
1320b–2 note	45 Part 95
1382e	20 Part 416
1382g	20 Part 416
1382h	20 Part 416
	42 Part 435
	45 Part 1396
1383c	20 Part 416
1396	20 Part 416
1396d	42 Part 442
1437 et seq	24 Part 200
1437j	29 Parts 1, 5

The second part of the *LSA's* Parallel Table section lists references to *USC, Statutes at Large* and Presidential documents deleted from the *CFR* since its *Index* was last published.

CFR Parts Affected:

The *CFR* Parts Affected, published daily in the *Federal Register*, lists amendments enacted from the beginning of a month through the present date. That is, the finding aid in the March 25, 1982 issue of the *Register* includes all changes incorporated into *CFR* parts between March 1 and 25. (figure 6-31) During this period, 24 *CFR* 868 was not amended.

Figure 6-31

Federal Register, March 25, 1982
CFR Parts Affected During March, 1981

24 CFR

201	17190
203	14743, 16893
207	14743, 16893
213	16893
220	14743, 16893
221	16893
232	16893
234	16893
235	16893
236	16893
241	16893
242	16893
244	16893
300	15505
803	17366
888	17366

Numbers in the right hand column refer to *Federal Register* page numbers. The Parts Affected section is preceded by a list of *Federal Register* page numbers and corresponding dates, enabling researchers to use this finding aid more easily. This cumulative list of parts affected should not be confused with a similar table printed at the beginning of the *Register*, *CFR* Parts Affected In This Issue. Citations in that table are limited to the daily issue in hand.

Secondary Sources That Describe The Regulatory Process:

Index To The Code of Federal Regulations, 1938-1976:

This series, which is published by Information Handling Services in fifty-nine volumes, is a comprehensive index to the *CFR*. Information is accessed through two primary indexes, the Subject Index and the Geographic Index. Both refer users to titles, chapters, parts and page numbers. In each case, the appropriate annual issue is indicated. Annual updated versions of the *Index To The Code of Federal Regulations,* covering 1977 to date, are available from the Congressional Information Service.

Calendar of Federal Regulations:

The *Calendar of Federal Regulations* has been published semiannually as a supplement to the *Federal Register* since 1979. The identical information is later reprinted by the Regulatory Information Center in a separate bound volume. The Calendar provides a non-technical overview of selected significant proposed regulations. The measures often have an annual effect on the economy of one hundred million dollars or more and create major cost increases to industry, government or geographic regions.

Entries in the May 1980 edition are arranged into the following twelve parts.

1. *CFR* citations affected by the proposed rule are indicated.

2. Statutory authority for the regulations are given.

3. Reasons for including the entries in the *Calendar* are stated.

4. Brief statements of the problems at hand are provided.

5. Descriptions of alternative solutions are given.

6. Summaries of benefits to the population, economy, government and other sectors of society are examined. A list of sectors which may be affected by the actions are also included.

7. Expected direct and indirect costs are discussed and sectors of society expected to bear these costs are listed.

8. Related regulations are discussed briefly.

9. Steps to coordinate the proposed rules with other government entities at all levels are examined.

10. Timetables for implementing the measures are given.

11. The availability of related documents are stated.

12. Names, addresses and phone numbers of agency contacts are given.

Information is located in the *Calendar* through various access points. The seven chapters of the May 1980 issue reflect broad subjects—energy; environment and natural resources; finance and banking; health and safety; human resources; trade practices and transportation and commerce. Within each chapter, the proposals are arranged alphabetically by agencies' names.

The *Calendar* has three indexes. The first, Sectors Affected By Regulatory Action, lists proposed rules in sequence by page numbers. The various economic sectors, local government entities, special populations and geographic areas affected by the measures are shown. (figure 6-32)

Figure 6-32

Calendar of Federal Regulations, May 1980
Index I, Sectors Affected By Regulatory Action

INDEX I: SECTORS AFFECTED BY REGULATORY ACTION

Index II. Date of Next Regulatory Action, illustrates when and how agencies are expected to act on their proposals. (figure 6-33)

Figure 6-33
Calendar of Federal Regulations, May 1980
Index II, Date of Next Regulatory Action

This index graphically displays the anticipated date of the next regulatory action that the agency plans to take for each proposed regulation the agency has described in this edition of the Calendar. The index is organized alphabetically by agency, unit within the agency, and then by the title of the regulation.

The actions we note fall into four general categories: ANPRM (the date on which the agency plans to publish an Advance Notice of Proposed Rulemaking in the Federal Register), NPRM (the date on which the agency or department plans to publish a Notice of Proposed Rulemaking in the Federal Register), Final Rule (the date on which the agency plans to publish the final rule in the Federal Register), and Other (the category that indicates the date of any other important next action that does not fall into the above three categories). Independent agencies are most likely to have "Other" actions, such as Staff Recommendations or Commission Decisions.

To see the schedule which the agency anticipates for all future actions on a regulation, the reader should turn to the Calendar entry for that regulation and refer to the Timetable section of the entry.

NOTE: In most cases, the Agencies can only estimate these dates. For current information on any action, please call the agency contact listed in the specific entry.

INDEX II: DATE OF NEXT REGULATORY ACTION

AGENCY	TITLE OF REGULATION	PAGE NO.	MAY '80	JUN '80	JUL '80	AUG '80	SEP '80	OCT '80	NOV '80	DEC '80	JAN '81	FEB '81	MAR '81	APR '81	MAY '81	JUN '81	JUL '81 and beyond
USDA-AMS	Amendments to Federal Seed Act Regulations	547															
USDA-AMS	Proposed Federal Milk Order for the Southwestern Idaho-Eastern Oregon Marketing Area (Boise, Idaho) .	552						O									

The final index, Dates For Public Participation Opportunities, is more useful for the public who wish to comment upon rules, than researchers who are attempting to locate information. (figure 6-34)

Figure 6-34

Calendar of Federal Regulations, May 1980
Index III, Dates For Public Participation Opportunities

INDEX III: DATES FOR PUBLIC PARTICIPATION OPPORTUNITIES

This index provides the basic timetable information needed by readers who are interested in participating in the development of regulations. The index is organized alphabetically by agency, by unit within the agency, and then by the title of the regulation.

The index graphically displays the dates of public comment periods, meetings, and hearings on proposed regulations which agencies describe in this edition of the Calendar. Where possible, we indicate the length and closing dates of the comment periods, where the public should send their written comments, the dates and locations of public hearings and meetings, and the next regulatory action for the entry. The index also indicates whether the agencies provide funding or technical assistance for each regulation.

Not all regulations described in the Calendar are included here; only those with present or future opportunities for public participation. Those which are not listed usually had public comment periods, meetings, or hearings that have passed.

For more information about public participation opportunities, the reader should consult Appendix II: Public Participation in the Federal Regulatory Process. For further information on each regulation the reader should refer to the text of the entry in the appropriate Chapter of the Calendar.

AGENCY	TITLE OF REGULATION	PAGE	MAY 80	JUN 80	JUL 80	AUG 80	SEP 80	OCT 80	NOV 80	DEC 80	JAN 81	FEB 81	MAR 81	APR 81	MAY 81	FUNDING, TECHNICAL ASSISTANCE AVAILABLE (YES/NO)	NEXT REGULATORY ACTION	COMMENTS
USDA-AMS	Amendments to Federal Seed Act Regulations	547			C									C		Funding - No Assistance - Yes	NPRM	Public meetings-September 1979 Public hearing-Planned following NPRM, if USDA decides to amend regulations
USDA-AMS	Proposed Federal Milk Order for the Southeastern Idaho-Eastern Oregon Marketing Area (Boise, Idaho)	552														Funding - No Assistance - Yes	Period Recommended Decision	Public hearing-December 1979 Reopened-hearing-February 1980

The May 1980 *Calendar* has five appendices. The first is a brief explanation of President Carter's program for regulatory reform. The second, Public Participation In The Regulatory Process, is an extremely useful one which outlines statutes and executive orders governing the regulatory process. The third appendix indicates the current status of measures described in the previous November 1979 *Calendar*. A list of expected publication dates for *Regulatory Agendas* appears in the fourth appendix. The fifth is a list of Important Regulations Scheduled For Agency Review. Agencies are required to review their regulations periodically to determine whether or not they are fulfilling intended goals.

Federal Regulatory Directory:

The *Federal Regulatory Directory,* published annually since 1980, is a fine secondary source that considers the regulatory process in a non-technical, lucid manner. The 1981/82 edition includes profiles of thirteen major agencies, plus ninety-three other executive and independent ones. Their responsibilities, histories and recent backgrounds, powers and authorities, and organizations, including names and phone numbers of relevant contacts, are given. Also provided are the names of Congressional committees that deal with similar issues, and names and phone numbers of the Chairmen and staff members. The Information Sources section of the profiles describes publications by and about the agencies, cites names and phone numbers of Freedom of Information Officers, and cites statutory and regulatory authorities. Information is accessed through a comprehensive index that includes subjects, popular names of acts and agency names. Appended material provides a brief description of how the *Federal Register* and the *Code of Federal Regulations* are best used.

Sources of Further Information:

How To Find U.S. Statutes and U.S. Code Citations, fourth revised edition published in 1980, is a nine page pamphlet that summarizes the subject. Information is presented in a chart format and is supplemented by a brief annotated bibliography.

The *Federal Register: What It Is and How To Use It,* distributed by the Office of the Federal Register, is a detailed guide to the *Register,* as well as to the *Code of Federal Regulations.* Ample illustrations and examples are included. The *Document Drafting Handbook,* designed for use by agencies when preparing texts of regulations, is a fine explanation of the various parts of regulations and their relationships. A third source, *Federal Regulation: Administrative Rules and Rulemaking,* written by Rita Ann Reimer and published by the Congressional Research Service, is also extremely useful.

On-Line Availability of Legislation and Regulations:

The *Federal Register* data base is available on-line from Capitol Services Incorporated for March 1977 to date. Selected information about *United States Code, Code of Federal Regulations* and *Federal Register* citations are available in a second data base, the *Federal Index,* which is also prepared by Capitol Services.

Chapter 6 Footnotes

[1]The *Statutes at Large* should be used only for its primary purpose, to cite laws. The sources described in Chapters 3 and 4 are more appropriate references for legislative histories. The legislative history of Public Law 94-375 as cited in the *Statutes* is incorrect. Figure 6-1 mentions two bills, H.R. 12,945 and H.R. 9852. S. 3295, the bill which eventually became PL 94-375, is not listed. The legislative history, as seen in the illustration, fails to indicate that it was S. 3295 which the Senate passed on April 27 and that the House passed that same bill on May 26 in lieu of H.R. 12,945. Also, citations to the conference reports are omitted.

BIBLIOGRAPHY

Calendar of Federal Regulations. Regulatory Information Center. Washington, D.C.: GPO, 1979-semiannual. Issued by the United States Regulatory Council between 1979 and 1980.

Code of Federal Regulations. National Archives and Records Service. Office of The Federal Register. Washington, D.C.: GPO, 1949-annual. Between 1938 and 1948 supplements to the first edition were issued irregularly.

Code of Federal Regulations, LSA, List of CFR Sections Affected. National Archives and Records Service. Office of The Federal Register. Washington, D.C.: GPO, September 1977-monthly. Published under various titles prior to September 1977. Original date of publication could not be determined.

Corpus Juris Secundum: A Complete Restatement of the Entire American Law As Developed By All Reported Cases, comp. by William Mack and Donald J. Kiser. Brooklyn, N.Y.: American Law Book Co., 1936-74. 101 numbered vols. in a set of 136.

Document Drafting Handbook. National Archives and Records Service. Office of The Federal Register. Rev. ed. Washington, D.C.: GPO, 1980.

Executive Orders and Proclamations: Study of Use of Presidential Powers. House Government Operations Committee. Committee Print. 85th Cong., 1st sess. Washington, D.C.: GPO, 1957.

Federal Register. National Archives and Record Service. Office of The Federal Register. Washington, D.C.: GPO, 1936-daily except Saturday, Sunday and Federal holidays.

The Federal Register: What It Is and How To Use It, A Guide For the User of the Federal Register—Code of Federal Regulations System. Ed. by Judie Craine. Office of the Federal Register. Washington, D.C.: National Archives and Records Service, 1980.

Federal Regulation: Administrative Rules and Rulemaking. Rita Ann Reimer and David R. Siddall. Report number 79-30 A. Washington, D.C.: Congressional Research Service, 1979. Reprinted in: *Major Studies and Issue Briefs of the Congressional Research Service, 1978-79 Supplement.* Washington, D.C.: University Publications of America, 1979.

Federal Regulatory Directory. Washington, D.C.: Congressional Quarterly Inc., 1979/80-annual.

How To Find U.S. Statutes and U.S. Code Citations. Dorothy Muse. Updated by Marie F. Faria Yeast. 4th ed. National Archives and Records Service. Office of The Federal Register. Washington, D.C.: GPO, 1980.

Index To The Code of Federal Regulations, 1938-1976. Englewood, Colorado: Information Handling Services, 1978-   .

Index To The Code of Federal Regulations. Washington, D.C.: Congressional Information Service, Inc., 1977-annual. (First issues covering 1977-1981 published in 1982).

Revised Statutes of the United States, Passed at the First Session of the Forty-Third Congress, 1873-74; Embracing the Statutes of the United States, General and Permanent In Their Nature, In Force Dec. 1, 1873. 2nd ed. Washington, D.C.: GPO, 1878.

United States Code. House Office of the Law Revision Counsel. Washington, D.C.: GPO, 1926-approximately every six years. Supplements issued annually.

United States Code Annotated. St. Paul: West Publishing Company, 1927-irregular. Pocket supplements issued annually. Replacement volumes issued irregularly.

United States Code Congressional and Administrative News. St. Paul: West Publishing Company, 1942-semimonthly when Congress is in session and monthly when Congress is not in session.

United States Code Service: Lawyers' Edition. Rochester, N.Y.: The Lawyers' Co-Operative Publishing Co., 1972-   . Updated with annual cumulative pockets. Replacement volumes are cumulated as necessary.

United States Statutes at Large. National Archives and Records Service, Office of the Federal Register. Washington, D.C.: GPO, 1937-annual. Earlier volumes covering 1789-1936 published irregularly. Published by Department of State between 1873 and 1950.

Chapter 6 Questions

Your community is considering construction of a bikeway along a highway that is being built with Federal funds. Your job is to investigate Federal legislation and regulations on this topic.

1. The *United States Code* is a good starting point. Questions 1A-D refer to the 1976 edition.

    A. In which volume and on what page of the General Index is appropriate information listed under "bicycles"?

    B. Where in the *USC* is appropriate information located? Note the title and section.

    C. In which volume and on what pages is this citation printed?

    D. The *USC* cites three laws that affect bikeways. Indicate their public law numbers.

    E. Consult the most recent supplement to the 1976 edition of the *United States Code* to determine if this same title and section has been revised. If yes, note the relevant public law number(s).

2. Public Law 93-87 appears in volume _____ of the *Statutes at Large*

on pages _____ through _____ .

3. Which Congressional report(s) relating to PL 93-87 are reprinted in the *United States Code Congressional and Administrative News.*?

4. Into which title and section of the *USC* has section 137 of PL 93-87 been incorporated?

5. Use Table 1 of the *CFR Index and Finding Aids* to locate relevant CFR

sections relating to 23 USC 217. The regulations appear in _____ CFR _____

and _____.

6. When did 23 CFR 652 appear in the *Federal Register?* Note the date, volume, and page number.

7. How would you confirm if the rules have been amended since the *CFR* was last distributed?

Chapter 6 Answers

    1A. Volume 13, page 607.

    B. 23 USC 217.

    C. Volume 6, pages 892-893.

    D. PL 93-87, PL 93-643, and PL 94-280.

    E. The most recent supplement currently available, that of 1980, indicates that PL 95-599 amended 23 USC 217. (Volume 2, page 1687).

    2. Volume 87, pages 250-296.

    3. House Report 93-118 and Senate Report 93-355.

    4. Table III of the *USC* indicates that section 137 was incorporated into 23 *USC* 103. (Table III, page 1227).

    5. 23 CFR 652 and 655.

    6. April 26, 1978. 43 FR 17814.

    7. Two sources are used to confirm this information, the List of CFR Sections Affected and the "CFR Parts Affected During (month)," which appears in each *Federal Register*. At the time of this writing (April 1981), 23 CFR 652, effective April 1, 1980, had not since been amended.

CHAPTER 7

LOCATING FEDERAL STATISTICS

The Federal government is the most prolific publishers of statistics in the world. Washington distributes over 7,500 statistical documents annually. The first section of this chapter describes the *American Statistics Index (ASI)*, the most comprehensive guide to United States government statistics currently available. Like the *Congressional Information Service*, the *ASI* is a commercial source issued in two parts, the *Abstract* volume and the *Index* volume. Both have been published monthly since 1973. The *Abstracts* are cumulated annually, while the *Indexes* are cumulated quarterly and annually. The first annual cumulated edition, the *1974 Annual and Retrospective Edition*, is especially important because it cites documents in print as of January 1, 1974 and also indexes significant statistical publications issued since the early 1960's. The chapter's second section describes selected quick reference statistical sources available in many libraries.

American Statistics Index:

The *American Statistics Index* provides access to data that relate primarily to social, economic, demographic and environmental topics. Periodicals, annual reports, special studies and irregular publications are among the major types of documents indexed. Press releases and related materials are indexed when they contain information not readily available in another form. Scientific, technical, and experimental statistics are included when they have significant social or economic implications. Documents issued by sub-agencies are cited when their information is unavailable in agency-wide reports. For instance, the annual reports of the Department of Labor will be indexed and abstracted, but those of the Department's Office of Mine Safety and Health will be included only when they contain unique data. Congressional publications, excluding appropriation hearings due to their voluminous natures, are also indexed. Appropriation hearings are indexed very adequately in the *CIS Index*.

To use the *ASI*, first consult the *Index* volume and then refer to the *Abstract* volume. The *Index* volume consists of five parts—the Index by Subjects and Names, the Index by Categories, the Index by Titles, and the Index by Agency Report Numbers. The fifth part, the Guide To Selected Standard Classifications, describes briefly statistical classifications used by the Federal government and indicates where more detailed information about them are located. When using the indexes, note the *ASI* entry numbers which follow each citation. References are listed in the *Abstract* volume in numerical order according to these numbers.

Index of Subjects and Names, Subject Approach:

To locate data pertaining to the public housing situation, search appropriate subject headings in the Index of Subjects and Names. Figure 7-1 shows excerpts from entries listed under "Low-income housing."

Figure 7-1

ASI, Index of Subjects and Names, 1979.
Subject Approach

Low-income housing
Aged and handicapped persons housing,
  HUD low-cost financing program (Section
  202), occupant and project characteristics,
  and finances and cost effectiveness,
  1959-77, 5188-51
Allowances for low-income families to
  obtain housing, experimental HUD
  program in 12 metro areas, series,
  5186-2
Developing countries housing conditions and
  housing sector activity, detailed data, and
  summary socioeconomic data, country rpt
  series, 7206-5
HUD housing and community dev
  programs, related research and policies,
  analytical paper series, 5186-8
Low-rent public housing program status,
  quarterly rpt, 5002-1.6
Multifamily HUD-assisted housing project
  residents satisfaction with mgmt and
  facilities, related to sociodemographic
  characteristics, 1972-77, 5188-57
Municipal bond issues for lower-interest
  home mortgage loans, Illinois, as of June
  1, 1979, article, 9375-1.804

"Low-rent public housing program status, quarterly report" is used as an example.

Refer to figure 7-1 when answering the following:

The *ASI* entry number for the citation in question is ———————— .

    5002-1.6

This document is part of a serial that is issued ———————— .

    quarterly

Index of Subjects and Names, Subject Approach:

Abstract Volume:
    Entry number 5002-1.6 appears as indicated in the *Abstract* volume. (figure
7-2)

Figure 7-2

ASI, Abstract Volume, 1979

1.————— 5002-1   HOUSING AND URBAN ————————2.
                        DEVELOPMENT TRENDS
3.—————————————Quarterly. Approx. 50 p. ——————4.
                        HUD 316-(nos.)-UD.——————5.
6.————————————— •Item 581-E-10. †
                        ASI/MF/4
                        *HH1.14:(v.nos.&nos.) ————————7.
8.————————————— MC 79-1153.

Quarterly report on current housing production
and finance and HUD program activities and
funding. Most data are shown by month through
the cover date quarter and for last 2-4 years.
  Contents consist of 43 tables, listed below.
Issues covered during 1979: Sept. 1978-Mar. 1979
(D) (Vol. 31, Nos. 3, 4; Vol. 32, No. 2).

TABLES:

5002-1.1: Production of Housing Units
  ["Type of structure" is single- and multiunit.]
  NEW HOUSING STARTS
  A1. Total, private and public.
  A2. Private, by census region.

5002-1.6: Other HUD Housing Programs
  E9. FHA property improvement loans: total
  and mobile homes insured.
  E10. FHA rent supplement program: reserva-
  tions and contracts executed.
  E11. Low rent public housing programs.
  E12. Community development block grant
  program: approvals.
  ‖ E13. Rehabilitation loans: approvals.

Reproduced with permission from *American
Statistics Index,* published and copyrighted by
Congressional Information Service, Inc., 4520
East-West Highway, Washington, D.C. 20014.

1. *ASI* entry number.   5. Series number.
2. Title.   6. Depository status.
3. Frequency.   7. Superintendent of Documents number.
4. Pagination.   8. *Monthly Catalog* entry number.

The decimal point, ".6," is used for more specific indexing. This enables
researchers to locate their data more easily. To obtain the bibliographic information, the Superintendent of Documents number, and the depository status, refer
from the decimal point to the whole number, "5002-1."

Refer to figure 7-2 when answering the following:

  The title of this document is ————————————————— .

Housing and Urban Development Trends

Each issue has approximately _____ pages.

50

Is this publication a depository or a non-depository one?

depository

Its SuDoc number is _____ .

HH1.14: (To complete the SuDoc number, fill in the volume and issue numbers of the editions needed.)

Tables _____ and _____ would probably have information relevant to public housing.

E10 and E11

Other parts of the bibliographic heading need explanation. The cross immediately following the item number indicates that the document may be available from the publishing agency, the Department of Housing and Urban Development. "ASI/MF/4" is a price code indicating the cost of a microfiche edition of the document. Fiche availability is mentioned below. "MC 79-1153" shows that this document was entry number 1153 in the 1979 *Monthly Catalog*.

To obtain further practice using the *American Statistics Index,* answer the following questions which relate to figure 7-3. This article compares social welfare expenditures among various functions, including housing.

Figure 7-3
ASI, Abstract Volume, 1979

4742-1   SOCIAL SECURITY
         BULLETIN
         Monthly. Approx. 90 p.
         SSA (yr.)-11700. ●Item 523.
         GPO: $14.00 per yr.; single
         copy $1.35. ASI/MF/3
         S/N 017-070-80001-7.
         *HE3.3:(v.nos.&nos.)
         MC 79-971.   LC 40-29327.

Monthly journal providing information and statistics on current social security developments and programs, and historical data from 1940 or year of initiation of program.

Contains feature articles, individually described below; and the following regular monthly departments:

a. Social security in review, including program operations summary.

b. Notes and brief reports, including social security abroad.

c. Recent publications.

d. Current operating statistics, 48 tables, listed below.

JUNE 1979
Vol. 42, No. 6

4742-1.812: Social Welfare Expenditures Under Public Programs, FY77

By Alma McMillan (p. 3-12). Annual article on expenditures for social services programs, selected years FY50-77. Covers Federal and State/local outlays for social insurance, public assistance, health and medical programs, veterans programs, education, and housing.

Includes 1-chart and the following 5 tables with data for selected years, FY50-77:

1. Social welfare expenditures under public programs [by detailed function]. (p. 4-6)

2. Total and per capita social welfare expenditures under public programs in the U.S., in actual and 1977 prices. (p. 9)

3. Social welfare expenditures under public programs as percent of GNP. (p. 10)

4. Social welfare expenditures under public programs: Federal funds as percent of total. (p. 12)

e. Quarterly statistics, 33 tables, also listed be-low, appearing in Mar., June, Sept., and Dec. issues.

Issues covered during 1979: Jan.-Oct. 1979 (P) (Vol. 42, Nos. 1-10).

5. Social welfare expenditures from public funds in relation to government expenditures for all purposes, by type of fund. (p. 12)

Previous report included data on private ex-penditures for social services (see ASI 1977 Annual, 4742-1.601).

Entry number 4742-1.812 is an article entitled " _____

_____ ."

Social Welfare Expenditures Under Public Programs, FY77

It is published __(frequency) .__

annually

Its author is _____ _____ .

Alma McMillan

The article is printed on pages _____ through _____ .

3 through 12

Statistics relating to social welfare expenditures under public programs as a

percent of the Gross National Product are printed on page_____, table_____.

page 10, table 3

It was cited in the 1979 *Monthly Catalog*, entry number _____ .

79-971

The stock number, _____ , is used when purchasing docu-ments from the Government Printing Office.

017-070-80001-7

The article in question appeared in the _____ , 1979 issue of _____

_____ .

June, *Social Security Bulletin*

Its SuDoc number is _____ .

HE3.3:42/6

Index By Subjects and Names—Name Approach:

The Index of Subjects and Names lists personal authors, in addition to subject headings. Alma McMillan, the author of the article seen in figure 7-3, is indicated as follows. (figure 7-4) Underline the appropriate citation.

Figure 7-4

ASI, Index Volume, 1979
Index of Subjects and Names
Name Approach

McLain, William H.
"Role of Fire Prevention and Control on
Building Construction and Regulations",
2218-51

McLemore, Thomas
"1977 Summary: National Ambulatory
Medical Care Survey", 4146-8.47

McMillan, Alma
"Social Welfare Expenditures, FY77",
4746-16.1
"Social Welfare Expenditures Under Public
Programs, FY77", 4742-1.812

McMillan, B. C.
"Hepatitis-B Surface Antigen and Antibody:
Prevalence and Persistence in
Institutionalized and Noninstitutionalized
Persons", 4102-1.824

McMillan, Carl H.
"Soviet Investment in the Industrialized
Western Economies and in the
Developing Economies of the Third
World", 23848-113.2

Reproduced with permission from *American
Statistics Index,* published and copyrighted by
Congressional Information Service, Inc., 4520
East-West Highway, Washington, D.C. 20014.

Index By Titles:

The Index by Titles includes the titles of all documents that are abstracted, plus the titles of articles and essays that appear in edited volumes and periodicals. The article seen in figure 7-3, "Social Welfare Expenditures Under Public Programs" and the periodical it appeared in, *Social Security Bulletin,* are illustrated below. (figure 7-5) Underline the appropriate *ASI* entry numbers.

Figure 7-5

ASI, Index Volume, 1979
Index by Titles

Social Security Benefits for Women in the
Federal Republic of Germany, Switzerland,
and the United Kingdom, 4748-28
Social Security Bulletin, 4742-1
Social Security Disability Insurance Program,
9373-1.804
Social Security Farmworker Statistics, 1975,
4746-16.11

Social Security in a Changing World,
4748-28

Social Security Legislation, 23844-4.3

Social Service Insurance Dilemma: Problems,
Analysis, and Proposed Solutions,
7308-138

Social Services U.S.A.: Statistical Tables,
Summaries and Analyses of Services Under
Social Security Act Titles XX, IV-B, and
IV-A/C for Fifty States and D.C., 4882-1

Social Welfare Expenditures, FY77,
4746-16.1

Social Welfare Expenditures Under Public
Programs, FY77, 4742-1.812

Index By Categories:

The Index by Categories divides all data into twenty-one categories falling within three broad groups—geographic, economic and demographic breakdowns.

GEOGRAPHIC BREAKDOWNS

By Census Division	By Outlying Area
By City	By Region
By County	By SMSA
By Foreign Country	By State
	By Urban-Rural

ECONOMIC BREAKDOWNS

By Commodity	By Industry
By Federal Agency	By Occupation
By Income	
By Individual Company or Institution	

DEMOGRAPHIC BREAKDOWNS

By Age	By Marital Status
By Disease	By Race
By Educational Attainment	By Sex

Statistics in each category are then separated into the following sub-headings.

Agriculture and Food
Banking, Finance, and Insurance
Communications and Transportation
Education
Energy Resources and Demand
Geography and Climate
Government and Defense
Health and Vital Statistics
Housing and Construction

Industry and Commerce
Labor and Employment
Law Enforcement
Natural Resources, Environment, and
    Pollution
Population
Prices and Cost of Living
Public Welfare and Social Security
Recreation and Leisure
Science and Technology
Veterans Affairs

For instance, citations broken down "By Age" and subdivided by "Population" refer to statistics that measure population comparatively among various age groups. To give a second example, researchers interested in locating data pertaining to the income characteristics of individuals receiving supplemental rent payments can locate appropriate information in the breakdown "By Income" subdivided by "Housing and Construction." (figure 7-6)

Figure 7-6
ASI, Index Volume, 1979
Index by Categories

BY INCOME

Housing and Construction
Black Americans migration from central cities
    to suburbs, and other intra-SMSA mobility,
    compared to whites, by income, education,
    region, and selected SMSA, 1955-78,
    5188-53
Home mortgages FHA-insured, financial,
    property, and mortgagor characteristics, US
    summary quarterly rpt, 5142-1
Home mortgages FHA-insured, financial,
    structural, property, and mortgagor
    characteristics, 1978, annual summary rpt.
    5144-17
HUD housing and community dev programs,
    related research and policies, analytical
    paper series, 5186-8
Low-rent housing HUD projects, problems,
    and project, tenant, and neighborhood
    characteristics, 1978, 5188-65
Minority and other population subgroups
    housing conditions, flaws, and affordability
    of adequate housing, series, 5186-6
Mortgagors demographic characteristics,
    HUD housing programs, selected years
    1955-77, annual statistical yearbook,
    5004-1.13
Rent subsidies for low-income families, HUD
    Section 8 Assistance Program participating
    households and landlords characteristics,
    experiences, and attitudes, 1976 survey and
    evaluation, 5188-52

Index By Agency Report Numbers:

The Index by Agency Report Numbers indexes documents by report numbers within each agency. When report numbers are known, this approach provides more direct access to the abstracts than that of subjects. For instance, report number HUD-PDR-473-2 appears in the index as seen in figure 7-7.

Figure 7-7

ASI, Index Volume, 1979
Index by Agency Report Numbers

DEPARTMENT OF HOUSING AND URBAN DEVELOPMENT

HUD-PDR-413	5186-6.4
HUD-PDR-444	5186-11.1
HUD-PDR-463	5188-65
HUD-PDR-469	5188-66
HUD-PDR-473-2	5182-1
HUD SOR-3	5144-1

Reproduced with permission from *American Statistics Index*, published and copyrighted by Congressional Information Service, Inc., 4520 East-West Highway, Washington, D.C. 20014.

According to figure 7-7, the *ASI* entry number for HUD-PDR-473-2 is

_____ .

5182-1

Using The Quarterly Cumulative Indexes:

Figure 7-8 is a typical example of the quarterly cumulative indexes. The bold faced numbers in parentheses preceding the *ASI* entry numbers indicate which monthly abstract volume researchers must consult. For example, articles pertaining to characteristics of households appear in the October, November and December *Abstract* volumes.

Figure 7-8

ASI, Quarterly Index, 1978

Public housing
Characteristics of housing and households, and unit and neighborhood quality and deficiencies, 20 SMSAs, 1976, annual survey series, **(10)(11)(12)** 2485-6
Govt revenues by source, expenditures by function, debt, and assets, detailed data by State or large cities or counties, FY77, annual rpt series, **(12)** 2466-2
Inventory and costs of Fed Govt-owned real property, detailed worldwide listing, by location, agency, and use, Sept 30, 1978, annual rpt, **(10)** 9454-20

Public attitudes about public services and
govt efficiency and fiscal responsibilities
in central cities, suburbs, small towns, and
rural areas, by sociodemographic
characteristics, 1978 natl survey,
(12) 5188–47.5

Reproduced with permission from *American
Statistics Index*, published and copyrighted by
Congressional Information Service, Inc., 4520
East-West Highway, Washington, D.C. 20014.

ASI Microfiche Library:

Practically all documents indexed in the ASI are available on microfiche as part of the *ASI Microfiche Library of Statistical Publications of the US Government*. Microfiche are sold either on a subscription or a demand basis. The "ASI/MF" code that appears in most abstract citations indicates the price of fiche copies when purchased on a demand basis. Contact the publisher to obtain current price information.

On-Line Availability of ASI:

The *American Statistics Index* is available on-line from 1973 to date through the Lockheed and the Systems Development Corporations.

Further Information:

Consult the *American Statistics Index User Guide* for more detailed information. It is available from the Congressional Information Service for a nominal fee.

> 4520 East-West Highway
> Suite 800
> Washington, D.C. 20014

The introductions to both the *Index* and *Abstract* volumes also provide valuable insight. A third source, the *ASI Search Guide*, a two page flier distributed by the publisher, is a fine summary of the reference tool.

Selected Quick Reference Statistical Sources:

Very often, researchers must incorporate quick reference statistics into their work. Detailed bibliographic searching can sometimes be avoided in such cases. The Federal government publishes many reference tools that include this type of data. Twelve selected sources that provide a general statistical overview of society are described below.

Statistical Abstract of The United States

Pocket Data Book

Historical Statistics of The United States: Colonial Times To 1970

County and City Data Book, 1977

Congressional District Data Book

State and Metropolitan Area Data Book, 1979

Directory of Federal Statistics For Local Areas: A Guide To Sources, 1976.

Directory of Federal Statistics For Local Areas: A Guide To Sources, Urban Update, 1977-1978.

Social Indicators III: Selected Data on Social Conditions and Trends In The United States.

Federal Statistical Directory

A Statistical Portrait of Women In The United States, 1978

The Social and Economic Status of The Black Population In The United States: An Historical View, 1790-1978.

Following that, additional sources that pertain to seven popular topics are considered.

Education

Energy, environment, and natural resources

Health

Housing and construction

Labor, business, and economics

Law enforcement and crime

Transportation

The sources are, for the most part, serial publications issued at pre-determined intervals. Thus, most data is relatively recent. A limited number of monographs and other serials published irregularly, are included due to their special significance.

General Statistical Overviews:

The *Statistical Abstract of The United States,* distributed by the Bureau of the Census, is the single most important handbook to current Federal data. It has been published annually since 1879. The 1980 edition's thirty-four chapters are arranged topically. Population, banking, finance and insurance, social welfare, environment, energy, agriculture and manufacturing are examined, among other topics. Though most data relates to the national scene, chapter thirty-three depicts comparative international statistics. Each chapter is preceded by an introductory section where appropriate definitions are given. From its first issue through the current one, footnotes following each table indicate the sources from which the information was extracted. The notes are, consequently, not only a significant resource for researchers involved with contemporary issues, but for historians as well. The appendices include two major bibliographies. One lists both public and private sources of additional information in a topical arrangement, while the other lists names and addresses of state agencies which publish state statistical abstracts. The index to the *Statistical Abstracts* is an extremely comprehensive one.

Five supplements to the *Statistical Abstracts* are published by the Bureau of the Census. The *Pocket Data Book,* issued in 1979, is an abridged version of the *Abstracts.* Its twenty-five chapters include current data, plus historical trends. The introductory section is a fine statistical summary of the American socioeconomic picture. Government agencies and private entities from which the data was obtained are noted following each table, but specific titles are omitted. The *Pocket Data Book's* index is a fairly comprehensive one.

The two volume set, *Historical Statistics of The United States: Colonial Times To 1970,* is a second important *Statistical Abstract* supplement. All facets of American life are covered in twenty-six chapters. Each one is preceded by an introduction that cites both public and private sources for further study. Again, the index is an excellent finding device.

The three remaining supplements to the *Abstracts* depict data at local levels. The ninth edition of the *County and City Data Book, 1977* includes nearly two hundred data items relating to regions, states, counties, and cities whose populations are 25,000 or more. Data pertaining to standard metropolitan statistical areas (SMSA's) are also considered. In most simplified terms, SMSA's are census divisions that include central cities of at least 50,000 people and their surrounding suburbs, all of which form a socioeconomic whole. The *County and City Data Book* concentrates upon population, vital statistics, labor force, health, income, social welfare, housing, local government finance, election, crime and business statistics. The data is extracted from government and private sources. The *Congressional District Data Book,* the fourth supplement, is similar to the *County and City Data Book,* except that its data pertains to congressional districts.

The first edition of the *State and Metropolitan Area Data Book, 1979,* which was published in 1980, is the newest *Statistical Abstract* supplement. National, regional and state information is described in two thousand and eight data series, whereas those for SMSA's are deliniated in four hundred and forty data items. Current information and historical trends are given. The three major tables are each indexed separately. Five appendices list SMSA's in rank order according to twenty-one categories, describe effects of population trends and changes upon standard metropolitan statistical area definitions, list components of SMSA's by square miles and populations, indicate names of local agencies that prepare population estimates and provide population data by congressional districts. Source notes to further references which provide more detailed information are given. Although the *State and Metropolitan Data Book* covers the national, regional, state, and metropolitan scene in greater detail than the *County and City Data Book,* it excludes the cities located outside SMSA's that are considered in the latter volume.

While on the subject of local data, the *Directory of Federal Statistics For Local Areas,* a bibliographic guide issued in 1976, should be mentioned. Reports that include national data broken down by areas smaller than states are included. The sixteen chapters cover agriculture, banking, commerce, transportation, law enforcement, environment, government and revenue sharing, housing, income and prices, plus other topics. The information is presented in a tabular format as seen in figure 7-9.

Figure 7-9

Directory of Federal Statistics For Local Areas

Subject	Tabular Detail	Areas to Which Data Apply	Frequency	Sources (See Bibliography, pp. 329-339.)
GOVERNMENT FINANCES— Con.	Local government finances:—Con. Property Sales and gross receipts General: selective Other Current charges Miscellaneous Water supply; other utility revenue General expenditure, all functions			150. *County Government Finances, 1974-75,* tables 4, 5. (Also later issues.) 148. *City Government Finances, 1974-75,* tables 5, 6. (Also later issues.) Census Bureau

| Revenue and Expenditures, in Detail | Local government finances, in detail
  Total revenue
  General revenue
   Intergovernmental
    From State
     In 5 to 7 functions[a]
    From Federal
     General revenue sharing
    From local
   From own sources
    Taxes.
     Property | Counties of 500,000 or more; 48 largest cities | Annual | 150. *Current Government Reports, County Government Finances in 1974-75,* table 6. (Also later issues.) 148. *City Government Finances, 1974-75,* table 7. (Also later issues.) Census Bureau. |

More complete bibliographic citations are provided in the bibliography section where the references are listed in numerical sequence. Sources for unpublished data are also given. The index to this *Directory* is a thorough one.

The 1977-78 update to the *Directory of Federal Statistics For Local Areas* emphasizes urban areas. Information pertaining to special areas, such as engineering or fishery districts, which was included in the 1976 volume, is omitted from the updated one. The *Update's* cumulative index refers researchers to the 1976 edition.

Social Indicators III: Selected Data on Social Conditions and Trends In The United States, published in 1980, is the third edition in a series that measures the quality of American life. Social conditions and their trends and developments are examined through narrative discussions and are illustrated in charts and tables. Most data is aggregate for the U.S., but selected statistics relate to race, sex and age groups. The eleven chapters cover population and family, health, work, social participation (voting, volunteerism, group memberships) and utilization of leisure time, plus additional issues. The introduction includes an extensive bibliography on social indicators, their uses and the quality of life. Every chapter has a concluding section on international comparisons, in addition to bibliographies and contracts for further information. The index is small, but adequate.

The former Office of Federal Statistical Policy and Standards within the Department of Commerce had been charged with coordinating Federal statistical activities. Effective April 1, 1981, this function was transferred to the Office of Information and Regulatory Affairs, a division of the Office of Management and Budget. The new agency has yet to distribute significant reference material. The *Federal Statistical Directory,* a valuable tool issued by the former body, is a phone book listing the major statistical agencies in the Federal government. It has usually been published biennially since 1935. Entries, which are arranged by agencies, include the names, phone numbers and addresses of appropriate personnel. Researchers must be familiar with the Washington bureaucracy to use the *Directory* most effectively because it lacks a subject index. This source should be used in conjunction with the *Federal Executive Telephone Directory,* a bimonthly commercial publication, to obtain the latest changes in personnel and phone numbers.

Researchers sometimes require general statistical overviews of significant sectors of the population. Two important groups, women and blacks, are the focus of much attention. A *Statistical Portrait of Women In The United States, 1978,* distributed in 1980, is a fine compilation. The fourteen topical chapters compare the socioeconomic condition of females to males during the 1970's with historical trends since the 1950's. Data concerning black, Hispanic, Native American and Asian females in comparison to Caucasian women is also given. Information is presented in charts, graphs and tables. An earlier edition published in 1976 includes selected trends since 1900. Those studying this subject should also be aware of *Issues in Federal Statistical Needs Relating To Women,* a compendium of papers presented at an April 1978 Bureau of the Census conference.

Regarding the black population, *The Social and Economic Status of The Black Population In The United States: An Historical View,* published in 1979, is the tenth such report. Census data, plus other selected public and private statistics, document historical changes in demographic, economic and social characteristics. Part I covers 1790-1975, while part II emphasizes 1975-1978. Additional sources of information for further study are cited.

Education:

The *Digest of Education Statistics* and *The Condition of Education* are two significant statistical publications that provide overviews of education. The former has been issued annually since 1962. Data from both public and private sources that relate to the pre-kindergarten period through graduate education is included. The most current 1980 volume is divided into six chapters that differentiate between instructional levels. The sixth section, which covers special studies, incorporates information on education and work, libraries, museums, public television and the international picture. References to further information follow each table. The data is accessed through a comprehensive subject index.

The *Condition of Education* is an annual publication distributed since 1975. It delineates educational conditions in perspective of the larger social picture. Data from Federal, state and private concerns are provided. This volume differs from the *Digest* in that it includes more narrative discussion and a greater number of charts. Sources for further study are cited. The 1980 issue has a small glossary and a fairly comprehensive subject index that cumulates information from editions published between 1977 and 1980.

Energy, Environment and Natural Resources:

The Department of Energy's Energy Information Administration is responsible for the collection, processing and dissemination of statistics concerning energy reserves, production, consumption and related issues. Its three Volume *Annual Report To Congress* describes historical, current, and projected energy data. Though Volume I, primarily a description of the agency's activities, contains limited statistics, Volumes II and III are particularly important to researchers requiring data. The second volume examines retrospective figures and provides current information whereas, the third, which incorporates much narrative discussion, concentrates upon statistical projections. Most data is in tabular format, but charts and graphs are also used. The second volume's index is more comprehensive than that of the last volume. Concerning bibliographic references, Volume I lists Energy Information Administration publications issued during the previous year and Volumes II and III cite sources for additional statistics.

The *Monthly Energy Review,* distributed since October 1974, is an excellent source for current information. Its various sections cover types of energy, such as coal, electricity, nuclear power and natural gas, plus other issues relating to consumption, prices and international comparisons. The tables include annual historical trends for eight years. Monthly figures are given for the most recent two years. Footnotes are appended to each section and conversion factors, which state approximate heat content of various fuels and indicate units of measure, are provided. Selected issues also include feature articles.

Turning to natural resources other than those used for energy, the *Minerals Yearbook,* published annually since 1882/83, is a major three volume statistical source. Volume I is a topical arrangement that considers specific minerals in separate essays. Production, consumption, uses, prices and foreign trade are emphasized. The number of tables in each chapter varies depending upon the significance of the mineral under discussion. Many footnotes are included.

Volumes II and III are area reports that relate respectively to the United States and foreign nations. The domestic volume has separate chapters on each state. Its tables measure county production by value and relationships of mining to the states' general business climate. Relevant local legislation and programs are mentioned, and lists of major producers within each county by kinds of minerals and type of production are given. Volume III consists of essays that summarize mineral and mining conditions in countries throughout the world. Imports and exports to and from specific nations are sometimes indicated.

Health:

The National Center for Health Statistics within the Department of Health and Human Services is the agency primarily responsible for the collection and dissemination of health related statistics. Its annual publication, *Health United States*, has been issued since 1976. A narrative discussion is supplemented by graphs, charts and small tables. Comprehensive lists of further references are provided. Detailed statistics appear following the descriptive information. Among the subjects included are utilization of health resources, expenditures for health care and physician supply and demand. The 1980 edition included a new section, "Preventive Profile," which will henceforth appear every third year. It evaluates economic burdens that preventive medicine could reduce, successes and failures of preventive controls and methods of tracking future progress in the field.

The third edition of *Facts At Your Fingertips: A Guide To Sources of Statistical Information on Major Health Topics* was published by the Center For Health Statistics in 1978. Under each topic, appropriate contacts, their addresses and their phone numbers are indicated. Personnel with the Department of Health, Education, and Welfare (since changed to the Department of Health and Human Services), other Federal agencies and private concerns are cited.

Housing and Construction:

The *HUD Statistical Yearbook* has been issued annually since 1966. It covers data relating to Department of Housing and Urban Development programs and financial operations, plus other housing and urban activities. The information is based upon statistics compiled by HUD, other Federal agencies, and private sources. Most data reflects national and state conditions. Community planning and development, fair and equal housing, insurance programs, new construction, housing sales, mortgage financing and occupancy, among other issues are examined. The index is moderately comprehensive.

Labor, Business and Economics:

The *Economic Report of The President,* published annually since 1947, provides a fine statistical overview of the national economy. The first two sections include annual reports of the President and the Council of Economic Advisors. The Presidential statement is a brief one, whereas that of the Council is far more extensive and includes limited tables. The third part of the *Report* consists of detailed statistics covering national income and expenditures, employment, wages, productivity, price indexes, credit, government finance, corporate profits and finance, agriculture and international comparisons. Selected information includes historical trends since 1929.

Two major publications distributed by the Bureau of Labor Statistics depict the conditions of workers, the *Handbook of Labor Statistics,* issued annually since 1924/26 and the *Monthly Labor Review,* published monthly since 1915. The former is a compilation of the Bureau's data series, plus selected figures produced by other agencies and nations. Employment, unemployment, marital and family characteristics, work experience, earnings, educational enrollment and attainment, productivity, prices and living conditions, labor relations, occupational illness and foreign labor statistics are among the topics covered. Historical and current statistics are given. Each section includes technical notes which define terms and lists sources of reference. These notes sometimes describe historical and/or current comparability with other data. Further references for additional information are appended to many tables and are listed at the end of the *Handbook.*

The *Monthly Labor Review* also provides quick reference data on major Bureau of Labor Statistics programs. Though trends generally through one or two years are provided, emphasis is upon current statistics. Employment, hours, earnings, unemployment insurance, price indexes, productivity and labor-management relations are covered. Most information relates to the national level, but selected state data is provided. The "Notes on Current Labor Statistics" section describes the availability of more detailed data.

A second monthly publication, *Economic Indicators,* first issued in 1948, is another very useful compendium of economic statistics. Income, spending, employment and unemployment, wages, production, prices and Federal finance, plus selected international data pertaining to foreign trade, prices and production are considered. The information, which is presented in graphs, charts, and tables, usually covers eight through ten years.

The *1980 Supplement To Economic Indicators: Historical and Descriptive Background* describes how data in *Economic Indicators* is derived, its relation to other statistics and its uses and limitations. The narrative background defines significant concepts in laymen's terms and provides citations to sources for additional explanations. The *Supplement* also gives historical data relating to the identical topics covered in its monthly counterpart, in some cases going as far back as 1929.

The *Survey of Current Business,* published since 1921, is a third significant monthly periodical. The data relates to commodity prices, construction, retail and wholesale trade, earnings and transportation, among other topics. Since its initial edition in 1932, the biennial supplement to this periodical, *Business Statistics,* has incorporated comparable figures for historical periods. Depending upon dates, the statistics are presented in annual, quarterly, and monthly configurations. The index to *Business Statistics* is a comprehensive one.

Much in the economy depends upon the production, sale and consumption of agricultural products. *Agricultural Statistics,* an annual publication first distributed in 1936, is a fine quick reference guide to related data. Separate chapters deal with farm income and resources, price supports, conservation, taxes and insurance, production and total as well as percapita consumption, plus other issues. Most statistics relate to the national level, but limited data pertains to international, state and local areas. Informative footnotes are appended to most tables. Regarding further references, names of agencies are cited without mention of specific titles. The thorough index emphasizes commodities and subjects.

Law Enforcement and Crime:

The primary Federal statistical compendia pertaining to law enforcement and crime are two annual publications issued by the Department of Justice, the

Uniform Crime Reports and the *Sourcebook of Criminal Justice Statistics.* The former title, which has been issued since 1930, incorporates data collected by local agencies. The type and number of crimes committed, arrests, convictions, acquittals, and law enforcement personnel are considered. In selected cases, ten year trends are given.

The *Sourcebook of Criminal Justice Statistics* has been distributed since 1973. Previously published data is compiled conveniently in this important reference tool. Characteristics of the criminal justice system, public attitudes towards crime, natures and distributions of known offenders, characteristics of those arrested, and judicial processing are among the issues examined. Definitions and methodological descriptions are considered in the appendices. Further references are provided in the notes that follow the tables and in the annotated bibliography. The relatively comprehensive index is an effective finding device.

Transportation:

National Transportation Statistics, published annually by the Department of Transportation since 1971, is an excellent source of national data. The information is taken from both public and private sources. Specific types of transportation, such as air, automobile and rail, relationships between transportation and the economy at large, and energy consumption by the transportation sector are considered. Though this document is not indexed, sources of further information and a glossary are included.

What Does The Future Hold?

The Federal government's collection and dissemination of statistics are evolving functions that change to meet new needs of Washington, as well as the public at large. *A Framework For Planning Statistics For the 1980's* presents an overview of potential directions that might be followed during the current decade. Subjects for which data is compiled, such as agriculture and employment, among other topics, are discussed in separate chapters. Typical chapters describe the many agencies that collect data in the respective areas, needs of data users and recommendations for change. Other sections pertain to user access, methodological standards and Federal-state cooperative data collection. The footnotes and bibliography refer researchers to additional references.

The *Statistical Reporter,* currently issued by the Office of Federal Statistical Policy and Standards, has been published monthly by various agencies since 1961. It describes the latest trends and developments in Federal statistics through feature articles, addresses and announcements of new programs and publications. The *Reporter* is indexed in the *Index To U.S. Government Periodicals.*

BIBLIOGRAPHY

Agricultural Statistics. Department of Agriculture. Washington, D.C.: GPO, 1936-annual.

American Statistics Index: A Comprehensive Guide and Index To The Statistical Publications of The U.S. Government. Washington, D.C.: Congressional Information Service, Inc., 1973-monthly.

American Statistics Index: A Comprehensive Guide and Index To The Statistical Publications of The U.S. Government, Users Guide. Washington, D.C.: Congressional Information Service, Inc., 1976.

American Statistics Index: ASI Search Guide. Washington, D.C.: Congressional Information Service, Inc. 1978.

American Statistics Index Microfiche Library of Statistical Publications of the US Government. Washington, D.C.: Congressional Information Service, Inc., 1973-monthly.

American Statistics Index 1974 Annual and Retrospective Edition: A Comprehensive Guide To The Statistical Publications of The U.S. Government. Washington, D.C.: Congressional Information Service, Inc., 1974.

Annual Report To Congress. Energy Information Administration. Washington, D.C.: GPO, 1977-annual.

Business Statistics. Bureau of Economic Analysis. Washington, D.C.: GPO, 1932-biennial.

Condition of Education Statistical Report. National Center For Education Statistics. Washington, D.C.: GPO, 1975-annual.

Congressional District Data Book. Bureau of the Census. Washington, D.C.: GPO, 1961-irregular.

County and City Data Book: 1977, A Statistical Abstract Supplement. Bureau of the Census. 9th ed. Washington, D.C.: GPO, 1978.

Digest of Education Statistics. National Center For Educational Statistics. Washington, D.C.: GPO, 1962-annual.

Directory of Federal Statistics For Local Areas: A Guide To Sources, 1976. Bureau of the Census. Washington, D.C.: GPO, 1978.

Directory of Federal Statistics For Local Areas: A Guide To Sources, Urban Update, 1977-1978. Bureau of the Census. Washington, D.C.: GPO, 1980.

Economic Indicators. Joint Economic Committee. Washington, D.C.: GPO, 1948-monthly.

Economic Report of The President. Washington, D.C.: GPO, 1947-annual.

Facts At Your Fingertips: A Guide To Sources of Statistical Information on Major Health Topics. National Center For Health Statistics. 3rd ed. Washington, D.C.: Department of Health, Education, and Welfare, 1978.

Federal Executive Telephone Directory. Washington, D.C.: Carroll Publishing Company, 1976-bimonthly.

Federal Statistical Directory. Department of Commerce. Office of Federal Statistical Policy and Standards. Washington, D.C.: GPO, 1935-irregular by various agencies. In 1981, functions of the Office of Federal Statistical Policy and Standards were transferred to the Office of Information and Regulatory Affairs within the Office of Management and Budget. The new agency has yet to issue this title.

A Framework For Planning Statistics For The 1980's. Department of Commerce. Office of Federal Statistical Policy and Standards. Washington, D.C.: GPO, 1978.

Handbook of Labor Statistics. Bureau of Labor Statistics. Washington, D.C.: GPO, 1924/26-annual.

Health United States. National Center For Health Statistics. Hyattsville, Maryland: Department of Health and Human Services, 1976-annual.

Historical Statistics of The United States: Colonial Times To 1970. Bureau of the Census. 3rd ed. Washington, D.C.: GPO, 1975. 2 vols.

HUD Statistical Yearbook. Department of Housing and Urban Development. Washington, D.C.: GPO, 1966-annual.

Index To U.S. Government Periodicals. Chicago: Infordata International Incorporated, 1974-quarterly. Retrospective issues cover 1970-1973.

Issues In Federal Statistical Needs Relating to Women. Bureau of the Census. Washington, D.C.: GPO, 1979.

Minerals Yearbook. Bureau of the Mines. Washington, D.C.: GPO, 1882/83-annual. Entitled *Mineral Resources of the United States* between 1882/83 and 1931.

Monthly Energy Review. Energy Information Administration. Washington, D.C.: GPO, October 1974-monthly.

Monthly Labor Review. Bureau of Labor Statistics. Washington, D.C.: GPO, 1915-monthly.

National Transportation Statistics. Department of Transportation. Washington, D.C.: GPO, 1971-annual. Entitled *Summary of National Transportation Statistics* between 1971 and 1977.

1980 Supplement To Economic Indicators: Historical and Descriptive Background. Joint Economic Committee. 8th ed. Washington, D.C.: GPO, 1980.

Pocket Data Book USA, 1979. Bureau of the Census. 6th ed. Washington, D.C.: GPO, 1980.

The Social and Economic Status of The Black Population In The United States: An Historical View, 1790-1978. Bureau of the Census. Current Population Report P-23/80. Washington, D.C.: GPO, 1979.

Social Indicators, III: Selected Data on Social Conditions and Trends In The United States. Bureau of The Census. Washington, D.C.: GPO, 1980.

Sourcebook of Criminal Justice Statistics. Bureau of the Census. Washington, D.C.: GPO, 1973-annual.

State and Metropolitan Area Data Book, 1979: A Statistical Abstract Supplement. Bureau of the Census. Washington, D.C.: GPO, 1980.

Statistical Abstract of The United States. Bureau of the Census. Washington, D.C.: GPO, 1878-annual.

A Statistical Portrait of Women In The United States, 1978. Bureau of the Census. Current Population Report P-23/100. Washington, D.C.: GPO, 1980.

Statistical Reporter. Office of Management and Budget. Office of Information and Regulatory Affairs. Washington, D.C.: GPO, 1961-monthly by various agencies.

Survey of Current Business. Bureau of Economic Analysis. Washington, D.C.: GPO, 1921-monthly.

Uniform Crime Reports For The United States. Federal Bureau of Investigation. Washington, D.C.: GPO, 1930-annual.

American Statistics Index, Questions:

Use the 1980 cumulative bound edition of the *American Statistics Index* to answer the following questions:

1. The Federal Aviation Administration publishes an annual report that provides ten year projections for air traffic, airport activity, fuel consumption by aircraft, and numbers of airplanes, plus other related data.

   A. Locate the citation in the Index of Subjects and Names.

   Subject heading _____ Page _____

   B. The *ASI* entry number is _____ .

   C. The title of the document is _____ .

   D. This document is a (depository/non-depository) publication whose

   SuDoc number is _____ .

   E. It has _____ tables.

   F. A glossary is printed on pages _____ through _____ .

   G. Information concerning estimated fuel consumption in general aviation by types of aircraft is located on table _____ , page _____ .

   H. Does this document include a narrative section that explains the data?

2. Gene D. Sullivan wrote an article about food prices.

   A. Locate the author's name in the *Index* volume.

   Page _____ .

   B. The title of the article is " _____ ."

   C. Where and when was this article published? Cite the title of the journal, the issuing agency, the date, and the volume and issue numbers.

   Journal title _____

   Issuing agency _____

   Date _____

   Volume and issue numbers _____

   D. The article appeared on pages _____ through _____ .

   E. The periodical is a (depository/non-depository) one.

   F. Is the SuDoc number given?

   G. Did Sullivan publish other articles that included statistics during 1980? If yes, note the following information:

   ASI entry number(s) _____

   Title of article(s) _____

   Title of journal(s) _____

Date(s) _____

Volumes and issue numbers _____

3. Use the Index by Categories to locate information concerning Palestin-
ian and mid-Eastern population.

    A. This information is located under geographic breakdowns by ___

    _____ , subdivided by _____ .

    B. The SuDoc number is _____ .

4. Locate the ASI entry number and the title to a document issued by the
Health Care Financing Administration. The report number is HCFA 03059.

    ASI entry number _____

    Title _____

American Statistics Index, Answers to Questions:

1. A. The document is indexed under the following subject headings.

"Air traffic control"	page 28
"Air travel"	page 28
"Aircraft"	page 29
"Airlines"	page 30
"Airports and airways"	page 31
"Aviation fuels"	page 57

   B. 7504-6.

   C. *FAA Aviation Forecasts, FY81-92.*

   D. Depository publication whose SuDoc number is TD4.32/11:80-8.

   E. 24 tables.

   F. Pages 63 through 65.

   G. Table 9, page 47.

   H. Yes, pages 1-35.

2. A. Page 804.

   B. "Basic Questions on Food Prices."

   C. Journal title: *Economic Review. Federal Reserve Bank of Atlanta.*
   Issuing agency: Federal Reserve Bank of Atlanta.
   Date: March/April, 1980.
   Volume and issue numbers: Volume 65, number 2.

   D. Pages 16 through 22.

   E. Non-depository.

   F. No.

   G. ASI entry number: 9371-1.907
   Title of article: "Rising Energy Costs Hit Southeast Crop Production.
   Title of journal: *Economic Review, Federal Reserve Bank of Atlanta.*
   Date: July/August, 1980.
   Volume and issue numbers: Volume 65, number 4.

3. A. Foreign country, subdivided by Population.

   B. Y4.F76/1:W52/4.

4. ASI entry number: 4657-2.

   Title: *Medicare: Health Insurance For The Aged and Disabled, Selected State Data, 1973-77.*

CHAPTER 8

CENSUS INFORMATION

Special consideration should be given to the Bureau of the Census when discussing Federal government statistics. That agency is the nation's most prolific publisher of data. Besides distributing information under its own imprint, the Bureau also compiles many figures for other agencies. For instance, employment and unemployment statistics issued by the Department of Labor are compiled and tabulated by the Bureau of the Census as part of its monthly Current Population Report series.

This chapter considers four significant Bureau programs relating to population and housing, economics, government and foreign trade. Special consideration is given to each of the eight economic counts, the Censuses of

      Manufacturers
      Mineral Industries
      Retail Trade
      Wholesale Trade
      Service Industries
      Construction Industries
      Transportation
      Agriculture

The importance of these statistics to researchers, government officials, businessmen and the public at large is explained. General reference guides that consider information relating to both the population and housing, as well as the economic enumerations, are described in the next section. Following that, more specialized sources relating to specific programs are examined. In addition to distributing information in print format, the Census Bureau also disseminates machine-readable data. This activity is also described and appropriate reference materials are mentioned.

Range of Census Bureau Programs:

Census of Population and Housing:

Many Americans have misconceptions about the Census Bureau. They believe incorrectly that the agency every ten years merely counts people and reports upon the number of inhabitants. While that is part of its function, the Bureau does much more as well. Decennial census statistics, which reflect the country's socioeconomic configuration, measure income, employment and unemployment, occupations, educational attainment, housing conditions, age, race, ethnic origins and languages spoken, among other variables. Moreover, selected information published in the decennial census is updated by continuous current population surveys conducted by the Bureau between the ten year studies.

Population information is particularly important to local government officials and others who are concerned with Federal grants. Many programs depend upon this data to determine eligibility requirements and amounts of allocations. After the 1980 census was taken, several big city mayors sued the Census Bureau claiming that the statistics failed to reflect their cities' actual population figures. Such undercounts would result in smaller distribution of revenue-sharing monies, as well as funds sponsored through other programs. A 1978 Congressional study identified one hundred and seven Federal programs that depend upon population distribution for funding.¹ A more recent study indicated that during the 1979 fiscal year one hundred and twenty-two billion dollars, approximately a fifth of the Federal budget, was obligated for one hundred and fifty domestic assistance programs.² The following table indicates selected variables collected as part of the decennial census and their frequency of use in determining allocation and eligibility requirements.

DECENNIAL CENSUS OF POPULATION AND HOUSING
FACTORS AND FREQUENCY OF USE³

Factor	Number of Assistance Programs Using Factor
Total Population	20
Population by Age	11
Population by Race	1
Migration	6
Density	4
Urban Population	1
Rural Population	13
Urbanized Population	3
Farm Population	4
Income	32
Land Area	14
Housing Condition	12
Educational Attainment	1

Population and housing data are also used in other ways. Reapportionment of Congressional and state election districts are based upon this information. Government officials apply these figures when forecasting housing, health, employment and school enrollment, among other variables.

The statistics are valuable to businessmen, scholars and the general public as well. Characteristics of communities must be studied carefully prior to opening new retail outlets or marketing new products. Demographers, sociologists, economists, and historians often incorporate census information into their research to illustrate points and to formulate hypotheses. Data is used by individuals to compare their situations to that of the community at large. Furthermore, statistics are often consulted by home buyers to understand characteristics of areas prior to making their purchases.

Economic Programs:

The economic censuses, except for that of agriculture, are conducted during years which end with the digits 2 and 7. For instance, the 1977 enumeration is the most current one, while the forthcoming figures will be based upon 1982 data. The most recent Census of Agriculture was taken in 1978, but beginning in 1982, this enumeration will be issued concurrently with the other economic statistics. Monthly, quarterly and annual current surveys update selected parts of the quinquennial program as is the case with the decennial one. The chart below summarizes the scope of each economic count, notes selected topics for which figures have been collected, and discusses how various sectors of society apply the data.

SCOPE OF THE ECONOMIC CENSUS PROGRAMS, THE TYPE OF DATA COLLECTED AND THE USES OF THE DATA

Census of	Scope	Selected Variables Collected	Uses of the Data
Manufacturers	Establishments that create new materials or products either mechanically or chemically.[a]	Number of employees, sizes of payrolls, inventories, assets, capital expenditures, quantities of fuels consumed and their costs.	Used by Federal government to compile Gross National Product and monthly indexes of industrial productivity; by State and local officials, chambers of commerce and businessmen who must study their area's economies to compare them to other places, measure markets and determine locations of new plants and warehouses.
Mineral Industries	Establishments that extract minerals, including solids, liquids and gases.	Employment, hours, payrolls, operating expenses, capital expenditures, electricity consumed and mineral development and exploration costs.	Used by Federal government to compile Gross National Product, evaluate and plan conservation and energy related policies, monitor the environment and oversee research and development; by lower level jurisdictions to analyze local energy situations; by trade associations, mining firms, manufacturers, university researchers, financial institutions and transportation concerns in planning and forecasting.
Retail Trade	General merchandise stores, plus other retail outlets dealing in durable and nondurable goods.	Payrolls, employment, sizes of establishments and sales. Sales data is subdivided by over 200 merchandise categories.	Data is essential for comprehending current market conditions and forecasting future ones. Used by all sectors of the business community in planning for expansion and in advertising.
Wholesale Trade	Wholesale distributors of both durable and nondurable goods.	Sales by over 500 commodity categories, payrolls, employment, operating expenses, year end inventories and warehouse spaces.	Statistics needed to understand current economic conditions and anticipate future ones. Used by trade associations, chambers of commerce, market researchers and businessmen to forecast and analyze sales and to compare economic situations in their communities to those elsewhere.

SCOPE OF THE ECONOMIC CENSUS PROGRAMS, THE TYPE OF DATA COLLECTED AND THE USES OF THE DATA

Census of	Scope	Selected Variables Collected	Uses of the Data
Service Industries	Service oriented concerns, such as hotels, movies, museums, health facilities and social service facilities.	Payrolls, employment, revenues, fixed assets, capital expenditures, numbers of admissions and legal forms of organizations.	Used by Federal government for compiling national income accounts and forecasting trends; by manufacturers and distributors to study potential markets, project sales and plan additional outlets; by local officials to compare their areas to others.
Construction Industries	Establishments that act as general and special trade contractors, builders and land developers.	Employees, payments for sub-contracted work, costs of materials, payments for renting of leasing equipment, fixed assets and depreciations and classes of construction (new or maintenance and repair work).	Used by government officials to analyze housing and non-residential building situations, transportation, utilization of natural resources and employment; by contractors, bankers, retailers, wholesalers, chambers of commerce and utility companies to evaluate and forecast markets.
Transportation [b] consists of four parts: 1. National Travel Survey	Civilian travel on trips in excess of 100 miles.	Means of transportation, purpose of trips, distances traveled, overnight accommodations and selected socio-economic characteristics of travelers.	Used by government officials, trade associations, transportation concerns, economists, market researchers and manufacturers for planning and forecasting trends; by planners for highway and airport improvements and extensions.
2. Truck Inventory And Use Survey	Truck resources.	Number of trucks by size and use, fleet sizes, local and short/long range uses, products carried and average miles per truck.	Same

SCOPE OF THE ECONOMIC CENSUS PROGRAMS, THE TYPE OF DATA COLLECTED AND THE USES OF THE DATA

	Scope	Selected Variables Collected	Uses of the Data
3. Commodity Transportation Survey	Intercity commodity shipments in continental United States.	Volume of shipments, means of transportation, length of hauls and areas of origins and destinations.	Used by government officials, trade associations, transportation concerns, economists, market researchers and manufacturers for planning and forecasting trends; by planners for highway and airport improvements and extensions.
4. Nonregulated Motor Carriers And Public Warehousing Survey[c]	Motor carriers of persons and property not subject to Federal Regulations.	Payrolls, revenues, employment, operating expenses, capital expenditures and warehouse storage spaces.	Same
Agriculture	Places from which $1,000 agricultural products were sold or normally would have been sold.	Acreage and values, uses of fertilizers and pesticides, production, uses of machinery, payrolls and employment, farm debts and values of products sold.	Used by government officials for planning rural development and agricultural research; by agricultural and food processing industries and appropriate wholesalers and retailers to ensure orderly marketing and distribution.

[a] Establishments are considered separate manufacturing facilities. Two plants at different locations are still recognized as two establishments, though they are owned and operated by the same firm.

[b] What is generally referred to as the Census of Transportation is in reality four separate surveys. A census differs from a survey in that the former is a complete enumeration, while the latter is a sample count.

[c] This report was included in the 1963 Census of Transportation. During 1967 and 1972 comparable statistics were issued as part of the Census of Service Industries. However, in 1977 it was again incorporated into the transportation program.

Census of Governments:

The Census of Governments is the only comprehensive uniform analysis of American state and local governments. Tax valuations and receipts, other government receipts, expenditures, indebtedness, public employment and labor-management policies are among the many topics measured. Officials at all levels use the data for planning and administering fiscal policy, appraising the effectiveness of intergovernmental programs and comparing property taxes. These statistics are also essential to researchers and public interest groups who study trends and natures of government.

Foreign Trade Statistics:

Import data covers merchandise worth $250.00 or more that has been brought into the United States and Puerto Rico, while export figures deal with movements of merchandise from the United States and Puerto Rico, whether or not a commercial transaction is involved. Summary statistics are printed in selected publications. However, other series include breakdowns by commodities, quantities and values at ports of departures and entries, plus other variables. The Federal government uses this data to evaluate trends in international trade and planning agricultural and other assistance programs. The private sector uses this information for marketing research, transportation planning, planning new products and appraising economic outlooks.

Guides To Census Bureau Publications and Programs:

General Guides:

Data User News, a monthly newsletter, includes brief informative articles which describe the most recent developments in census programs and publications. It is essential reading for all serious census users. This publication should be read in conjunction with the *Statistical Reporter,* a journal which summarizes statistical programs of all Federal agencies.

New Census Bureau publications are listed in a monthly bibliography, *Monthly Product Announcements.* Documents concerning economic, geographic, government, housing and population programs are included. Reference materials that enhance the use of Bureau data and other technical documentation are also cited. Government Printing Office stock numbers are given when appropriate.

The annual *Bureau of the Census Catalog of Publications* provides annotated descriptions of all publications and data files issued during the previous year. Older census publications are described in the *Bureau of The Census Catalog of Publications 1790-1972.* Part I covers those printed between 1790 and 1945 and part II deals with more recent documents issued between 1946 and 1972. Most entries include valuable annotations. Many citations in this *Catalog* are available in microformats. Research Publications issued a microfilm version of the decennial series covering 1790 through 1970 and Greenwood Press prepared a microfiche edition of the non-decennial reports dated between 1790 and 1945.

Two significant general reference sources include sample tables and much descriptive information about the statistics. The *Guide To County Census Data For Planning Economic Development* was designed for planners who use county level data. Illustrations are taken from the *1970 Census of Population and Housing,* the *1972 Economic Censuses,* the *1974 Census of Agriculture* and appropriate current surveys. The introductory section describes Bureau programs and evaluates accuracy of data. Bibliographic references are cited throughout the text. Two annotated bibliographies cover Census Bureau publications and sources published by other agencies.

The second document, *Environmental Socioeconomic Data Sources,* was issued by the Air Force to assist its planners in completing human environmental parts of environmental impact statements. The introductory section explains the significance of census information, as well as data available from other Federal agencies, local jurisdictions, chambers of commerce and banks. The following section, "Getting Started," which is limited to the Census of Population and Housing, includes questions and answers, plus sample tables. Part three, "Helpful Hints," is a tabular guide to locating specific information in both the population and housing counts and the economic enumerations. The conclusion is a detailed description of census data and other figures compiled by various Federal agencies. Again, sample tables are reproduced. This very readable source is a fine introduction to the subject.

Factfinders For The Nation are a set of approximately twenty pamphlets that describe Census Bureau programs and activities. In most issues, illustrative tables are reproduced, data collection methods and various applications of the statistics are described, reports are cited and sources of further information are noted.

Current Survey Statistics Available From The Bureau of The Census describes data sources about related programs. Titles of series are listed under relevant subject headings. Scopes of the surveys, frequencies, geographic areas covered, sources of data and contacts for further information are provided. Selected reference publications and statistical compendia are cited.

Aside from the references described above, most census publications include much explanatory information. Introductions and appendices give background to their subjects, provide definitions, depict data collection methods and compare data to that in other reports. Many documents also include very useful table finding guides. Two such guides reprinted from the *1970 Census of Population: General Social and Economic Characteristics* and the *1978 Census of Agriculture* are illustrated below. (figure 8-1)

Figure 8-1

1970 Census Of Population: General Social and Economic Characteristics,
Table Finding Guide

Subject	The State				Standard metropolitan statistical areas		Places of—				Counties		
	1970 and 1960	Total Urban Rural nonfarm Rural farm	Size of place	Metropolitan nonmetropolitan residence	Urbanized areas		50,000 or more	10,000 to 50,000	2,500 to 10,000		Total	Rural nonfarm Rural farm	
SUMMARY CHARACTERISTICS													
Social	–	–	–		40		40		40	42	43		
Economic	–	–			41		41		41	42	44		–
GENERAL CHARACTERISTICS													
Age	–	48	59	70	96'		96'		112'	–	129'	134, 136	
Relationship to head of household	–	48	59	70	96'		96'		112'	–	129'	134, 136	
Families by presence of own children under 18 years	–	48	59	70	96'		96'		112'	–	129'		
SOCIAL CHARACTERISTICS													
Nativity and parentage	45	49	60	71	81		81		102		119		
State of birth	45	50	61	72	82. 91', 97'		82, 91', 97'		102, 108', 113'	117	119, 125', 130'		
Country of origin	45	49	60	71	81		81		102	–	119		
Mother tongue	–	49	60	71	81		81		102	–	119		

(Asterisks—*—refer to tables about the Black population and crosses—†—refer to tables about Spanish heritage population.)

1978 Census of Agriculture
Index

	ɔunty tables	
State tables	Summary	County report
A		
Abnormal farms.	10,34	7	2
Age of operator	4, 29–35	6	4
Agricultural products sold, value.	10, 13 17 29–35	9–11	2
Agricultural service income . . .	12 ,29–35	37	–
Alfalfa hay.	25 ,26, 28–35	30	10
Alfalfa seed	25, 26	30	10
Almonds.	28–35	32	–
Alsike clover seed.	–	30	–
Angora goats.	23	22	–
Animal health costs.	6 ,29–35	12	5
Apples	25, 28–35	32	10
Apricots	–	32	–

The guides list variables being measured and indicate on which tables information relating to types of geographic areas can be located.

Refer to figure 8-1 when answering the following questions:

Census of Population and Housing
Statistics that compare nativity and parentage of the population on a state-wide basis between 1960 and 1970 are located on table _____ .

45

Summary economic statistics that deal with places having populations between 10,000 and 50,000 people are found in table _____ .

41

Census of Agriculture:
Statewide data concerning the production of apples is located on tables

_____ and _____ through _____ .

25 and 28 - 35

Summary statistics by counties relating to the production of apples are found on table _____

32

More detailed data for counties are located on tables listed in the "county report" column. The data dealing with apples appears on table _____ .

10

Guides To The Census of Population and Housing:

Except for the following sources, few guides to the 1980 Census have been published to date.

1980 Census of Population and Housing: Users Guide

Census '80: Continuing The Factfinder Tradition

Census '80: Projects For Students

1980 Census Update

The other guides discussed in this section relate to the 1970 enumeration. Though some differences exist between the two counts, many generalizations about 1980 can be made when studying the previous census.

The *1980 Census of Population and Housing: Users Guide* is a comprehensive study. Included among the topics discussed are census history and objectives, analysis of the questions asked, data collection and processing procedures, geography, both print and non-print products, data limitations and sources for further information. Illustrative maps and tables are reproduced. The Census Bureau intends to issue supplements as funds become available.

Census '80: Continuing The Factfinder Tradition is a well written college level text that introduces readers to the Bureau and its activities. The agency's history and organization, demographic concepts, components of population change and basic statistical concepts are discussed. Emphasis is placed upon planning, collection and publication of figures and the various ways demographers, planners, businessmen and others utilize the statistics. Numerous illustrations, charts and bibliographies are included. This volume is much more a descriptive guide about the Census Bureau and the decennial enumeration than a handbook for locating specific data.

Census '80: Projects For Students is a workbook intended to supplement *Census '80: Continuing The Factfinder Tradition.* Practical exercises deal with data collection, fieldwork experiences, manipulation of variables to form more meaningful data and applications of statistics in the public and private sectors. Numerous tables and maps are reprinted. A similar, but more concise volume, *A Student's Workbook On The 1970 Census,* is most valuable for its questions and answers which provide practical experience in the use of data. The collection and dissemination of statistics, geographic concepts and hints for reading tables are covered as well.

Changes have occurred in plans for the 1980 census since the above was published in January 1980. These modifications, as well as additional developments in data coverage, are noted in *1980 Census Update.* This supplement to *Data User News* appeared quarterly between January 1977 and July 1981. Typical articles are one or two pages, are very informative and often cite further references. Issue nineteen, the final one, includes an index to the entire series. Consult *Data User News* and/or *Statistical Reporter* for post-July 1981 developments.

The *Index To Selected 1970 Census Reports* provides access to major series for which separate volumes have been issued for states and standard metropolitan statistical areas (SMSA's). That is, cities of at least 50,000 population which are integrated, both socially and economically, with their surrounding suburbs. *1970 Census of Population: Detailed Characteristics,* report number PC(1)-D, is an example of the type of information included. This series consists of fifty-three volumes, a national summary and a separate issue for each state, the District of Columbia and Puerto Rico.

The *Index* has three parts. The first is a users guide that cites reports included, provides definitions and deciphers abbreviations. The second section, a "Cross Reference Guide," is a thesaurus of subject headings used in the index section, part three. That section lists in alphabetical order variables measured and reports and table numbers where appropriate information can be located.

Suppose you are researching the number of people born in foreign countries who were living in Buffalo, New York in 1970. Consult proper headings in the alphabetical index. (figure 8-2)

Figure 8-2

Index To Selected 1970 Census Reports

```
COUNTRY OF ORIGIN (29) BY NATIVITY AND PARENTAGE
     (2) BY RACE (4)
   UNIVERSE:  PERSONS OF FOREIGN STOCK -- FOR:
       STATE:  U/RNF/RF                          PC(1)-C  49

COUNTRY OF ORIGIN (82) B" RACE (2) BY NATIVITY
     AND PARENTAGE (2)
   UNIVERSE:  PERSONS OF FOREIGN STOCK -- FOR:
       STATE, PLACES 100,000+               PC(1)-D  141

COUNTRY OF ORIGIN (29) BY RACE (4) BY NATIVITY
     AND PARENTAGE (2)
   UNIVERSE:  PERSONS OF FOREIGN STOCK -- FOR:
       STATE:  U/RNF/RF                          PC(1)-C  49

COUNTRY OF ORIGIN (29) BY RACE (3) BY
     CITIZENSHIP (2)
   UNIVERSE:   FOREIGN BORN PERSONS -- FOR:
       STATE, SMSA'S 250,000+, PLACES 250,000+  PC(1)-D  144
```

The last citation in figure 8-2 will help answer the question. "Country of origin (29)" indicates that twenty-nine nationalities are considered in this table. Three variables relating to race and two elements dealing with citizenship are also noted. The "universe," or the type of entries being counted is "foreign born persons." Geographic coverage is limited to states, SMSA's and places of at least 250,000 people. Since the 1970 Buffalo population exceeded 250,000, your information is located on table 144 in the New York State issue of PC(1)-D, the *Detailed Characteristics* series noted above. This table will have comparable data in each volume of the series, except the *National Summary* issue. Table numbers in that source fail to correspond to those in the other volumes.

The *Reference Manual on Population and Housing Statistics From The Census Bureau* is a well written introduction to the 1970 enumeration and related current surveys. Its ten chapters cover subject contents of the census, geographic concepts, availability of both published and machine readable data, data limitations and hints for locating specific information. The numerous illustrations, bibliographic references and index enhance the document's value.

The importance of small area data, which relate to census tracts and blocks, is discussed in *Census Data For Community Action*. Tracts are subdivisions of standard metropolitan areas forming homogeneous communities usually inhabited by approximately four thousand people, whereas blocks represent the physical boundaries of streets in urbanized areas. This source is more appropriate for beginning students than advanced researchers.

Housing Data Resources: Indicators and Sources of Data For Analyzing Housing describes concepts and sources of statistics that evaluate neighborhood socioeconomic conditions and trends. Federal, local and non-government information is examined. An annotated bibliography and footnotes supplement the fine text.

General Guides To The Economic Programs:

Mini-Guide To The 1977 Economic Censuses is a fine introduction to the subject. The Censuses of Retail Trade, Wholesale Trade, Service Industries, Manufacturers, Mineral Industries and Transportation, plus other enumerations, are considered. Historical backgrounds, geographic concepts, availability of data and the standard industrial classification—a Census Bureau scheme for organizing related industries and products—are covered. Bibliographic citations and illustrative maps and tables increase the usefulness of this source.

Consult *History of The 1977 Economic Census* for a detailed methodological study of the topic. Initial planning, geographic coding, mailings, the public information program and the collection and processing of data, among other issues, are examined. Chapter nine, which deals with the publications program, is especially useful. Contents of reports and the availability of microfiche and public use tapes are described. Comparable information is noted in *1977 Economic Censuses Publication Program,* a concise pamphlet more suited for those who are interested only in access to data rather than related methodology.

Five practical guides to quinquennial economic data have been published as part of the *Data Finder* Series.

Industrial Statistics Data Finder examines the 1972 Censuses of Manufacturers and Mineral Industries.

Business Statistics Data Finder deals with the 1972 Censuses of Retail and Wholesale Trade and Service Industries.

Construction Statistics Data Finder covers the 1972 Census of Construction Industries.

Agricultural Statistics Data Finder considers the 1974 Census of Agriculture.

Foreign Trade Statistics Data Finder deals with periodical and annual reports.

Titles of reports, frequencies of publication, geographic areas covered, selected variables measured and their levels of detail are noted in tabular format. Current surveys updating selected quinquennial figures are cited whenever appropriate. Two additional sources are arranged similarly. The *Economic Survey Division Data Finder* describes statistics printed in *County Business Patterns, Minority Owned Businesses, Women Owned Businesses, Truck Inventory and Use Survey, Commodity Transportation Survey* and *Enterprise Statistics,* among other series. The *Energy Statistics Data Finder* notes energy related information found in population and housing, economic, government and foreign trade counts.

Guides To The Censuses of Manufacturing and Mineral Industries:

The *Guide To Industrial Statistics* is a detailed how-to-source for locating data about manufacturing and mineral industries. Definitions, geographic concepts, current surveys, energy related industrial data and Census Bureau special tabulation services are among the topics discussed. Numerous tables are provided. The explanation of the standard industrial classification is especially good. Related sources published by the Census Bureau, plus other agencies are cited in an annotated bibliography. Though this *Guide* is based upon the 1972 enumeration, many applications are still appropriate when using the more recent 1977 information.

Guides To The Censuses of Retail Trade, Wholesale Trade and Construction Industries:

Excluding the *Factfinders* and *Data Finders* discussed above, separate guides to these censuses have not been published by the Census Bureau. Refer to Appendix A, "General Explanations," in the *1977 Censuses of Retail Trade, Wholesale Trade* and *Service Industries* for information concerning scopes and methodologies, comparabilities with 1972 data, relevant definitions and kinds of businesses covered in the respective reports. The introduction to the *1977 Census of Construction Industries* describes kinds of establishments included, appropriate standard industrial classifications, reliability of data and geographic concepts. Definitions are provided in Appendix A, "Explanation of Terms." The "Users Guide For Locating Statistics By Table Number," which appears immediately following the Introduction, is also a valuable reference tool.

Guide To The Census of Transportation:

The *Census Bureau Guide To Transportation Statistics,* issued in 1976, describes the three surveys that encompassed the 1972 enumeration, the *National Travel Survey,* the *Truck Inventory and Use Survey* and the *Commodity Transportation Survey.* Generalizations concerning this data can be applied to the 1977 count. The latter statistics include these reports, plus an additional one, the *Nonregulated Motor Carriers and Public Warehousing Survey.* Consult the introduction to that document for an explanation of its scope, definitions, a description of census coverage and methodology and a statement concerning data limitations.

Guides To The Census of Agriculture:

Changes in methods of data collection between the 1974 and the 1978 Censuses are discussed in *Factfinder For The Nation: Agricultural Statistics.* However, differences in contents are not elaborated. A brief explanation of data comparability and differences between the two enumerations is given in Appendix A to the 1978 *State Report* series. Researchers should also be familiar with Appendix C, "Comparison of 1974 Farm Counts With 1978 Farm Counts." The forthcoming *Procedural History* to the 1978 count will contain more detailed information concerning the dissimilarities.

Guides To The Census of Governments:

Illustrative tables from the 1977 count are reprinted in *Guide To 1977 Census of Governments.* An introductory section describes the contents of the quinquennial reports and related quarterly, annual and special studies. The publication program is discussed in the last section. A second reference tool, *Guide To Recurrent and Special Government Statistics,* which is arranged in a similar fashion, is also a very useful source.

Guide To Foreign Trade Statistics:

The *Guide To Foreign Trade Statistics, 1979* is a detailed handbook on the subject. The "Information Locator" at the beginning of the volume is a fine summary indicating types of data found in the various reports. Statistical applications are considered in part one. The second section is a detailed analysis of foreign trade programs describing import and export data, seasonally adjusted variations and trade with outlying areas, among other issues. Special Census Bureau services, such as the compilation of unique tabulations, are noted in part three and significant reference materials are described in part four. Sample tables from both printed, as well as microfiche, reports are reproduced. Microfiche include more detailed information than the printed or bound studies.

Availability of Machine-Readable Data From The Bureau of The Census:

Four types of information are produced by the Census Bureau in machine-readable formats.

Summary tapes	Geographic files
Microdata tapes	Software

Summary tapes provide aggregated data. For instance, suppose the unit of measurement is households and the geographic coverage is by states. Aggregated statistics will refer to all households within each state. Factors that refer to individual units are available on microdata tapes. Using the example above, microdata refers to each household within the states. Microdata tapes are programmed to preserve the respondents' confidentiality, since Federal law prohibits the Bureau from disseminating information that can be either directly or indirectly associated with particular answers.

Geographic files contain boundary and area coordinates, plus additional kinds of related information. The fourth type of file, software, was developed to aid researchers in generating tables and to assist them in better utilizing other census tapes.

Machine-readable data is accessed through three sources. The public can purchase tapes from the Census Bureau's Customer Services Branch for $110.00 per reel. The same office will also prepare special tabulations at cost.

The National Clearinghouse For Census Data Services is comprised of summary tape processing centers, groups providing access to machine readable information and offering consultation services. The centers, which are independent of the Census Bureau, maintain their own operating procedures and cost structures. A directory of processing centers noting services each provide, the *National Clearinghouse For Census Data Services: Address List,* is published by the Bureau.

Machine-readable data is also available through the State Data Center program. Unlike the National Clearinghouse For Census Data Services, this is supported through the Census Bureau. Participating states choose central agencies, which are called data centers, to disseminate census figures in their respective jurisdictions. To assist them, the state agencies designate municipal bodies, universities and other research institutions data center affiliates. Affiliates are responsible for meeting the statistical needs of local governments, businesses and researchers within their areas. The Census Bureau provides participants with printed reports, tapes, training, technical assistance and consultation services through the central state agencies. A comprehensive list of data centers and affiliates appeared in the March and April 1982 issues of *Data User News.*

The *Directory of Data Files,* published in 1979 and updated quarterly, describes tapes available from the Census Bureau. Summary, microdata, geographic and softwear files dealing with all Bureau programs are included. Entries cite titles of tapes, their types, subject matters, geographic coverages, file sizes, appropriate reference materials, related print, plus machine-readable information, and availability. The index is arranged by titles of files.

Sources of Further Information:

Consult the Bureau of the Census for further information. Phone numbers are indicated on lists that are published periodically by the Bureau and in appendices to the Census Bureau's annual *Catalogs of Publications.* Relevant phone numbers can also be obtained from the *Federal Executive Directory.*

Footnotes

[1]United States. Congress. House. Committee on Post Office and Civil Service. Subcommittee on Census and Population. *The Use of Population Data In Federal Assistance Programs.* Washington, D.C.: GPO, 1978. P.

[2]Danuta Emery et al. "Distributing Federal Funds: The Use of Statistical Data (Preliminary Report)," *Statistical Reporter* (December 1980), pages 73-90.

[3]*Ibid,* page 81.

BIBLIOGRAPHY

Agricultural Statistics Data Finder. Washington, D.C.: Bureau of The Census, 1978.

Bureau of The Census Catalog of Publications. Washington, D.C.: GPO, 1946-annual. Published quarterly and cumulated annually between 1946 and 1979.

Bureau of The Census Catalog of Publications, 1790-1972. Bureau of The Census. Data User Services Office. Washington, D.C.: GPO, 1974.

Business Statistics Data Finder. Bureau of The Census. Washington, D.C.: GPO, 1978.

Census Bureau Guide To Transportation Statistics. Bureau of The Census. Washington, D.C.: GPO, 1976.

Census Data For Community Action. Rev. ed. Washington, D.C.: GPO, 1975.

Census '80: Continuing The Factfinder Tradition. Charles P. Kaplan and Thomas L. Van Valey. Bureau of The Census. Washington, D.C.: GPO, 1980.

Census '80: Projects For Students. Data User Services Division. Washington, D.C.: Bureau of The Census, 1981.

Construction Statistics Data Finder. Washington, D.C.: Bureau of The Census, 1978.

Current Survey Statistics Available From The Bureau of The Census. Bureau of The Census. Data Access Description 38 rev. Washington, D.C.: GPO, 1977.

Data User News. Bureau of The Census. Washington, D.C.: GPO, 1946-monthly. Title varies.

Directory of Data Files. Washington, D.C.: Bureau of The Census, 1979-quarterly.

"Distributing Federal Funds. The Use of Statistical Data (Preliminary Report)," by Danuta Emery et al. *Statistical Reporter.* 80-12 (December, 1980), pp. 73-90.

Economic Surveys Division Data Finder. Washington, D.C.: Bureau of The Census, 1979.

Energy Statistics Data Finder. Data User Services Division. Washington, D.C.: Bureau of The Census, 1980.

Environmental Socioeconomic Data Sources. Department of The Air Force and Bureau of The Census. Washington, D.C.: Department of Defense, 1976.

Factfinder For The Nation. Washington, D.C.: Bureau of The Census, Series of twenty pamphlets issued during the indicated times.

1. *Minority Statistics.* 1979.
2. *Availability of Census Records About Individuals.* 1980.
3. *Agricultural Statistics.* 1979.
4. *History and Organization.* 1979.
5. *Reference Sources.* 1981.
6. *Housing Statistics.* 1981.
7. *Population Statistics.* 1981.
8. *Geographic Tools.* 1980.

9. *Construction Statistics.* 1979.
10. *Retail Trade Statistics.* 1979.
11. *Wholesale Trade Statistics.* 1979.
12. *Statistics on Service Industries.* 1979.
13. *Transportation Statistics.* 1979.
14. *Foreign Trade Statistics.* 1978.
15. *Statistics on Manufacturers.* 1980.
16. *Statistics on Mineral Industries.* 1979.
17. *Statistics on Governments.* 1980.
18. *Census Bureau Programs and Products.* 1979.
19. *Enterprise Statistics.* 1979.
20. *Energy and Conservation Statistics.* 1980.

Federal Executive Telephone Directory. Washington, D.C.: Carroll Publishing Company, 1976-bimonthly.

Foreign Trade Statistics Data Finder. Rev. ed. Washington, D.C.: Bureau of The Census, 1978.

Guide To County Census Data For Planning Economic Development. Bureau of The Census and Economic Development Administration. Washington, D.C.: Bureau of The Census, 1979(?).

Guide To Foreign Trade Statistics, 1979. Washington, D.C.: Bureau of The Census, 1980.

Guide To Industrial Statistics: Industrial Statistics Program Locator Guide To Published Data, Types of Data Presented, Publications of Major Censuses, Other Sources of Statistics. Bureau of The Census. Washington, D.C.: GPO, 1978.

Guide To 1977 Census of Governments. Bureau of The Census. 1977 Census of Governments, vol. 7. Washington, D.C.: GPO, 1980.

Guide To Recurrent and Special Governmental Statistics. Bureau of The Census. State and Local Government Special Study no. 78. Washington, D.C.: GPO, 1976.

History of The 1977 Economic Censuses. Bureau of The Census. Washington, D.C.: GPO, 1980.

Housing Data Resources: Indicators and Sources of Data For Analyzing Housing and Neighborhood Conditions. Bureau of The Census. Washington, D.C.: GPO, 1980.

Index To Selected 1970 Census Reports. Comp. by Paul T. Zeisset. Bureau of The Census. Washington, D.C.: GPO, 1974.

Industrial Statistics Data Finder. Washington, D.C.: Bureau of The Census, 1978.

Mini-Guide To The 1977 Economic Censuses. Bureau of The Census. Washington, D.C.: GPO, 1978.

Monthly Product Announcements. Washington, D.C.: Bureau of The Census, 1981-monthly.

National Clearinghouse For Census Data Services: Address List. Washington, D.C.: Bureau of The Census, 1981.

1980 Census of Population and Housing: Users Guide, Part A, Text. Washington, D.C.: Bureau of The Census, 1982.

1980 Census Update. Washington, D.C.: Bureau of The Census, published quarterly between January 1977 and July 1981.

1977 Economic Censuses Publication Program. Washington, D.C.: Bureau of The Census, 1979.

Reference Manual on Population and Housing Statistics From The Census Bureau. Rev. ed. Washington, D.C.: Bureau of The Census, 1978.

Statistical Reporter. Office of Management and Budget. Office of Information and Regulatory Affairs. Washington, D.C.: GPO, 1961-monthly by various agencies.

A Student Workbook On The 1970 Census. Bureau of The Census. Washington, D.C.: GPO, 1978.

The Use of Population Data In Federal Assistance Programs. House Committee on Post Office and Civil Service. Subcommittee on Census and Population. 95th Cong., 2nd sess. Committee Print. Washington, D.C.: GPO, 1978.

CHAPTER 9

LOCATING TECHNICAL REPORTS

Until now, the discussion has emphasized publications available through the Government Printing Office. The GPO is a major source for information published by government departments, but it is not the only one. The National Technical Information Service (NTIS), a division of the Department of Commerce, is another extremely important agency that provides many information services. This chapter describes the functions of NTIS with emphasis upon the indexing and dissemination of research reports. The nature of technical reports—the most predominate literature distributed by NTIS, a description of *Government Reports Announcements and Index (GRA&I)*—the index to NTIS documents, the weekly abstract newsletters issued by the agency and selected indexes that are similar to *GRA&I* are discussed. Relationships between NTIS and GPO are considered in the final section.

Nature and Development of NTIS:

Following World War II, the United States realized the need to create a central clearinghouse for dissemination of government sponsored research to business and industry. Executive Order 9568, issued in June 1945, created the Publications Board to fulfill this responsibility. Since that time the agency has been renamed three times. It became the Office of Technical Services in 1947 and the Clearinghouse for Scientific and Technical Information in 1964 before becoming the National Technical Information Service in 1970.

Research reports on all aspects of science and technology, the social sciences, and the humanities are indexed and sold by NTIS in paper, as well as microfiche, formats. In 1979, approximately fifty-nine thousand documents were made available to the public by the Information Service, the majority of which were technical reports prepared by the Departments of Defense and Energy, and the National Aeronautic and Space Administration.[1] Moreover, during that same year, NTIS sold 3,189,704 copies of its documents, 722,490 in paper format and 2,467,214 on microfiche.[2]

NTIS does more than merely index and distribute research reports. The agency is the central source for United States government machine readable tapes and programs for sale or lease to the public. As of 1981, approximately twelve hundred data files prepared by a wide array of Federal agencies were available from NTIS.[3] The Information Service is also a central source for information about government owned patents and patent applications.

Technical Report Literature:

Technical reports describe results of investigations in the sciences, the social sciences, and to a far lesser extent, the humanities. Citations to reports generally have the following six characteristics.

personal authors
corporate authors or the names of institutions
    where the research was performed
titles
contract or grant numbers
alphanumeric report codes
dates of publication

Places of publication and names of publishers are rarely given.

Technical reports should be considered when studying government information because two significant types of documents, contract progress reports and contract final reports, are very often prepared at public expense. Moreover, NTIS, a government agency, is the primary source for indexing and disseminating this information. Progress reports are interim statements that are submitted periodically to foundations or, in most cases, to governing jurisdictions that sponsor research. Final reports, usually the most widely distributed technical reports, are submitted after the work has been completed.

Technical reports are sometimes of dubious quality. An editorial in the well respected journal, *Nature,* stated:

> Some . . . are humdrum documents, reviews of the literature in
> some narrow field, reports on particular experiments or
> calculations more suitable for the backs of envelopes than for
> the solemn stationery on which they are distributed. Some,
> however, turn out to be important and distinguished con-
> tributions to understanding . . .[4]

There are a number of reasons for this. Reports are often prepared hurriedly by technical experts for other technical experts in the sponsoring agencies, rather than for the entire scientific community. Moreover, they are usually intended to serve as temporary working documents, rather than permanent contributions to the literature. Since technical experts are not generally trained in preparing reports, their writing sometimes lacks appropriate editing and fails to meet recognized style.

Locating Technical Reports in Government Reports Announcements and Index (GRAI):

Government Reports Announcements and Index has been published semi-monthly since April 1975. Comparable predecessor titles have been issued since 1946.

Bibliography of Science and Industrial Reports, January 1946-June 1949.

Bibliography of Technical Reports, July 1949-December 1954.

United States Government Research Reports, January 1955-December 1964.

United States Government Research and Development Reports, January 1965-February 1971.

Government Reports Announcements, March 1971-March 1975.

Prior to April 1975, the index to *Government Reports Announcements, Government Reports Index,* had been published separately. At that time, both were combined to form GRA&I.

Government Reports Announcements and Index is divided into two sections, the abstracts and the indexes. The former is separated into twenty-two major subject areas that are further divided into one hundred and seventy-eight subcategories. Information is located in the abstract section through five indexes for keywords, corporate authors, personal authors, contract/grant numbers and NTIS order/report numbers. NTIS publishes quarterly index cumulations on microfiche and annual cumulations in bound format. The *Retrospective Index,* issued by NTIS on microfiche in 1980, covers July 1964 through December 1978.

Keyword Index:

The Keyword Index is arranged alphabetically according to subject headings. Entries provide titles of documents, pages on which the abstracts are located and NTIS accession numbers or alphanumeric acquisition codes. The code used most often, "PB," which relates to the former Publications Board, is applied to materials prepared outside NTIS, but indexed and abstracted by that agency. Since 1980, two digits representing the year in which the reports were entered into the NTIS system have followed the PB's. Other common accession schemes are:

AD—Department of Defense reports

DOE—Department of Energy reports

E—NASA reports relating to LANDSAT, a satellite mapping program

EIS—environmental impact statements

N—NASA reports other than those relating to LANDSAT

NTIS—reports prepared by NTIS prior to 1980. Since that time PB has been applied to these documents.

NUREG—Nuclear Regulatory Commission reports. Both PB and NUREG codes were assigned to these documents between 1975 and June 1979. Since then, NUREG has been used exclusively.

As in previous chapters, you are searching for information concerning public housing, in this case, as it relates to crime. Consult the Keyword Index under appropriate subject headings. Entries cited under "Public Housing" are reproduced below. (figure 9-1)

Figure 9-1
GRA&I, Volume 81, number 11
Keyword Index

PUBLIC HOUSING
Housing Allowances and Other Rental Housing Assistance Programs-A Comparison Based on the Housing Allowance Demand Experiment. Part 2: Costs and Efficiency,
PB81-151813   2146

Housing Allowances and Other Rental Housing Assistance Programs-A Comparison Based on the Housing Allowance Demand Experiment, Part 1: Participation, Housing Consumption, Location, and Satisfaction,
PB81-151979   2147

Factors Influencing Crime and Instability in Urban Housing Developments.
PB81-169856   2152

PUBLIC LANDS
Economic Impacts in Idaho of Changing Federal Land Management Policies.
PB81-151516   2134

PUERTO RICO
Counterbalance: An Analysis of Scientific and Technical Information Requirements to Support the Legislative Task in Puerto Rico, Project Report, Volume 1.
PB81-149064   2129

The following refers to figure 9-1:

The title of this document is _____

_____.

Factors Influencing Crime and Instability
In Urban Housing Developments

The abstract is located on page _____.

2152

The NTIS accession number is _____.

PB81-169856

Abstracts:

Consult the Abstract section to obtain full bibliographic information and summaries of the documents after noting relevant entries in the index. Abstract citations usually have nine parts.

1. Accession numbers.

2. Availability statements and price codes: Indicates if documents are available from NTIS in paper (PC) and/or microfiche (MF). Tables on the back covers of *GRA&I* decipher the price codes.

3. Issuing agency.

4. Titles.

5. Personal authors.

6. Dates of publication.

7. Paginations.

8. Report numbers.

9. Abstracts.

Grant or contract numbers are sometimes indicated as well.

PB81-169856, the citation referred to in figure 9-1, appears in the abstract section as indicated in figure 9-2.

Figure 9-2

GRA&I, Abstracts, Volume 81, number 11

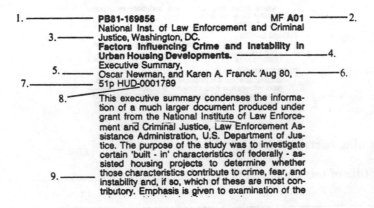

role played by physical factors such as entry ways, adjacent common grounds, building layout and site design, real barriers (fences, locks, intercoms), and the presence of security personnel. Newark, St. Louis, and San Francisco provided the 63 federally - assisted, moderate - income developments studied. The developments consist of row house, walk - up, and high - rise buildings with a varied composition of rent - subsidized residents. Path analysis is used to estimate the model and to calculate total, direct, and total indirect effects. Major findings, directions for future research, and policy implications are discussed. Tables, graphs, and references are included.

Refer to figure 9-2 when answering each question:

Underline the accession number.

    PB81-169856

This report was written by two personal authors, _____

and _____ .

    Oscar Newman and Karen A. Franck

The research was funded by the _____

_____ .

    National Institute of Law Enforcement
    and Criminal Justice

This report was published in _____ _____.

    August 1980.

Its report number is ____ _____.

    HUD-0001789

(Although the corporate author is a subdivision of the Department of Justice, the document has a HUD report number because the research was partially funded by that agency. Chances are the publication was submitted to NTIS by the Department of Housing and Urban Development, rather than the Justice Department.)

Is this report available in both paper and microfiche formats or is its availability limited to one or the other?

    Microfiche only.

Corporate and Personal Author Indexes:

Factors Influencing Crime and Instability In Urban Housing Developments is also cited in the Corporate and Personal Author Indexes. (figure 9-3)

Figure 9-3

GRA&I, Volume 81, number 11

Corporate Author Index	Personal Author Index

NATIONAL INST. OF ALLERGY AND INFECTIOUS DISEASES, BETHESDA, MD.

DHEW/NIH/PUB-81-2215
New Initiatives in Immunology.
PB81-157844   2162

NATIONAL INST. OF LAW ENFORCEMENT AND CRIMINAL JUSTICE, WASHINGTON, DC.

Factors Influencing Crime and Instability in Urban Housing Developments.
(HUD-0001789)
PB81-169856   2152

NATIONAL LIBRARY OF MEDICINE, BETHESDA, MD.

NLM-MED-81-01
List of Serials and Monographs Indexed for Online Users, 1981.
PB81-159469   2133

NATIONAL MARINE FISHERIES SERVICE, GALVESTON, TX. GALVESTON LAB.

NOAA-TM-NMFS-SEFC-20
Commercial Brown, White and Pink Shrimp Tail Size: Total Size Conversions.
(NOAA-80110710)
PB81-148488   2154

NEWMAN, J. B.

Thermomechanical Theory of Materials Undergoing Large Elastic and Viscoplastic Deformation (AWBA Development Program).
WAPD-TM-1472   2281

NEWMAN, OSCAR

Factors Influencing Crime and Instability in Urban Housing Developments.
PB81-169856   2152

NEWMAN, THOMAS H.

Reprint: Organosilyl Substituted Phosphoranyl Radicals.
AD-A093 892/8   2185

NEWNAM, B. E.

Multiple-Shot Laser Damage Thresholds of Ultraviolet Reflectors at 248 and 308 Nanometers.
LA-UR-80-3429   2287

NEWTON, MURRAY

State Administrative Models for Toxic Substances Management. Toxics Integration Policy Series,
PB81-147373   2179

NICHOLS, HENRY

Site Symmetry of Surface Adsorbed Molecules.
AD-A093 804/3   2184

NICHOLSON, FRANCIS H.

Vortex Modeling.
AD-A093 793/6   2125

Underline the appropriate information in each case. Note that only the Corporate Author Index cites report numbers.

NTIS Order/Report Number Index:

The same document is indexed in the NTIS Order/Report Number Index as illustrated below. (figure 9-4)

Figure 9-4

GRA&I, Volume 81, number 11
NTIS Order/Report Number Index

NTIS Order or Accession Number	Report Number

PB81-169849

Soviet Housing and Urban Design,
PB81-169849   2252 PC A05/MF A01

PB81-169856

Factors Influencing Crime and Instability in Urban Housing Developments.
PB81-169856   2152 MF A91

PB81-802084

Library Management. 1978-January, 1981 (Citations from the NTIS Data Base).
PB81-802084   2133 PC N01/MF N01

HUD-0001789

Factors Influencing Crime and Instability in Urban Housing Developments.
PB81-169856   2152 MF A01

HUD-0001796

Survey of Homeowner Experience with New Residential Housing Construction,
PB81-151821   2146 PC A10/MF A01

HUD-0001811

Intrajurisdictional Property-Tax Capitalization.
PB81-151839   2134 PC A10/MF A01

HUD-0001824

How Housing Allowances Affect Housing Markets: Supply Experiment Interim Findings. Housing Assistance Supply Experiment,
PB81-151847   2146 PC A03/MF A01

Again, underline the relevant information. In addition to providing titles, accession numbers and page numbers for abstracts, this Index also indicates the availability of documents and their price codes.

Contract/Grant Number Index:

Since a contract or grant number was excluded from the abstract to the document in question, a second citation is used to illustrate the Contract/Grant Number Index. (figure 9-5)

Figure 9-5

GRA&I, Volume 81, number 11

Contract/Grant Number Index   Abstracts

HUD-H-2664
HUD USER, Germantown, MD.
PB81-169724   2151
PB81-169732   2151
PB81-169740   2151

HUD-H-2878
Abt Associates, Inc., Cambridge, MA.
PB81-151854   2146

HUD-H-2882
Urban Inst., Washington, DC.
PB81-151888   2146

HUD-H-2915RG
John F. Kennedy School of Government, Cambridge, MA.
PB81-151839   2134

HUD-H-5040
Department of Housing and Urban Development, Washington, DC. Office of Policy Development and Research.
PB81-169831   2152

HUD-H-5088RG
National Opinion Research Center, Chicago, IL.
PB81-169781   2131

HUD-H-5108G
Woodrow Wilson International Center for Scholars, Washington, DC.
PB81-169849   2252

HUD-H-5233
Northeast Ohio Areawide Coordinating Agency, Cleveland.
PB81-151920   2147

PB81-169831   **PC A07/MF A01**
Department of Housing and Urban Development, Washington, DC. Office of Policy Development and Research.
Residential Energy Efficiency Standards Study.
Final rept.
Jul 80, 144p HUD/PDR-614, HUD-0001733
Contract HUD-H-5040

This is the final report to the Congress on the Residential Energy Efficiency Standards Study conducted by HUD in coordination with other Federal agencies as directed in Section 253 of the National Energy Conservation Policy Act of 1978 (Public Law 95 - 619). Six major issue areas address the concerns raised in the legislation, including the feasibility of developing an energy efficiency standard for existing units, the amount of energy that would be saved by the implementation of a mandatory standard over and above the energy savings estimated as resulting from current programs, and the impact of such a standard on individual households. Other concerns are how the implementation would affect credit availability and related financial matters, how it would affect the building community, and what major administrative options are available to implement the Section 253 requirement. This document integrates and highlights the findings of the principal support contractors. It presents contractors' findings and recommendations concerning the feasibility of a mandatory regulatory action as described in Section 253 and on related energy conservation policies and initiatives. Based on this technical work, the HUD recommendation does not favor a federally mandated time - of - sale program. The legislation and technical analysis information are appended.

Observe, this Index cites corporate authors, instead of titles as the other finding aids do.

On-Line Accessibility of GRAI:

The National Technical Information Service Bibliographic Data File, the on-line version of *Government Reports Announcements and Index,* is available from July 1964 to date. As of December 1979, the data base included approximately 750,000 titles.[5]

Weekly Abstract Newsletters:

The weekly abstract newsletters summarize reports within three weeks after they have been entered into the NTIS system. Twenty-six separate newsletters cover agriculture and food, energy and environment, health planning, transportation, business and economics, medicine, engineering and computer technology, among other areas. Except for *NASA Earth Resources Survey Program* which is published bimonthly, all other newsletters are issued weekly.

**Selected Indexes To Technical Reports
That Are Similar To GRAI:**

Three significant sources that index information in a similar fashion as *Government Reports Announcements and Index* are *EPA Publications Bibliography: Quarterly Abstract Bulletin, Scientific and Technical Aerospace Reports (STAR)*, and *Energy Research Abstracts (ERA)*.

The first title, which has been issued quarterly since 1977, includes technical reports and journal articles that the Environmental Protection Agency submitted to NTIS during the previous three months. All indexing is similar to that in *GRA&I*, except for the Title Index and the Sponsoring EPA Office Index, which are added features of *EPA Publications Bibliography*. The fourth issue of each volume has annual cumulative indexes. For retrospective coverage of EPA publications, consult *EPA Cumulative Bibliography, 1970-1976* and *ORD Publications Summary* which covers 1967-1976. The *Environmental Protection Agency Reports System*, a database operated by the Agency, covers publications issued between 1960 and the present.

Scientific and Technical Aerospace Reports has been distributed semimonthly since 1963. All aspects of space and aeronautic research published by the National Aeronautic and Space Administration (NASA), NASA contractors and grantees, United States government agencies other than NASA, domestic and foreign universities, research institutes and the private sector are indexed. Information is accessed in *STAR* by subjects, personal and corporate authors, report and order numbers and contract numbers. The indexes are cumulated semiannually and annually. A special section, "On-Going Research Projects," lists current NASA grants and university contracts, as well as other related projects. However, this information is not indexed. Unlike *EPA Publications Bibliography*, whose citations are available from NTIS, only selected items indexed in *STAR* are available from that agency. Other sources include the Government Printing Office, the Department of Energy, University Microfilms, the United States Geological Survey and Her Majesty's Stationery Office—the British government publisher. Sources included in *STAR* are available on-line through two data bases operated by NASA. The automated version of *Scientific and Technical Aerospace Reports* and *NASA STI Database* are both available from 1962 through the present.

Energy Research Abstracts (ERA), a semimonthly source first distributed in 1976, indexes technical reports, journals, conference papers and proceedings, books, patents, theses, and monographs produced by the Department of Energy and its laboratories, energy centers and contractors. Technical reports prepared by other U.S. agencies, state and local governments, foreign governments and universities and research centers funded by sources outside the Energy Department are also included. All Department of Energy reports, plus additional ones indexed in *ERA*, are available from both the National Technical Information Service and the Energy Department's Technical Information Center in Oak Ridge, Tennessee. The Government Printing Office hopes to make this information available to depository libraries soon. Other availability indications in *Energy Research Abstracts* include the Energy Technology Engineering Center, the Energy Department's Grand Junction, Colorado office and the Nuclear Standards Office. Though not distributed by the above sources, the non-report literature cited in *ERA* can often be obtained in university and research libraries. Documentation cited in *Energy Research Abstracts*, plus other energy related sources, are available on-line through the *DOE Energy Data Base*, which covers literature published since the late 1800's.

The following chart summarizes the similarities and differences among *GRA&I, EPA Publications Bibliography, STAR* and *ERA*.

	GRA&I	EPA Publications Quarterly	STAR	ERA
Abstracts	✓	✓	✓	✓
Indexes by Subjects	✓	✓	✓	✓
by Corporate Authors	✓	✓	✓	✓
by Personal Authors	✓	✓	✓	✓
by Contract/Grant Numbers	✓	✓	✓	✓
by Report/Accession Numbers	✓	✓	✓	✓
by Titles				✓
by Sponsoring Agencies				✓
On-line Availabilities	1964-Present	1960-Present	1962-Present	Late 1800's-Present

GPO and NTIS, A Comparison:

Differences exist between the Government Printing Office and the National Technical Information Service. The Printing Office is a legislative body established in 1860 to meet Federal printing needs. Except for its sales program, which is self-sustaining, GPO operations are funded with public monies. On the other hand, all NTIS activities are self-sustaining. When enacting PL 81-776, which gave the former Office of Technical Services statutory authority, Congress was concerned that no public funds be made available to an agency whose purpose is to serve a specific sector of society—businessmen, as opposed to the public at large. Moreover, unlike GPO documents which eventually go out of print, publications available through NTIS are always accessible upon request. Equally as important, NTIS is the only agency of the two that distributes automated data files. Regarding types of materials distributed, NTIS is the only agency of the two that distributes automated data files. Though GPO indexes in the *Monthly Catalog* and distributes to depository libraries selected technical reports, NTIS does not deal with the non-report literature handled by the Printing Office.

Much information indexed in *GRA&I* is also indexed by the Government Printing Office in its *Monthly Catalog*. Using the September 1980 *Monthly Catalog* as an example, the two thousand and ninety-seven entries in that issue included four hundred and thirty-two or over twenty percent that were indicated as being for sale from NTIS. The same citations are also listed in *Government Reports Announcements and Index*.

The *Monthly Catalog,* however, does not always include NTIS availability statements. Again, using the September 1980 *Catalog* as an example, seven out of a random sample of eleven entries having technical report numbers but no NTIS availability statement were indexed in *GRA&I*. Although the Government Printing Office sometimes indicates in the *Monthly Catalog* when publications are available from NTIS, the latter agency omits comparable information from *GRA&I* for those materials also available from GPO.

NTIS and GPO have recently agreed to a sales arrangement. Those maintaining GPO deposit accounts can order materials from the other agency and charge their purchases against their accounts. Such orders should be submitted to GPO, rather than NTIS. Likewise, individuals with NTIS accounts can order materials from GPO by submitting purchase requests to the Information Service.

When fortunate enough to have a choice of purchasing materials from either agency, note that the identical information can usually be obtained from GPO at less expense. Five of the seven citations considered above that were listed in the *Monthly Catalog* without NTIS availability indications are for sale from both agencies. Paper copies can be purchased from the Printing Office at an average price of $2.50, whereas comparable copies from NTIS are available at an average cost of $7.50. Moreover, NTIS microfiche editions average $3.50, a dollar more than those in paper from GPO.

Further Information About NTIS:

For more information about NTIS, consult *National Technical Information Service: General Catalog of Information Services No. 7a, 1981,* distributed gratis by the Information Service. A second pamphlet available from NTIS without charge, *A Reference Guide To The NTIS Bibliographic Data Base,* is a fine description of the subject.

Footnotes

[1]*A Reference Guide To The NTIS Bibliographic Data Base, 1980.* (Springfield, Virginia: NTIS, 1980). p. 4.

[2]*Departments of State, Justice, and Commerce, The Judiciary, and Related Agencies Appropriations For 1981.* Hearings before House Committee on Appropriations. Subcommittee on The Departments of State, Justice, and Commerce, The Judiciary, and Related Agencies. 96th Cong., 2nd sess. (Washington, D.C.: GPO, 1980), p. 389.

[3]*Op. cit.* at 1, p. 1.

[4]"Do Technical Reports Belong To The Literature," CCXXXVI (April 7, 1972), p. 275.

[5]*Op. cit.* at 1, p. 2.

BIBLIOGRAPHY

Departments of State, Justice, and Commerce, The Judiciary, and Related Agencies Appropriations For 1981. Hearings before House Committee on Appropriations. Subcommittee on The Departments of State, Justice, and Commerce, The Judiciary, and Related Agencies. 96th Cong., 2nd sess. Washington, D.C.: GPO, 1980.

"Do Technical Reports Belong To The Literature," *Nature.* CCXXXVI (April 7, 1972), p. 275.

Energy Research Abstracts. Technical Information Center. Oak Ridge, Tennessee: Department of Energy, 1976-semimonthly.

EPA Cumulative Bibliography, 1970-1976. Springfield, Virginia: NTIS, 1976. 2 parts.

EPA Publications Bibliography: Quarterly Abstract Bulletin. Library Systems Staff. Washington, D.C.: Environmental Protection Agency, 1977-quarterly.

Government Reports Announcements and Index. Springfield, Virginia: NTIS, 1975-semimonthly. Published under various titles since 1946.

National Technical Information Service: General Catalog of Information Services No. 7a. Springfield, Virginia: NTIS, 1981.

NTIS Title Index (Current). Springfield, Virginia: NTIS, 1979-quarterly.

NTIS Title Index (Retrospective, 1964-1978). Springfield, Virginia: NTIS, 1980.

ORD Publications Summary. Office of Research and Development. Report number EPA-600/9-76-013d. Cincinnati: Environmental Protection Agency, 1976.

A Reference Guide To The NTIS Bibliographic Data Base, 1980. Springfield, Virginia: NTIS, 1980.

Scientific and Technical Aerospace Reports. Scientific and Technical Information Branch. Washington, D.C.: National Aeronautics and Space Administration, 1963-semimonthly.

Government Reports Announcements and Index, Questions:

A survey of state criminal justice innovations was conducted in March 1980.

A. In which issue of Government Reports Announcements and Index is this document cited?

B. The abstract appears on pages _____ and _____.

C. The title of the document is _____

_____

_____ .

D. Its NTIS accession number is _____ .

E. The corporate author is the _____

_____ .

F. The personal author of this document is _____

_____ .

G. This document's report number is _____

and its grant number is _____ .

H. Is this document available in both paper and microfiche editions or merely one or the other format?

Government Reports Announcements and Index, Answers:

A. Volume 81, number 4, February 13, 1981.
B. Pages 557 and 558.
C. *A Review of Innovative State Criminal Justice Programs (Innovations).*
D. PB81-115339.
E. Council of State Governments.
F. Scott Seymour.
G. Report number: BUE-80, NSF/RA-80093; grant number: NSF-ISR75-21176.
H. The document is available in both paper and microfiche formats.

CHAPTER 10

LOCATING MAPS AND AUDIO-VISUAL MATERIALS

Besides preparing information in print format, the United States government also produces large numbers of maps and other audiovisual materials. This chapter's initial section describes the services and products of three significant agencies concerned with cartography, the United States Geological Survey, the National Ocean Survey and the Defense Mapping Agency. Major map series available through the Government Printing Office are also noted. A chart illustrating selected map products available through these agencies, plus additional ones, is included. The second section, which emphasizes services and functions of the National Audiovisual Center, deals with non-print materials other than maps.

Maps:

United States Geological Survey (USGS):

The United States Geological Survey, a part of the Interior Department, is the Federal government's largest map producer. Topographic, geologic and hydrologic maps are the three basic types distributed by this agency. Topographic maps illustrate relief data, such as mountains and valleys and geologic maps depict the structures and compositions of geologic features and ages of surficial rocks. Hydrologic maps portray water resources.

The Geological Survey maintains a system of map depository libraries independent from that of GPO.[1] Institutions throughout the nation generally obtain this status upon written request. Topographic maps are forwarded to all depository libraries, but geologic and hydrologic ones are provided on a depository basis only to colleges and universities offering degrees in geology. Full depository libraries receive as many as four through five thousand maps per year.

Geological Survey maps are accessed through various catalogs published by the agency. Separate issues of the *Index To Topographic Maps* are published irregularly for each state. The same topographic maps, along with geologic and hydrologic ones, are cited in a monthly bibliography, *New Publications of The Geological Survey*. This source is cumulated annually. Two multiyear cumulative editions entitled *Publications of The Geological Survey* have also been issued, the first covering 1879-1961 and the second 1962-1970. Maps of areas East of the Mississippi River, including Minnesota, Puerto Rico and the Virgin Islands, are obtained from the:

> Distribution Branch
> USGS
> 1200 South Eads Street
> Arlington, Virginia 22202

Those for areas West of the Mississippi River, including Alaska, Hawaii, Louisiana, Guam and American Samoa, are available from the:

> Distribution Branch
> USGS
> Box 25286
> Federal Center
> Denver, Colorado

National Ocean Survey (NOS):

The National Ocean Survey, which is within the National Oceanic and Atmospheric Administration, produces and distributes aeronautical and nautical charts, and bathymetric and topographic-bathymetric maps. NOS aeronautical charts are the primary ones used by Federal Aviation Administration air traffic controllers and pilots of both civilian and military aircraft during domestic flights. Nautical charts are used by maritime navigators. Bathymetric maps outline water depths and underwater topography, whereas topographic-bathymetric maps are coastal illustrations combining both land and water features. The latter are prepared jointly by NOS and the Geological Survey. All materials are revised regularly.

NOS nautical charts are listed in *Nautical Chart Catalogs 1-5,* a set of five bibliographies each dealing with a different area. The *Catalog of Aeronautical Charts and Related Publications* cite Ocean Survey publications pertaining to those subjects. The National Oceanic and Atmospheric Administration also distributes *World, United States and Historical Maps,* an extremely useful title. Charts and their indexes are available from the:

> National Ocean Survey
> Distribution Division (C44)
> 6501 Lafayette Avenue
> Riverdale, Maryland 20840

Defense Mapping Agency (DMA):

The Defense Mapping Agency prepares topographic and thematic maps, plus aeronautical and nautical charts, for areas outside the United States and its possessions. Thematic maps, which are sometimes called geographic, special-purpose or distribution maps, portray a single subject, such as geology, climatology, crop distribution or population distribution, among numerous other topics.

Three DMA offices are most significant, the Topographic, Aerospace and Hydrographic Centers. The Topographic Center administers the College Depository Program. New depositories are accepted only when existing ones leave the program.[2] A waiting list has been established for such eventualities. The Aerospace Center, which does not have a depository program, prepares aeronautical charts and the Hydrographic Center produces charts of the world's oceans, coastlines and islands, plus bathymetric maps and schematic plans of foreign port cities.

The *Numerical Listing of Charts and Publications* is a comprehensive bibliography of all DMA maps, charts and related products. It is available from the:

> Defense Mapping Agency Depot
> Clearfield, Utah 84106
>
> and
>
> Defense Mapping Agency
> 5801 Tabor Avenue
> Philadelphia, Pennsylvania 19120

Two of the three Centers also publish catalogs noting their respective publications. Each of the nine volumes of the *Catalog of Nautical Charts* deal with different world regions. These Hydrographic Center publications are available from the DMA's Clearfield and Philadelphia offices. Topographic

Center materials are cited in the *Price List of Maps and Charts For Public Sale,* available without charge from the:

> DMA Topographic Center
> 6500 Brooks Land
> Attn: 55510
> Washington, D.C. 20315

Since January 1982, *New Publications of The Geological Survey* have also included DMA topographic maps.

Charts prepared by the Aerospace Center are distributed through the National Ocean Survey and are indexed in that Agency's Catalog of *Catalog of Aeronautical Charts and Related Publications.*

Government Printing Office:

Census Bureau and Central Intelligence Agency maps are among the most significant distributed by the Government Printing Office.[3] Census maps portray population distribution, percapita retail sales and selected characteristics of major urban areas, among many other themes. The CIA's multi-colored General Reference Maps illustrate roads, population density, industries and natural resources, plus additional features, for countries throughout the world. Under the Keyword "Maps," the *Publications Reference File* includes a complete list of those available for sale from the Government Printing Office. Subject Bibliography 102, *Maps (United States and Foreign),* also has a comprehensive list.

Further Sources of Information About U.S. Government Maps:

Three sources of great value are *Maps For America, A Guide To Obtaining Information From The USGS* and *Map Data Catalog.* The purpose of the first title, which is an excellent introductory text, is to inform users of various kinds of maps, their characteristics and sources of information about cartography. Color inserts, illustrations, tables and charts, a glossary and a select bibliography are included. *A Guide To Obtaining Information From The USGS* describes the Agency's offices and publications and give instructions for ordering them. A very detailed table, "List of USGS Products and Sources Where They May Be Obtained," is most informative. *Map Data Catalog* describes special services provided by the National Carteographic Information Center (NCIC), a division of the Geological Survey whose goal is to become a central clearinghouse for all carteographic information produced by the Federal government.

The chart reproduced below, "Map Products and Sources," provides an overview of the kinds of carteographic products and their availabilities. A key to the agency abbreviations and their addresses follow the chart. Consult the most recent issue of the *United States Government Manual* for address changes.

MAP PRODUCTS AND SOURCES*

TABLE 1. Map products and sources

[Addresses of Federal, State, and other agencies identified by acronyms in this table begin on page 247.]

Products	Producing agency	Available from	Products	Producing agency	Available from
Aeronautical charts	NOS	NOS	Civil subdivisions and reservations State/Federal	BLM DOS	BLM DOS
Boundary information:					
United States and Canada	IBC	IBC	Census data (social and economic)	BC	GPO
United States and Mexico	IBWC	IBWC			
Boundary and annexation surveys			Climatic maps	NWS	NWS
of incorporated places with 2,500					
or more inhabitants	BC	GPO	Earthquake hazard maps	USGS	USGS

TABLE 1. Map products and sources (continued)

Products	Producing agency	Available from	Products	Producing agency	Available from
Federal property maps:			**Photographic products:**		
Water and Power Resources Service	WPRS	WPRS	Aerial photographs	ASCS	ASCS
Fish and Wildlife Service	FWS	FWS		BLM	BLM
National Aeronautics and Space				BLM	EDC
Administration	NASA	NASA		BPA	BPA
National forests	FS	FS		DMA	DMA
National Park Service	NPS	NPS		NASA	EDC
Military reservations:				FHWA	FHWA
Air Force	USAF	USAF		FS	EDC
Army	USA	USA		FS	NCIC
Coast Guard	USCG	USCG		FWS	EDC
Marines	USMC	USMC		FWS	NCIC
Navy	USN	USN		NOS	NOS
State maps of lands administered				NPS	NPS
by Bureau of Land Management	BLM	BLM		SCS	SCS
U.S. maps of lands administered by				USCE	USCE
Bureau of Land Management	BLM	BLM		FS	FS
				USGS	NCIC/
Flood-plain maps	DRBC	DRBC			EDC
	FIA	FIA			
	MRC	MRC	Orthophotomaps	BIA	BIA
	NOS	FIA		NOS	NOS
	SCS	SCS		USGS	USGS
	USCE	USCE	**Space imagery:**		
	USGS	USGS	Landsat (ERTS)	NASA	ASCS
Geodetic control data	NOS	NOS		NASA	EDC
	USCE	USCE		NASA	EDIS
	USGS	NOS/	NASA manned spacecraft	NASA	EDC
		NCIC	Nimbus	NWS	NWS
Geologic maps:			Skylab	NASA	ASCS
Coal investigations	USGS	USGS		NASA	EDC
General geologic	SGA	SGA	Tiros	NWS	NWS
	USGS	USGS	**Recreation maps**	BLM	BLM
Geophysical investigations	NOAA	EDIS		HCRC	HCRC
	NOAA	ERL	**Seismicity maps and charts**	ERL	ERL
	USGS	USGS		USGS	USGS
Mineral investigations	USGS	USGS			
Mines	BM	BM	**Soils**	SCS	SCS
Oil and gas investigations	USGS	USGS			
Geographic maps:	NOS	NOS	**Soils—substation quality**	BPA	BPA
Land use	USGS	USGS	**Topographic maps**	USGS	USGS
Highway maps:				MRC	MRC
Indian lands	BIA	BIA		NASA	NASA
Federal lands	FHWA	FHWA			
Federally funded roads	FHWA	GPO	**Utilities:**		
Federal primary and secondary	FHWA	GPO	Ground conductivity maps of the		
Interstate	FHWA	FHWA	U.S.	FCC	GPO
Federal highway maps of the U.S.	FHWA	GPO	Principal electric-facilities maps of		
Historical maps and charts	LC	LC	the U.S.	ERC	GPO
	All Federal		Principal natural-gas-pipelines		
	agencies	NARS	maps of the U.S.	ERC	GPO
			Water resources development data	USGS	USGS
Hydrographic charts and bathymetric					
maps:	NOS	NOS	**Miscellaneous data:**		
	USCE	USCE	Clinometric (slope) maps	USGS	USGS
	USGS	USGS	Gravity survey charts	EDIS	EDIS
Hydrographic surveys	NOS	NOS		NOS	NOS
	USGS	USGS		USGS	USGS
Nautical charts	NOS	NOS	Income distribution maps	BC	GPO
	USCE	USCE	Isogonic charts	USGS	USGS
Navigable waterways maps	USCE	USCE	Isomagnetic charts	NOS	NOS
River and stream surveys	MRC	MRC	Magnetic charts	EDIS	EDIS
River basin watershed studies	ERC	ERC	National science trail maps	SCS	SCS
	SCS	SCS	State indexes of fish hatcheries and		
	USGS	USGS	national wildlife refuges	FWS	FWS
River surveys	WPRS	WPRS	Storm evacuation maps	NOS	NOS
	USGS	USGS	Tree danger (to powerlines)		
Wildlife and scenic river jurisdiction	BLM	BLM	detection maps	BPA	BPA
Hydrologic investigations atlases	USGS	USGS	U.S. location maps of fish		
Indian reservations:			hatcheries and national wildlife		
Land surveys	BIA	GPO	refuges	FWS	FWS
U.S. maps of Indian lands	BIA	GPO			
Land plats	BLM	BLM			
	BLM	NARS			
	NPS	NPS			
	USCE	USCE			
National Atlas of the U.S.	USGS	USGS			

*Reprinted from *Maps For America: Cartographic Products of The U.S. Geological Survey and others*, by Morris M. Thompson. United States Geological Survey. 2nd ed. (Washington, D.C.: GPO, 1981), pp. 18-19.

MAP PRODUCTS AND SOURCES*
Key To Agencies Abbreviations and Addresses

Agricultural Stabilization and Conservation Service (ASCS)
Aerial Photography Field Office
Agricultural Stabilization and Conservation Service
Department of Agriculture
(2222 West, 2300 South)
P.O. Box 30010
Salt Lake City, Utah 84125

Bonneville Power Administration (BPA)
Bonneville Power Administration
Department of Energy
(1002 NE. Holladay Street)
P.O. Box 3621
Portland, Oreg. 97208

Bureau of the Census (BC)
Users Service Staff
Data Users Services Division
Bureau of the Census
Department of Commerce
Washington, D.C. 20233

Bureau of Indian Affairs (BIA)
Bureau of Indian Affairs
Department of the Interior
18th and C Streets, NW.
Washington, D.C. 20240

Bureau of Land Management (BLM)
Bureau of Land Management
Department of the Interior
18th and C Streets, NW.
Washington, D.C. 20240

Bureau of Mines (BM)
Environmental Affairs Field Office
Bureau of Mines
Department of the Interior
Room 3323
Penn Place
20 North Pennsylvania Avenue
Wilkes-Barre, Pa. 18701

Mine Map Repository
Bureau of Mines
Department of the Interior
Building 20
Denver Federal Center
Denver, Colo. 80225

Mine Map Repository
Bureau of Mines
Department of the Interior
4800 Forbes Avenue
Pittsburgh, Pa. 15213

Defense Mapping Agency (DMA)
Defense Mapping Agency
Building 56
U.S. Naval Observatory
Washington, D.C. 20305

Delaware River Basin Commission (DRBC)
Executive Director
Delaware River Basin Commission
(25 State Police Drive)
Post Office Box 7360
West Trenton, N.J. 08628

Department of Energy (DOE)
Public Affairs Director
Department of Energy
1000 Independence Avenue, SW.
Washington, D.C. 20585

Department of State (DOS)
Office of the Geographer
Bureau of Intelligence and Research
Department of State
8742 NS INR/GE
Washington, D.C. 20520

Environmental Protection Agency (EPA)
Office of Public Awareness
Environmental Protection Agency
401 M Street, SW.
Washington, D.C. 20460

Federal Energy Regulatory Commission (FERC)
Office of Public Information
Federal Energy Regulatory Commission
825 North Capital Street, NE.
Washington, D.C. 20426

Federal Highway Administration (FHWA)
Office of Public Affairs
Federal Highway Administration
Department of Transportation
Room 4208
400 7th Street, SW.
Washington, D.C. 20590

Aerial Surveys Branch
Highway Design Division
Federal Highway Administration
Department of Transportation
Room 3130A
400 7th Street, SW.
Washington, D.C. 20590

Federal Insurance Administration (FIA)
National Flood Insurance Program
Federal Insurance Administration
Federal Emergency Management Agency
P.O. Box 34294
Bethesda, Md. 20034

Heritage Conservation and Recreation Service (HCRC)
(formerly Bureau of Outdoor Recreation)
Federal Land Planning Division
Heritage Conservation and Recreation Service
130 Interior South Building
18th and C Streets, NW.
Washington, D.C. 20240

**International Boundary and Water Commission, United States
and Mexico (IBWC)**
U.S. Commissioner
International Boundary and Water Commission, United States and
Mexico
United States Section
(4110 Rio Bravo, Executive Center)
P.O. Box 20003
El Paso, Tex. 79998

**International Boundary Commission, United States and Canada
(IBC)**
U.S. Commissioner
International Boundary Commission, United States and Canada
United States Section
Room 150
425 I Street, NW.
Washington, D.C. 20001

Library of Congress (LC)
Geography and Map Division
Library of Congress
Washington, D.C. 20540

Mississippi River Commission (MRC)
Executive Assistant
Mississippi River Commission
(Mississippi River Commission Building)
U.S. Army Corps of Engineers
P.O. Box 60
Vicksburg, Miss. 39180

National Aeronautics and Space Administration (NASA)
Contact the facility office of the installation concerned.

National Archives and Records Service (NARS)
Cartographic Archives Division
National Archives and Records Service
General Services Administration
Archives Building
Pennsylvania Avenue at 8th Street, NW.
Washington, D.C. 20408

National Oceanic and Atmospheric Administration (NOAA)

Environmental Data and Information Service (EDIS)
National Oceanic and Atmospheric Administration
Department of Commerce
Page Building 2
3300 Whitehaven Street, NW.
Washington, D.C. 22023

Environmental Research Laboratories (ERL)
Environmental Research Laboratories
National Oceanic and Atmospheric Administration
Department of Commerce
3100 Marine Avenue
Boulder, Colo. 80302

National Ocean Survey (NOS)

   Aerial photographs and shoreline maps:
   Coastal Mapping Division, C3415
   National Ocean Survey
   National Oceanic and Atmospheric Administration
   Department of Commerce
   Rockville, Md. 20852

   Chart sales:
   Washington Science Center 1, C5131
   National Oceanic and Atmospheric Administration
   Department of Commerce
   Rockville, Md. 20852

   Charts:
   Distribution Division, C64
   National Ocean Survey
   National Oceanic and Atmospheric Administration
   Department of Commerce
   Riverdale, Md. 20840

   General cartographic information:
   Physical Science Services Branch, C513
   National Ocean Survey
   National Oceanic and Atmospheric Administration
   Department of Commerce
   Rockville, Md. 20852

   Geodetic control data:
   National Geodetic Information Center, C18
   National Ocean Survey
   National Oceanic and Atmospheric Administration
   Department of Commerce
   Rockville, Md. 20852

National Weather Service (NWS)

   National Meteorological Center
   National Weather Service
   National Oceanic and Atmospheric Administration
   Department of Commerce
   5200 Auth Road
   Camp Springs, Md. 20233

National Park Service (NPS)
   Office of Communications
   National Park Service
   3043 Interior Building
   18th and C Streets, NW.
   Washington, D.C. 20242

Soil Conservation Service (SCS)
   Cartographic Division
   Soil Conservation Service
   Department of Agriculture
   Federal Building
   6505 Belcrest Road
   Hyattsville, Md. 20782

State Geologic Agencies (SGA)
   Contact the State Geologist or
   other cognizant official in each State.

Tennessee Valley Authority (TVA)
   Mapping Services Branch
   Tennessee Valley Authority
   200 Haney Building
   Chattanooga, Tenn. 37401

U.S. Air Force (USAF)
   Contact the information officer of the base concerned.

U.S. Army (USA)
   Contact the commander of the base concerned.

   U.S. Army Corps of Engineers (USCE)
   Office of Chief of Engineers
   U.S. Army Corps of Engineers
   Washington, D.C. 20314

U.S. Coast Guard (USCG)
   Oceanographic Unit
   U.S. Coast Guard
   Building 159E, Washington Navy Yard Annex
   Washington, D.C. 20590

U.S. Fish and Wildlife Service (FWS)
   Division of Realty
   U.S. Fish and Wildlife Service
   Department of the Interior
   555 Matomic Building
   1717 H Street, NW.
   Washington, D.C. 20240

U.S. Forest Service (FS)
   U.S. Forest Service
   Office of Information
   Department of Agriculture
   P.O. Box 2417
   Washington, D.C. 20013

U.S. Geological Survey (USGS)

   All cartographic data:

   Branch of User Services
   National Cartographic Information Center (NCIC)
   U.S. Geological Survey
   Department of the Interior
   MS 507, National Center
   (12201 Sunrise Valley Drive)
   Reston, Va. 22092

   Photographs and remote sensor imagery:
   User Services Unit
   EROS Data Center (EDC)
   U.S. Geological Survey
   Department of the Interior
   Sioux Falls, S. Dak. 57198

   Maps and control data by mail:
   Alaska
   Distribution Section
   U.S. Geological Survey
   Department of the Interior
   101 12th Avenue
   Fairbanks, Alaska 99701

   States east of Mississippi River plus Puerto Rico
   Eastern Distribution Branch
   U.S. Geological Survey
   Department of the Interior
   1200 South Eads Street
   Arlington, Va. 22202

   States west of Mississippi River plus Hawaii, Guam, and American Samoa
   Western Distribution Branch
   U.S. Geological Survey
   Department of the Interior
   MS 306, Box 25286
   Denver Federal Center
   Denver, Colo. 80225

   Commercial dealers are listed on sales indexes which can be obtained from any of the above three offices.

U.S. Government Printing Office (GPO)
   Assistant Public Printer
   (Superintendent of Documents)
   U.S. Government Printing Office
   North Capitol and H Streets, NW.
   Washington, D.C. 20402

U.S. Marine Corps (USMC)
   Contact the commander of the base concerned.

U.S. Navy (USN)
   Contact the commander of the base concerned.

Water and Power Resources Service (WPRS)
   Chief, Publications and Photography Branch
   General Services Division
   7442 Interior Building
   18th and C Streets, NW.
   Washington, D.C. 20240

Reprinted from *Maps For America: Carteographic Products of The U.S. Geological Survey and Others,* by Morris M. Thompson. United States Geological Survey. 2nd ed. (Washington, D.C.: GPO, 1981). pp. 247-9.

Audiovisual Materials Other Than Maps:

Both civilian and military agencies produce and use audiovisual formats for training purposes and for emphasizing their services and functions to the public. Robert Lissit, an advisor to President Carter, estimated approximately $500,000,000 per year is spent by Federal agencies for audiovisual production and distribution.[6] The *Hope Reports,* an industry publication, claimed the annual amount is closer to $632,300,000.[7]

National Audiovisual Center:

The General Service Administration's National Audiovisual Center (NAC), created in 1969, is the Federal government's information clearinghouse in this area. The Center distributes audiovisual materials and related information to Federal agencies, as well as the general public.

NAC maintains a data bank developed in cooperation with other agencies that is accessible either by title or subject. Producers of A-V information are required to file preproduction and postproduction reports with NAC. This enables the Center to determine what is or will shortly become available. To supplement these reports, agencies are also required to file annual reports outlining A-V activities.

Motion pictures, which comprise eighty percent of NAC's collection, video and audio tapes and multi-media kits can be purchased from the agency. Multimedia kits are collections of more than one media used in cooperation, such as slide/tapes. 16mm films are available for rent and can be previewed prior to purchase. The Center refers agencies and people interested in borrowing items to appropriate offices responsible for preparing the information.

The Audiovisual Center publishes many catalogs describing government A-V products. Over six thousand items available for sale or rent are cited in *A Reference List of Audiovisual Materials Produced By The United States Government 1978.* Entries in the title section, the major part of the catalog, appear alphabetically. Types of media, producers, distributors if different from producers, brief summaries and intended audiences are indicated. The subject section, which is arranged by broad headings, facilitates access to information. A *Supplement* was published in 1980.

Quarterly Update is a periodical publicizing new materials and services. Arrangement is by topics, such as alcohol and drug abuse, business, government management, career and vocational education, history and science. Medical sources comprise the largest part of the journal. Titles and title numbers, prices, dates, types of formats, producers, abstracts and intended audiences are given. A title index is also included.

The *Directory of U.S. Government Audiovisual Personnel* is a central listing of related employees. Information is separated into five parts according to NAC, Congress, executive offices, independent agencies and boards, committees and commissions. Entries include titles, phone numbers and zip code addresses. Information is indexed by names of individuals and agencies. Though much of this volume, which was last published in 1977, is dated, some offices may still exist or comparable ones may have been created and selected phone numbers may not have changed.

NAC's Reference Section distributes information lists on many special subjects. Foreign language instruction, nursing, special education, business and government management are among the topics covered. The Reference Section also refers questions to other sources when NAC does not have materials relating to your interests.

The Government Printing Office's Subject Bibliography 73, *Motion Pictures, Films and Audiovisual Information* is a list of print sources describing Federal A-V products and services. Titles, dates, paginations, Superintendent of Document numbers, stock numbers and prices are given, along with brief one or two sentence annotations. Most documents are agency bibliographies, many of which were prepared by the Department of Health Education and Welfare. A related Subject Bibliography, *Photography* (SB 72), lists compilations of photos and other sources relating to photographic methods.

Despite efforts by the National Audiovisual Center, much audiovisual production and distribution remains extremely decentralized. Agencies can sell or loan materials without NAC's assistance, providing department heads determine that such actions are essential for efficient operations. In selected cases, the Center might be providing the same services for the identical items. Agencies are not required to forward copies of their productions to the Center or provide copies for duplication, unless NAC requests that they do so. The situation is further complicated since agencies often fail to submit production reports. NAC cannot request that materials be added to its collection when the Center is unaware of appropriate information.

However, a bright spot still lies on the horizon. The GPO, the Library of Congress and the National Audiovisual Center have recently reached an agreement whereby approximately six hundred audiovisual materials will be indexed in the *Monthly Catalog* annually.

Footnotes

[1] In his letter of July 26, 1982 to heads of GPO depository libraries, Senator Charles Mathias, Chairman of the Joint Committee on Printing, states the Federal government intends to incorporate the USGS and DMA map depository programs into that of GPO. He did not indicate when this might become effective.

[2] *Ibid.*

[3] *Ibid.*

[4] *Maps For America: Carteographic Products of The U.S. Geological Survey and Others.* Morris M. Thompson. United States Geological Survey. 2nd ed. (Washington, D.C.: GPO, 1981), pp. 18-19.

[5] *Ibid,* pp. 247-9.

[6] *Summary of Findings and Recommendations on Federal Audiovisual Activities.* Robert Lissit et al. In *Federal Audiovisual Materials Policy and Programs.* Hearings before the House Committee on Government Operations. Subcommittee on Government Activities and Transportation. 95th Cong., 2nd sess. (Washington, D.C.: GPO, 1979), p. 401.

[7] *Ibid.*

BIBLIOGRAPHY

Catalog of Aeronautical Charts and Related Publications. Riverdale, Maryland: National Oceanic and Atmospheric Administration, updated regularly.

Catalog of Nautical Charts. Hydrographic/Topographic Center. Rockville, Maryland: Defense Mapping Agency, updated regularly.

Directory of U.S. Government Audiovisual Personnel. 6th ed. Washington, D.C.: National Audiovisual Center, 1977.

Federal Audiovisual Materials Policy and Programs. Hearings before the House Committee on Government Operations, Subcomittee on Government Activities and Transportation. 95th Cong., 2nd sess. Washington, D.C.: GPO, 1979.

GPO Sales Publications Reference File Microform. Superintendent of Documents. Washington, D.C.: GPO, 1977-bimonthly.

A Guide To Obtaining Information From The USGS, 1981. Comp. by Paul F. Clarke et al. Geological Survey Circular 777. Alexandria, Virginia: United States Geological Survey, 1981.

Index To Topographic Maps. Arlington, Virginia: United States Geological Survey, separate index issued for each state, Puerto Rico, Guam, American Samoa and the Virgin Islands.

Map and Chart Catalog 5: United States, Bathymetric Maps and Special Purpose Charts. Riverdale, Maryland: National Oceanic and Atmospheric Administration, updated regularly.

Map Data Catalog. United States Geological Survey. National Carteographic Information Center, Washington, D.C.: GPO, 1980?

Maps and Atlases (United States and Foreign). Superintendent of Documents. Subject Bibliography 102. Washington, D.C.: GPO, 1981.

Maps For America: Carteographic Products of The U.S. Geological Survey and Others. Morris M. Thompson. United States Geological Survey. 2nd ed. Washington, D.C.: GPO, 1981.

Motion Pictures, Films and Audiovisual Information. Superintendent of Documents. Subject Bibliography 73. Washington, D.C.: GPO, 1981.

Nautical Chart Catalog 1: United States Atlantic and Gulf Coasts Including Puerto Rico and the Virgin Islands. Riverdale, Maryland. National Oceanic and Atmospheric Administration, updated regularly.

Nautical Chart Catalog 2: United States Pacific Coast Including Hawaii, Guam and Samoa Islands. Riverdale, Maryland: National Oceanic and Atmospheric Administration, updated regularly.

Nautical Chart Catalog 3: United States Alaska Including Aleutian Islands. Riverdale, Maryland: National Oceanic and Atmospheric Administration, updated regularly.

Nautical Chart Catalog 4: United States Great Lakes and Adjacent Waterways. Riverdale, Maryland: National Oceanic and Atmospheric Administration, updated regularly.

New Publications of The Geological Survey. Reston, Virginia: Department of The Interior, 1907-monthly.

Numerical Listing of Charts and Publications. Hydrographic/Topographic Center. Washington, D.C.: Defense Mapping Agency, updated regularly.

Photography. Superintendent of Documents. Subject Bibliography 72. Washington, D.C.: GPO, 1981.

Price List of Maps and Charts For Public Sale. Office of Distribution Services. Washington, D.C.: Defense Mapping Agency, 1978. Reprinted 1980.

Publications of The Geological Survey, 1879-1961. Washington, D.C.: United States Geological Survey, 1964?

Publications of The Geological Survey, 1962-1970. Washington, D.C.: GPO, 1972.

Quarterly Update: A Comprehensive Listing of New Audiovisual Materials and Services Offered by The National Audiovisual Center. Washington, D.C.: National Audiovisual Center, 1980-quarterly.

A Reference List of Audiovisual Materials Produced by The United States Government, Supplement, 1980. Washington, D.C.: National Audiovisual Center, 1980.

A Reference List of Audiovisual Materials Produced By The United States Government, 1978. Washington, D.C.: National Audiovisual Center, 1978.

World, United States and Historical Maps. Physical Science Services Branch. Scientific Services Division. Educational Pamphlet #1. 11th ed. Riverdale, Maryland: National Oceanic and Atmospheric Administration. Office of Program Development and Management, 1980.

CHAPTER 11

USING THE FREEDOM OF INFORMATION
AND PRIVACY ACTS

Until now, discussion has been limited to published information in print and other formats. This chapter considers two laws mandating that certain kinds of unpublished records be made available to individuals upon request, the Freedom of Information Act (FOIA) and the Privacy Act. The purpose of the FOIA, which was enacted in 1966 and amended in 1974, is to make government more open to the public. During House debates on the original legislation, Representative Rumsfeld quoted James Madison who stated:

> Knowledge will forever govern ignorance. And a people who mean to be their own governors, must arm themselves with the power knowledge gives. A popular government without popular information or the means of acquiring it, is but a prologue to a farce or a tragedy, or perhaps both.[1]

The Privacy Act, which was enacted in 1974, attempts to protect individuals rights to privacy by safeguarding the Federal government's use of personal information. In doing so, a balance was achieved, enabling the Federal government to use such files for legitimate purposes. The Freedom of Information Act is used by those requesting data of impersonal natures, while the Privacy Act is used by individuals seeking personal information.

The characteristics of each statute are discussed below. The rights of individuals and the responsibilities of government agencies are considered. Recommended procedures for requesting information under both laws are given and suggestions for appealing government decisions to withhold files are outlined. Sources of further information are also cited.

Freedom of Information Act:

Basic Provisions:

The Freedom of Information Act covers records adopted, issued or enacted by Federal government agencies after July 4, 1967. According to the law, agencies are defined as executive departments, the military, government corporations, government controlled corporations and independent regulatory bodies. The President's personal staff, Congress and the courts are excluded from the Act. Information compiled by government grantees also falls outside the law's domain. In *Forsham v. Harris,* the Supreme Court ruled that private concerns who receive Federal funding for research cannot be forced to release to the public information compiled during the same research. The fact that government agencies, in some cases, might have the right to request that records be transferred to their possession is irrelevant. The data remains private property when the government fails to exercise this right.

Many kinds of records are covered under the Freedom of Information Act. Records have been defined as "memorialization(s) of . . . fact(s), opinion(s), or idea(s) which (are) not . . . irreproducible physical object(s)."[2] Included among the data are:

Organizational structures of central and regional offices.

Substantive, as well as procedural, rules and regulations.

Final opinions, orders, policy statements and interpretations of law not published in the *Federal Register.*

Staff manuals and instructions to employees that affect the public.

Records appear in various mediums, such as computer, audio or video tapes, films and phonograph recordings, plus paper. In the past, files made available have covered wide ranges of subjects, including nutrition, effectiveness of drugs, pollution, affirmative action, occupational health and safety, automobile safety and Central Intelligence Agency and Federal Bureau of Investigation activities, among many other topics.

Records Exempt From Disclosure Under the Freedom of Information Act:

Nine types of records are exempt from disclosure under the Act.

1. Information classified for national defense purposes.

2. Information relating to internal agency functions, such as personnel rules and other housekeeping activities. Critics charge that this is contrary to the intent of the Act. For instance, 5 USC 552(a) (2) (c) requires agency manuals be published, yet this exemption can be interpreted to the contrary.

3. Records which government agencies are prohibited from making public under other laws, such as patent applications and census responses.

4. Business data regarding trade secrets and confidential financial and commercial trade information that might harm competitive positions.

5. Inter and intraoffice memoranda outlining policy options circulated during predecisional stages. This helps ensure free exchange of ideas among officials. However, related communications circulated in postdecisional stages must be disclosed upon request.

6. Data whose release might invade personal privacy.

7. Records compiled for law enforcement purposes when their release might:[3]

Interfere with law enforcement.

Inhibit due process.

Disclose identities of informants.

Endanger the safety of law enforcement officials.

8. Information relating to financial institutions prepared by, on behalf of or for the use of agencies responsible for the regulation or supervision of the institutions.[4]

9. Information concerning wells and other geologic and geophysical data that might reveal trade secrets.

Requesting Information Under The Freedom of Information Act, Initiating Requests:

Anyone can request records under the Freedom of Information Act, including non-citizens and residents of foreign nations. Contact in writing the agency head, the Freedom of Information Officer or the individual responsible for maintaining the files. A sample letter follows.[5]

Agency Head or FOIA Officer
Title
Name of Agency
Address of Agency
City, State, zip

Re: Freedom of Information Act
Request.

Dear _____:

Under the provisions of the Freedom of Information Act, 5 USC 552, I am requesting access to (identify the records as clearly and specifically as possible).

If there are any fees for searching for, or copying, the records I have requested, please inform me before you fill the request. (Or: . . . please supply the records without informing me if the fees do not exceed $ _____)

[Optional] I am requesting this information (state the reason for your request if you think it will assist you in obtaining the information.)

[Optional] As you know, the act permits you to reduce or waive fees when the release of the information is considered as "primarily benefiting the public". I believe that this request fits that category and I therefore ask that you waive any fees.

If all or any part of this request is denied, please cite the specific exemption(s) which you think justifies your refusal to release the information, and inform me of the appeal procedures available to me under the law.

I would appreciate your handling this request as quickly as possible, and I look forward to hearing from you within 10 days, as the law stipulates.

Sincerely,

Signature
Name
Address
City, State, zip

To assist the public in pinpointing records, government agencies are required to publish indexes at least quarterly and make these finding aids available either by sale or any other method. When it is impractical and/or unnecessary to publish indexes, notices to that effect must be placed in the *Federal Register*. After doing so, agencies still must provide individuals with appropriate finding aids upon request. Lists of indexes currently available are published in the *Federal Register*.

Agency Responses to Requests:

The law requires agencies to respond to inquiries within ten working days, excluding holidays and weekends. When unable to do so, they must inform requesters that an extension of time is needed. This cannot exceed an additional ten days.

The time periods should not be taken for granted. Depending upon the agencies and volumes of requests, the twenty days are sometimes extended to months before information is provided. Some believe few government agencies meet deadlines regularly. For instance, delays at the FBI are sometimes as long as eight months or more. These problems, plus others, are discussed in two recent hearings, *Oversight of The Administration of The Federal Freedom of Information Act* and *Freedom of Information Act Oversight*.

Government agencies are required to charge reasonable and uniform fees which cover research and reproduction costs when providing information. The fees can be waived when release of the records benefits the general public. Search fees usually range from approximately $5.00 per hour for clerical time to $10.00 through $18.00 per hour for professional time, while reproduction costs average about ten cents per page at most agencies.[6]

When denying requests, agencies must indicate their rationales for doing so, provide names and addresses of those responsible for the denials and cite names of àgencies' administrators to whom appeals can be made.

Appeal Procedures:

Appeals of denied requests must be filed within thirty days following receipt of the notices. Though agencies are usually required to respond to the challenges within twenty days, this time period is sometimes extended. If they fail to respond or elect to uphold the original denials, requesters can file suit in the United States District Court where they reside or work or where the records are stored. The burden of proof is upon the government agencies, rather than the individuals. That is, the agencies must prove why the information should be withheld. The court can award attorney's fees to requesters if their cases substantially prevail over the agencies'. Regarding bureaucrats who deny information requests arbitrarily, the Civil Service Commission is empowered to take disciplinary action against such employees.

Further Sources of Information About The Freedom of Information Act:

Senate and house reports and debates, selected cases and other materials relating to the original 1966 legislation are reprinted in *Freedom of Information Act Sourcebook: Legislative Materials, Cases, Articles.* The *Freedom of Information Act and Amendments of 1974 (PL 93-502), Source Book: Legislative History, Texts, and Other Documents* is similar to its earlier counterpart.

Both the Freedom of Information Act and the Privacy Act are discussed in three important publications. James T. O'Reilly's multi-volume study, *Federal Information Disclosure: Procedures, Forms, and The Law,* is a detailed analysis. Though it is intended for use by attorneys, laymen might find this source useful as well. O'Reilly also discusses the Government In The Sunshine Act and the Federal Advisory Committee Act in less detailed a fashion as the other legislation. Sample letters used to request information and to appeal denied requests are reprinted.

A *Citizens Guide on How To Use The Freedom of Information Act and The Privacy Act In Requesting Government Documents* is an excellent summary of the laws. Their backgrounds, scopes and procedures to follow when requesting files are outlined in a concise, well written manner. The texts of both acts, plus the names and addresses of selected government agencies are also included. The House Committee on Government Operations recommends the use of this guide by citizens exercising their rights under the laws.

The third source, *Basic Information on The Use Of The Privacy Act and The Freedom of Information Act,* prepared by Elizabeth Smith of the Congressional Research Service, is also a fine summary of the laws. Answers to twenty-three questions about the Privacy Act and fifteen related to the FOIA are given. As with the *Citizens Guide,* sample request letters are reprinted.

Several organizations provide assistance in using the Freedom of Information Act. The Freedom of Information Clearinghouse, P.O. Box 19367, Washington, D.C. 20036, (202-785-3704), provides legal and technical aid to public interest groups, citizens and journalists. The Clearinghouse will often go to court arguing for information disclosures under the Freedom of Information

Act, plus other access laws. The Fund for Open Information and Accountability, 36 West 44th Street, New York City 10036, (212-730-8095), consists of individuals and groups who support the FOIA. Besides aiding the public in obtaining documents, the Fund also sponsors seminars and workshops for attorneys, historians and public interest groups, maintains a speakers bureau and distributes audiovisual materials to interested parties. The Freedom of Information Center, Box 858, Columbia, Missouri 65205, (314-882-4856), is part of the University of Missouri's School of Journalism. Its services are oriented primarily towards journalists, but others with no media affiliations are also assisted.

Privacy Act:

The Privacy Act covers records held by executive departments, the military, government corporations, government controlled corporations and independent regulatory agencies. These agencies routinely collect in various ways files of personal information about those who have been or are employed by the Federal government or its contractors. Data also exists relating to recipients of benefits, such as veterans assistance, medical services or loans for education or mortgages. Considering activities of those arrested, the Federal Bureau of Investigation maintains files on individuals taken into custody by local, state and national authorities. These are just a few of the many ways government agencies collect personal data.

The Privacy Act guarantees the public certain rights regarding personal records held by government agencies. Both citizens and legal aliens have the right to know what kinds of data about their lives are being collected and why it is being collected. They also have the right to know what effects upon their lives this information might have were it withheld from them. Government agencies are prohibited from divulging personal data to third parties, either people or government bodies, without the written permission of the relevant individuals, except under one of the following conditions:

1. The FOIA requires disclosure of information.

2. The Census Bureau utilizes the data for either planning or taking a census or a survey.

3. Records are transferred to the National Archives.

4. Heads of law enforcement agencies submit written requests for records.

5. The health or safety of the subjects of the records necessitate that information be disclosed to other individuals.

6. Court orders require that the data be disclosed.

7. Congress or its General Accounting Office requests the information. Government agencies are required to provide to the public, upon request, lists of third parties to whom personal data has been divulged, unless the information was disclosed under one of the seven conditions cited above. Other rights under the Act include the right to revise agency records and amend misinformation.

The Office of Management and Budget oversees the Act's administration. It provides guidelines, suggests regulations for agencies and offers additional assistance as necessary. OMB Circular A-108, which is designed to assist agencies in implementing the law, plus other related documents, are reprinted in *Legislative History of The Privacy Act S. 3418 (Public Law 93-579): Source Book on Privacy.*

Fee schedules under the Privacy and Freedom of Information Acts differ. The Privacy Act allows agencies to determine reproduction costs, but unlike the FOIA, it prohibits the government from charging the public for time spent searching for requested information.

Exemptions Under The Privacy Act:

The following kinds of records are exempt from release under the Privacy Act. Note that government agencies are not required to withold information, but may do so if they choose to.

1. All files maintained by the Central Intelligence Agency.

2. Data compiled by Federal criminal law enforcement agencies from the time a suspect is arrested through his release.

3. Documents compiled during investigations for Federal employment, military service, military promotion and contract awards may be released only when the identities of confidential sources are protected.

4. Secret Service information pertaining to protection of the President and other high officials.

5. Information possibly having harmful effects upon the national security.

6. Records concerning the Federal examination procedures whereby divulgence would compromise objectivity or the testing process.

7. Records required by statute to be maintained and used solely for statistical purposes, such as census or income tax returns.

Requesting Information Under The Privacy Act:

Contact either the agency head or the individual responsible for maintaining the records and note "Privacy Act Request" on the envelope. A sample request letter appears below.[7]

Agency Head or Privacy Act Officer
Title
Agency
Address of Agency
City, State, zip

Re: Privacy Act Request.

Dear _____:

Under the provisions of the Privacy Act of 1974, 5 USC 522a, I hereby request a copy of (or: access to)_____(describe as accurately and specifically as possible for the record or records you want, and provide all the relevant information you have concerning them).

If there are any fees for copying the records I am requesting, please inform me before you fill the request. (Or: . . . . please supply the records without informing me if the fees do not exceed $ _____)

If all or any part of this request is denied, please cite the specific exemption(s) which you think justifies your refusal to release the information. Also, please inform me of your agency's appeal procedure.

In order to expedite consideration of my request, I am enclosing a copy of _____ (some document of identification).

Thank you for your prompt attention to this matter.

Sincerely,

Signature
Name
Address
City, State, zip

Inclusion of appropriate identification, such as documentation illustrating your name, address and/or social security number might be a good idea. The Privacy Act again differs from the FOIA in that agencies are not required to provide the information within ten working days, but need only acknowledge receipt of the request within that time period. The acknowledgement should indicate if the data will be released and when it will be done. The only other time limit pertains to requests to amend false or incomplete files. Agencies are required to make the necessary changes within thirty days.

To assist the public in locating files, the Privacy Act mandates that an annual guide to all personal records held by the Federal government be published. The multivolume *Privacy Act Issuances,* prepared by the Office of The Federal Register, includes descriptions of all record groups held on individuals and procedures government agencies use when filing information requests. Typical entries cite names of data systems, their locations, categories of individuals covered, statutory/regulatory authorities under which the files are collected, descriptions of routine uses of the records and policies relating to storing, accessing, retrieving, retaining and disposing of the records. Several research aids are found in the last volume of the series. These include two lists of records relating to Federal employment and non-personnel data and citations to Privacy Act materials published in the *Federal Register* and the *Code of Federal Regulations.* A list of Privacy Act publications appearing in the *Federal Register* is also published in the *Register's* index.

Appealing Agency Decisions:

There is no standard manner of appealing government decisions to withhold information, since the various agencies establish their own appeal procedures. Unlike the FOIA, under the Privacy Act, the public is entitled to appeal decisions through the courts, rather than agencies' channels, when the government denies requests for files. However, it would usually be wiser to exhaust all agency channels before turning to the courts due to the expense involved. When notifying the public of denied requests, government agencies should specify relevant appeal procedures and cite names and addresses of parties to whom challenges are to be addressed. Complainants should contact the agency heads when other officials are not mentioned. If the government continues to uphold its original denials, the exemptions under which the data is being withheld must be cited.

Procedures for challenging denied requests to amend records differ from those relating to the withholding of information. In the former case, complainants must utilize agencies' channels before initiating law suits. Though the government is required to respond to appeals within thirty days, agencies' heads can extend this period under exceptional conditions. The needs for extensions are challengable in the courts.

Complainants can file suit in Federal District Court where they reside or work, where the records are maintained or in district court in Washington, D.C. This action is justified under one of the following four grounds.

1. In cases pertaining to amendment of files, all agencies' procedures have been exhausted or the agencies have failed to comply with the thirty day time limit.

2. In cases concerning withholding of records, individuals disagree with the government's justifications for doing so.

3. Government agencies which have failed to maintain accurate records have made decisions affecting individuals on the basis of this incorrect information. These decisions, in turn, affect the people concerned adversely by dis-

qualifying them from benefits, employment or other entitlements or infringing upon their rights.

4. Failure by government agencies to comply with other sections of the Act or pertinent regulations result in adverse affects upon individuals.

Suit must be brought within two years of the violations or within two years after the violations are discovered. Under grounds one and three, the burden of proof is upon the public, rather than the government agencies because the complainants can best show that files concerning their lives and activities are incorrect or false. Also, under grounds three and four complainants must prove the causal relationships between the inaccurate information and related adverse affects.

The courts can order agencies to amend files or release records when the complainants prevail. In suits filed under grounds one and two, attorney's fees are sometimes awarded to plaintiffs. However, in suits filed under grounds three and four, when the courts determine that agencies' actions were willful or intentional, such fees, plus minimum liability damages of $1,000, must be awarded to the complainants.

Further Information About The Privacy Act:

Coverage of the Privacy Act in the following three sources mentioned when considering the FOIA is excellent.

Federal Information Disclosure,

A Citizens Guide on How To Use The Freedom of Information Act and the Privacy Act of 1974

Basic Information on The Use of The Privacy Act of 1974 and The Freedom of Information Act

Legislative History of The Privacy Act of 1974 S. 3418 (Public Law 93-579): Source Book on Privacy is equally as valuable. Besides a legislative history and the Office of Management and Budget guidelines described above, law review articles, significant cases and a lengthy bibliography are also included.

Footnotes

[1] *Congressional Record,* 89th Cong., 2nd sess., 112:10 (June 20, 1966), p. 13654.

[2] *Federal Information Disclosure: Procedures, Forms and The Law.* James T. O'Reilly, Vol. 1 (New York: Shepard's/McGraw Hill, 1981), p. 5-7.

[3] This exemption has been a controversial one. The General Accounting Office's study of thirteen law enforcement agencies indicates between fiscal years 1975 and 1977 most requests for information came from subjects of Federal investigations, some of whom were identified as criminals. (*Data on Privacy Act and Freedom of Information Act Provided by Federal Law Enforcement Agencies.* LCD-78-119 (Washington, D.C.: GPO, 1978), p. 2.) When the government attempts to deny information under this exemption, as is the case under the others, it must prove why records should be withheld. The agencies argue that criminal elements are often capable of utilizing the information in ways officials fail to foresee. This can result in impediments to law enforcement activities, identification of informers or any number of other adverse consequences.

[4] Congressional intent when enacting this exemption was to guarantee the security of banks and related institutions. The legislators believed indiscriminate release of sensitive financial data might cause great harm.

It has been argued this exemption is unnecessary, since appropriate files would be covered under the trade secret exemption. One critic states:

> It is possible that future amendments of the Act may delete the exemption as superfluous, though the banking lobby remains strong and little in the way of public interest justification has been raised to date against its continued validity. (*Federal Information Disclosure.* Op. Cit. at 2. Vol. 2. p. 18-2.

[5] *A Citizens Guide on How To Use The Freedom of Information Act and The Privacy Act in Requesting Government Documents.* House Committee on Government Operations. 95th Cong., 1st sess., H. Rpt. 95-793 (Washington, D.C.: GPO, 1977), pp. 8-9.

[6] *Oversight of The Administration of The Federal Freedom of Information Act.* Hearings before the Senate Governmental Affairs Committee. Subcommittee on Intergovernmental Relations. 96th Cong., 2nd sess. (Washington, D.C.: GPO, 1980), p. 38.

[7] *A Citizens Guide . . .* Op. cit at 5, pp. 19-20.

BIBLIOGRAPHY

Basic Information On The Use of The Privacy Act of 1974 and The Freedom of Information Act. M. Elizabeth Smith. Congressional Research Service. Washington, D.C.: Library of Congress, 1976. Reprinted in *Major Studies of The Congressional Research Service, 1975-76 Supplement.* Washington, D.C.: University Publications of America, Inc., 1977.

A Citizens Guide on How To Use The Freedom of Information Act and The Privacy Act In Requesting Government Documents. House Committee on Government Operations. 95th Cong., 1st sess. H. Rpt. 95-793. Washington, D.C.: GPO, 1977.

Data on Privacy Act and Freedom of Information Act Provided By Federal Law Enforcement Agencies. General Accounting Office. LCD-78-119. Washington, D.C.: GPO, 1978.

Federal Information Disclosure: Procedures, Forms and The Law. James T. O'Reilly. New York: Shepard's/McGraw Hill, 1981. 2 vols.

Freedom of Information Act and Amendments of 1974 (PL 93-502), Source Book: Legislative History, Texts and Other Documents. House Committee on Government Operations. Subcommittee on Governmental Information and Individual Rights and Senate Committee on the Judiciary. Subcommittee on Administrative Practice and Procedure. Joint Committee Print. 94th Cong., 1st sess. Washington, D.C.: GPO, 1975.

Freedom of Information Act Oversight. Hearings before the House Committee on Government Operations. Subcommittee on Government Information and Individual Rights. 97th Cong., 1st sess. Washington, D.C.: GPO, 1981.

Freedom of Information Act Source Book: Legislative Materials, Cases, Articles. Senate Committee on The Judiciary. Subcommittee on Administrative Practice and Procedure. Committee Print. 93rd Cong., 2nd sess. Washington, D.C.: GPO, 1974.

Legislative History of The Privacy Act S. 3418 (Public Law 93-579): Source Book on Privacy. Senate Committee on Government Operations and House Committee on Government Operations. Subcommittee on Government Information and Individual Rights. Joint Committee Print. 94th Cong., 2nd sess. Washington, D.C.: GPO, 1976.

Oversight of The Administration of The Federal Freedom of Information Act. Hearings before the Senate Governmental Affairs Committee. Subcommittee on Intergovernmental Relations. 96th Cong., 2nd sess. Washington, D.C.: GPO, 1980.

Privacy Act Issuances. Office of The Federal Register. Washington, D.C.: National Archives and Records Service, 1976-annual.

CHAPTER 12

CONCLUSION

This concluding chapter summarizes the most significant titles examined in the book. All citations in part I, which is arranged alphabetically by titles, are annotated. Part II consists of a series of tabular guides which describe the indexes and in selected cases, texts of the most significant sources noted in the previous section. The fifteen tables are separated into four major groups.

General Comprehensive Indexes
Legislative Histories
Legislation
Regulations

Chapters which contain more detailed information about the reference tools are indicated.

The following ten titles represent a select list of sources having special significance to researchers.

1. The *Monthly Catalog* is the most comprehensive index to United States government publications.

2. The *Congressional Information Service* is the most comprehensive index to Congressional committee publications. It is an excellent source to use when either compiling legislative histories or when answering more general information needs.

3. The *American Statistics Index* is the most comprehensive index to U.S. government statistics. A great deal of narrative information is also indexed.

4. The *Publications Reference File* is the Government Printing Office's sales catalog. Its alphabetic section is most useful when answering general reference questions, as well as when ordering materials.

5. The *Cumulative Title Index To United States Public Documents* is the only source of its type.

6. *Government Reports Announcements and Index* is the most comprehensive guide to technical reports. Most documents indexed are prepared either by or for Federal agencies.

7. The *CIS US Serial Set Index* is the best index to the Serial Set, which is probably the most significant collection of United States government publications.

8. The *United States Code* is the major subject codification of current Federal law.

9. The *Code of Federal Regulations* is a subject codification of Federal rules currently in effect.

10. The *Federal Register* includes texts of proposed and final regulations, Presidential orders and proclamations, and notices. Preambles to proposed rules and final ones provide background information to the issues involved. Considering the national trend towards revising and eliminating regulations, the *Calendar of Federal Regulations,* which is published semiannually in the *Register,* is a very important source. Background information, alternative solutions and cost benefit analysis, plus other items for the most significant regulations under study by all Federal agencies are outlined. Popular issues noted in the media are often discussed. Citations to the most recent issues are listed in the *PRF* under "Calendar of Federal Regulations."

Annotated Bibliography Section

American State Papers.
  See Serial Set.

American Statistics Index: A Comprehensive Guide and Index To The Statistical Publications of The U.S. Government. Washington, D.C.: Congressional Information Service, Inc., 1973-monthly.

The *ASI* is the most comprehensive guide to United States government statistics. It is issued in two parts, an *Abstract* volume and an *Index* volume. The abstracts are arranged consecutively by *ASI* entry numbers. The *Index* is divided into four parts: by subjects and names (names refer to personal authors and organizations), categories, titles and report numbers.

Calendar of Federal Regulations. Regulatory Information Center. Washington, D.C.: GPO, 1979-semiannual. Issued by the United States Regulatory Council between 1979 and 1980.

Overviews of significant proposed regulations are provided. Legal authorities, reasons for including the entries, statements of problems, alternative solutions and summaries of benefits and costs, plus additional information, is given. Data is arranged in chapters covering broad subjects (Energy, Environment and Natural Resources; Finance and Banking; Health and Safety; Human Resources; Trade Practices and Transportation; and Communication). Three indexes, which are barely adequate, deal with Sectors Affected by Regulatory Action, Date of Next Regulatory Action and Dates for Public Participation Opportunities.

Calendars of the United States House of Representatives and History of Legislation. Washington, D.C.: GPO, 1880(?)-daily when the House is in session.

The *House Calendar* is most useful for its concise and current legislative histories. Separate sections list House and Senate bills which have passed either or both chambers, or have been enacted. Additional features list bills in conference and those which have gone through conference, titles of bills that have become law and Presidential vetoes, plus other data. The Monday issues' weekly index is arranged by subject and popular names of acts and bills.

CIS Index To Publications of The United States Congress. Washington, D.C.: Congressional Information Service, Inc., 1970-monthly.

The *CIS Index* is the most comprehensive guide to Congressional publications. It is issued in two parts, an *Abstract* volume and an *Index* volume. The monthly *Abstract* volume is arranged in three sections for House, joint and Senate committee publications. The annual cumulative volume includes these parts, plus a fourth one for Legislative Histories. Information is indexed by subjects, names of witnesses who testified at hearings and names of organizations they represent, titles and bill, report and document numbers.

CIS U.S. Congressional Committee Hearings Index. Washington, D.C.: Congressional Information Service, Inc., 1981-1985(?). 8 parts.

This source is the most complete retrospective index to Congressional hearings. It is being published in eight parts, each one covering a different time period between the early 1800's when the initial Congressional hearings were held through 1969. Six indexes refer to subjects and names of organizations, names of witnesses, titles, bill numbers, Superintendent of Document numbers and report and document numbers. Complete bibliographic information is cited in the Reference Bibliography section which is arranged alphanumerically by reference bibliography numbers. Practically all hearings that are indexed are available on microfiche from the Congressional Information Service.

See also *Index of Congressional Committee Hearings (Not Confidential In Character)*.

CIS US Congressional Committee Prints Index From The Earliest Publications Through 1969. Washington, D.C.: Congressional Information Service, Inc., 1980. 5 vols.

This reference is the most complete guide to committee prints covering the indicated period. Indexes are arranged by subjects, personal authors, names of committees, titles, congresses and committees, bill numbers and SuDoc numbers. The Reference Bibliography section is arranged in alphanumeric order according to reference bibliography numbers and includes full bibliographic information.

CIS US Serial Set Index. Washington, D.C.: Congressional Information Service, Inc., 1975-1979. 12 parts.

1789 through 1969 is covered. The Index of Subjects and Keywords, the Private Relief and Related Actions section, which indexes names of individuals and organizations, and the Numerical List of Reports and Documents are useful finding aids.

See also Serial Set for a definition of this collection.

Code of Federal Regulations. National Archives and Records Service. Office of The Federal Register. Washington, D.C.: GPO, 1949-annual. Supplements to the original 1938 edition were issued irregularly through 1948.

The *Code of Federal Regulations* is a compilation of Federal regulations arranged in fifty titles, each one representing a broad subject area. The *CFR Index and Finding Aids,* which is revised semiannually, includes a subject index citing names of agencies, in addition to subject headings. Other finding aids include tables correlating *United States Code* and Presidential documents with *CFR* sections.

See also *Code of Federal Regulations: LSA, List of CFR Sections Affected*.
Federal Register.

Code of Federal Regulations: LSA, List of CFR Sections Affected. National Archives and Records Service. Office of The Federal Register. Washington, D.C.: GPO, September 1977-monthly. Published earlier under various titles.

The *List of Sections Affected* is a guide for locating new and amended regulations and proposed amendments to the *CFR*. The left hand column cites *CFR* sections affected, while the right hand one notes *Federal Register* page numbers on which relevant information was printed. A Table of Federal Register Issue Pages and Dates converts *Register* page numbers into dates, facilitating access to the data.

See also *Code of Federal Regulations*.
Federal Register.

Congress and The Nation: A Review of Government and Politics in The Postwar Years, Washington, D.C.: Congressional Quarterly, Inc., 1965-quadrennial. Vol. 1 covers 1945-1964.

Congress and The Nation is among the finest multiyear encyclopedic summaries of American politics. Legislation, socioeconomic issues, foreign affairs and Federal judicial activities are among the issues covered. When appropriate, bill, report and public law numbers and references to *Congressional Quarterly Almanacs* are cited.

See also *Congressional Quarterly Almanac.*

   CQ Weekly Report.

Congressional Index Service. Chicago: Commerce Clearing House, 1937-weekly while Congress is in session.

The *Congressional Index* is among the finest guides to legislative histories. The subject index, which is arranged in three parts, is a comprehensive one. The basic Subject Index covers the first session of a Congress, the Current one cites information relating to the second session and Headline Legislation deals with selected bills most often noted in the media. The Author Index is separated into basic and current ones as well. Additional features include bill sections where proposals are summarized, status sections where legislative actions are outlined and voting records sections.

Congressional Quarterly Almanac. Washington, D.C.: Congressional Quarterly, Inc., 1948-annual. Published quarterly between 1945 and 1947.

This annual summary of national political, social, economic, judicial and diplomatic developments is among the most important reference tools of its kind. When relevant, bill, report and law numbers are cited. Special features include legislative histories of public laws, voting records, references to earlier *Almanacs* and reprints of selected Presidential documents. The index is a comprehensive one.

See also *Congress and The Nation.*

   CQ Weekly Report.

Congressional Record. Congress. Washington, D.C.: GPO, 1873-daily while Congress is in session.

The debates and proceedings of Congress are printed in the *Congressional Record.* The subject index is a detailed one which includes names of Congressmen, Senators and personal names of authors whose works have been reprinted in the *Record.* Subject headings and numerous cross references are provided as well. The History of Bills and Resolutions section lists items in numerical order by chambers noting report numbers and pages on which the measures were debated.

Congressional Staff Directory. Indianapolis: New Bobbs-Merrill, 1959-annual.

Names, addresses, phone numbers and biographies of Congressmen, Senators and their staffs are given. Committee and subcommittee contacts are noted as well. This information is important when attempting to obtain Congressional publications because subcommittees will often distribute gratis copies of bills, committee prints, hearings, reports and documents upon request. Other special features include a list indicating Congressional districts and names of

Representatives for 9,900 cities and a directory of key officials in executive departments.

See also *Federal Executive Directory.*

United States Government Manual.

CQ Weekly Report. Washington, D.C.: Congressional Quarterly, Inc., 1945- weekly. Published under various titles between 1945 and 1950.

CQ Weekly Report is the weekly counterpart to the *Congressional Quarterly Almanac.*

See also *Congress and The Nation.*

Congressional Quarterly Almanac.

Cumulative Subject Index To The Monthly Catalog, 1900-1971. Washington, D.C.: Carrollton Press, 1973-1975. 15 vols.

Access to the *Monthly Catalog* is expedited through the use of this source. Following each entry, *Monthly Catalog* years are indicated in parentheses and *Catalog* entry numbers or page numbers follow the parentheses.

See also *Monthly Catalog of United States Government Publications.*

Cumulative Title Index To United States Public Documents, 1789-1976, Comp. by Daniel W. Lester et al. Arlington, Virginia: United States Historical Documents Institute, 1979-   . Completed series will include 16 vols.

Titles of documents published between the indicated dates are listed alphabetically. Following citations, SuDoc numbers are provided.

Digest of Public General Bills and Resolutions. Library of Congress. Congressional Research Service. Washington, D.C.: GPO, 1936-monthly.

Detailed abstracts of public laws and bills are given. Indexes are arranged by sponsor and cosponsor, short titles and subjects. A numerical table cites identical proposals introduced into both chambers of Congress. This source is far more valuable for its thorough abstracts than for its indexing, since other finding aids, such as the *Congressional Index,* index bills and resolutions equally as well.

Exhausted GPO Sales Publications Reference File.

See *GPO Sales Publications Reference File Microform.*

Federal Executive Directory. Washington, D.C.: Carroll Publishing Company, 1976-bimonthly.

Telephone numbers of officials in executive and independent regulatory agencies are given. Part I is arranged alphabetically by personal names, whereas Part II is arranged by agencies. The third section is a keyword index based upon titles of agencies. Unlike the *United States Government Manual,* agencies' functions and statutory authorities are excluded.

See also *Congressional Staff Directory.*

United States Government Manual.

Federal Register. National Archives and Record Service. Office of The Federal Register. Washington, D.C.: GPO, 1936-daily except Saturday, Sunday and Federal holidays.

Regulations, proposed rules and notices of all Federal agencies, plus Presidential executive orders and proclamations are printed in the *Federal Register*. Regulations or rules are statements issued by agencies which usually serve as guidelines for implementing legislation. Each monthly index cumulates information published between January and the most recent month. For example, the June index covers January through June. Regulations printed in the *Register* are codified in the *Code of Federal Regulations*.

See also *Code of Federal Regulations*.

   Code of Federal Regulations: LSA, List of CFR Sections Affected.

Federal Regulatory Directory. Washington, D.C.: Congressional Quarterly, Inc., 1979/80-annual.

The *Federal Regulatory Directory* is among the finest summaries of the Federal government regulatory process. The introductory section describes the history, development and current trends of regulatory activities. Responsibilities, powers and authorities, lists of regional offices, Freedom of Information officers and further references to government as well as private, sources, among other data, are provided for over one hundred agencies.

Government Periodicals and Subscription Services. Superintendent of Documents. Price List 36. Washington, D.C.: GPO, 1943-quarterly.

Periodicals published by the Government Printing Office are listed alphabetically by titles.

See also *Index To U.S. Government Periodicals*.

   Monthly Catalog of United States Government Publications: Serials Supplement.

Government Publications and Their Use. Laurence F. Schmeckebier and Roy B. Eastin. 2nd Rev. ed. Washington, D.C.: Brookings Institution, 1969.

Although somewhat dated, this textbook approach to U.S. documents is still a fine statement of the nature and use of government publications. Schmeckebier gives thorough descriptions of the histories and developments of executive, congressional and judicial materials.

See also *Introduction To United States Public Documents*.

Government Reports Announcements and Index. Springfield, Virginia: NTIS, 1975-semimonthly. Published under various titles since 1946.

GRA&I is the index to technical reports and other publications issued through the National Technical Information Service. The Keyword, Personal, Corporate, Contract/Grant Number and NTIS Order/Report Number Indexes note document accession numbers. These are listed in alphanumeric sequence in the Reports Announcements section where bibliographic information and abstracts are given. Though NTIS does not distribute its documents to depository libraries, selected publications are sometimes made available to these institutions by GPO.

GPO Sales Publications Reference File Microform. Superintendent of Documents. Washington, D.C.: GPO, 1977-bimonthly.

Publications available for sale from the GPO are cited. The first section is arranged numerically by stock numbers, the second alphanumerically by Superintendent of Document numbers and the third alphabetically by titles, keywords, selected subject headings and personal authors. Documents are in-dexed in the *PRF* sooner than in the *Monthly Catalog*.

A related series, the *Exhausted GPO Sales Publications Reference File* (Superintendent of Documents. Washington, D.C.: GPO, 1980-annual), which is arranged as the *PRF* is, includes materials no longer available for sale. The 1980 *EPRF* covers 1972-1978, whereas the 1981 issue deals with 1979 through June 1980.

House Journal.

See *Journal of The House.*

How To Find U.S. Statutes and U.S. Code Citations. Dorothy Muse. Updated by Marie F. Faria Yeast. 4th ed. National Archives and Records Service. Office of The Federal Register. Washington, D.C.: GPO, 1980.

This brief, but very informative guide, is a basic introduction to the subject. Besides describing the *Statutes at Large* and *U.S. Code,* the *Revised Statutes, U.S. Code Congressional and Administrative News, House Calendars, U.S. Code Annotated, U.S. Code Service* and *Shepard's Acts and Cases by Popular Name* are discussed as well.

Index of Congressional Committee Hearings (Not Confidential In Character) Prior to January 3, 1935 In The United States Senate Library. Rev. by James D. Preston et al. Senate Library. Washington, D.C.: GPO, 1935. Reprinted: Westport, Connecticut: Greenwood Publishing Company, 1971.

Congressional hearings held in the Senate Library are cited in part one by keywords, in part two by Committees, and in part three by bill numbers. The following supplementary volumes provide updated information through 1978.

Cumulative Index of Congressional Committee Hearings (Not Confidential In Character) From Seventy-Fourth Congress (January 3, 1935) Through Eighty-Fifth Congress (January 3, 1959) In The United States Senate Library. Indexed and comp. under direction of Felton M. Johnston. Washington, D.C.: GPO, 1959.

Quadrennial Supplement To Cumulative Index of Congressional Committee Hearings (Not Confidential In Character) From Eighty-Sixth Congress (January 7, 1959) Through Eighty-Seventh Congress (January 3, 1963) Together With Selected Committee Prints In The United States Senate Library. Comp. and indexed by Mary F. Sterrett. Washington, D.C.: GPO, 1963.

Cumulative Index of Congressional Committee Hearings (Not Confidential In Character): Second Quadrennial Supplement From Eighty-Eighth Congress (January 3, 1963) Through Eighty-Ninth Congress (January 3, 1967) Together With Selected Committee Prints In The United States Senate Library. Comp. under direction of Francis R. Valeo. Washington, D.C.: GPO, 1967.

Cumulative Index of Congressional Committee Hearings (Not Confidential In Character): Third Quadrennial Supplement From Ninetieth Congress (January 10, 1967) Through Ninety-First Congress (January 2, 1971) Together With Selected Committee Prints In The United States Senate Library. Comp. under direction of Francis R. Valeo. Washington, D.C.: GPO, 1971.

Cumulative Index of Congressional Committee Hearings (Not Confidential In Character): Fourth Quadrennial Supplement From Ninety-Second Congress (January 21, 1971) Through Ninety-Third Congress (December 20, 1974) In The United States Senate Library. Comp. under direction of Francis R. Valeo. Washington, D.C.: GPO, 1976.

Cumulative Index of Congressional Committee Hearings (Not Confidential In Character): Fifth Supplement Ninety-Fourth Congress (January 14, 1975 Through October 1, 1976) In The United States Senate Library. Comp. under direction of Francis R. Valeo. Washington, D.C.: GPO, ?

Cumulative Index of Congressional Committee Hearings (Not Confidential In Character): Sixth Supplement Ninety-Fifth Congress (January 4, 1977 Through October 15, 1978) In The United States Senate Library. Comp. under direction of William F. Hildenbrand. Washington, D.C.: GPO, ? .

This series will be superseded by the *CIS U.S. Congressional Committee Hearings Index,* which will be published in its entirety by 1985.

See also *CIS U.S. Congressional Committee Hearings Index.*

Index To United States Government Periodicals. Chicago: Infordata International Incorporated, 1974-quarterly. Retrospective editions published for 1970-1973.

This reference, which is the only current one devoted exclusively to U.S. government periodicals, cites articles in approximately 180 journals by subjects and personal authors.

See also *Government Periodicals and Subscription Services.*

Monthly Catalog of United States Government Publications: Serials Supplement.

Introduction To United States Public Documents. Joe Morehead. 2nd ed. Littleton, Colorado: Libraries Unlimited, Inc., 1978.

This textbook is the most current one describing the depository library system and the nature, development and use of Federal publications. Ample footnotes provide references for further study. A third edition will be published in 1983. Morehead's book should be used in conjunction with Schmeckebier's *Government Publications and Their Use* to obtain a thorough understanding of the subject.

See also *Government Publications and Their Use.*

Journal of The House of Representatives of The United States. Washington, D.C.: GPO, 1789-annual; *Journal of The Senate of The United States of America.* Washington, D.C.: GPO, 1789-annual.

Journals are the official records of proceedings of the House and Senate. Legislative histories, voting records, summaries of petitions and papers and presidential messages are among the information included. The History of Bills and Resolutions section, which is separated into two parts for Senate and House measures, and the Index, which includes subject headings and names of agencies, provide access to data.

Journal of The Senate.
See *Journal of The House of Representatives of The United States.*

List of Sections Affected.
See *Code of Federal Regulations: LSA, List of CFR Sections Affected.*

Monthly Catalog of United States Government Publications. Superintendent of Documents. Washington, D.C.: GPO, 1895-monthly. Title varies.

The *Monthly Catalog* is the most comprehensive index to U.S. government publications. Items issued by executive agencies, commissions, Congress, the Courts and special study groups are included. In its current format, the *Catalog* is indexed by subjects, personal and corporate authors, titles, keywords, series report numbers, stock numbers and Superintendent of Document numbers.

The GPO has published five sets of multiyear cumulative indexes to the *Monthly Catalog.*

> *United States Government Publications, Monthly Catalog: Decennial Cumulative Index 1941-1950.* Superintendent of Documents. Washington, D.C.: GPO, 1953.

> *Monthly Catalog of United States Government Publications: Decennial Cumulative Index 1951-1960.* Superintendent of Documents. Washington, D.C.: GPO, 1968. 2 vols.

> *Monthly Catalog of United States Government Publications: Cumulated Index, 1961-1965.* Superintendent of Documents. Washington, D.C.: GPO, 1976. 2 vols.

> *Monthly Catalog of United States Government Publications: Cumulated Index, 1966-1970.* Superintendent of Documents. Washington, D.C.: GPO, 1978. 2 vols.

> *Monthly Catalog of United States Government Publications: Cumulative Index 1971-1976.* Superintendent of Documents. Washington, D.C.: GPO, 1981. 2 vols.

Two additional indexes used in conjunction with the *Monthly Catalog* are the *Cumulative Subject Index To The Monthly Catalog, 1900-1976* and the *United States Government Publications. Monthly Catalog. Cumulative Personal Author Index, 1941-1975.*

See also *Cumulative Subject Index To The Monthly Catalog, 1900-1976.*

> *United States Government Publications. Monthly Catalog. Cumulative Personal Author Index, 1941-1975.*

Monthly Catalog of United States Government Publications: Serials Supplement. Superintendent of Documents. Washington, D.C.: GPO, 1961-annual. Published biennially between 1945 and 1960.

Depository and non-depository journals are listed in the *Monthly Catalog Serials Supplement.* Its indexing and format are identical to that in the *Monthly Catalog.* Periodical indexes that cite government journals are noted when appropriate and lists of monographic series are included.

See also *Government Periodicals and Subscription Services.*

> *Index To United States Government Periodicals.*

Numerical List and Schedule of Volumes. Superintendent of Documents. Washington, D.C.: GPO, 1934-annual.

Serial Set volume numbers are indicated for House and Senate reports and documents.

See also *CIS US Serial Set Index.*
> *Serial Set.*

Publications Reference File.
See *GPO Sales Publications Reference Microform.*

Senate Journal.
See *Journal of The House of Representatives of The United States.*

Serial Set.

The Serial Set is the compilation of House and Senate reports and documents issued by Congress since 1817. This series is probably the most significant collection of U.S. government publications. After the Serial Set began publication, Congress saw the need for a similar series covering 1789-mid 1817. The *American State Papers* (Ed. under authority of Congress. Washington, D.C.: Gales and Seaton, 1832-1861. 38 vols.) not only filled this gap, but also reprinted selected post-1817 materials excluded from the Serial Set.

See also *CIS U.S. Serial Set Index*
> *Numerical List and Schedule of Volumes.*

Statutes at Large.
See *United States Statutes at Large.*

Superintendent of Documents Microfiche Users Guide For Congressional House and Senate Bills. Washington, D.C.: GPO, 1979-irregularly while Congress is in session.

Microfiche copies of bills are accessed with this reference. House and Senate bills, resolutions, joint resolutions and concurrent resolutions are listed separately in numerical order. The Senate section also includes amendments to executive documents. Following each bill, fiche numbers and X-Y coordinates—notations representing vertical and horizontal rows on which the data is located—are given. Report numbers are cited whenever appropriate.

United States Code. House of Representatives. Office of the Law Revision Counsel. Washington, D.C.: GPO, 1926-approximately every six years. Supplements issued annually.

The *United States Code* is a subject compilation of Federal law. It is published in fifty titles, each one representing a broad subject category. Documentation includes references to the *Statutes at Large* and public laws. Information is accessed through a General Index, which is arranged alphabetically by subjects, a popular name index and nine tables citing the *Statutes at Large* and corresponding *USC* sections, Presidential proclamations, executive orders and reorganization plans, among other data.

See also *United States Code Annotated.*
> *United States Code Service.*
> *United States Statutes at Large.*

United States Code Annotated. St. Paul: West Publishing Company, 1927-irregular. Pocket supplements issued annually. Replacement volumes issued irregularly.

The *USCA* is a subject compilation of Federal law having the identical titles, sections and text as the *United States Code.* Following each section, the *Annotated* version provides relevant citations to *Corpus Juris Secundum (CJS),* a legal encyclopedia, and West's *Key Number Digests,* a comprehensive compilation of digested or summarized case law. References to and abstracts of local, state and Federal cases interpreting each section of the *USC* are also noted.

See also *United States Code.*

United States Code Service.

United States Code Congressional and Administrative News. St. Paul: West Publishing Company, 1942-semimonthly when Congress is in session and monthly when not in session.

Public laws and their legislative histories (excerpts or in selected instances, full texts of Congressional reports) are reprinted. The Public Laws section maintains identical pagination as the *Statutes at Large.* Proclamations, executive orders and reorganization plans are reprinted as well. The subject index and ten tables listing public law numbers and corresponding *USC* citations, *USC* sections affected by new legislation, legislative histories, bills enacted and popular names, among other data, are useful finding aids. The *Congressional and Administrative News* has two significant advantages over the *Statutes at Large.* The former is published sooner and it facilitates consultation of legislative histories. Remember, however, that the official law is printed in the *Statutes at Large,* not the *Congressional and Administrative News.*

United States Code Service: Lawyers Edition. Rochester, NY: The Lawyers Co-Operative Publishing Co., 1972- . Updated with annual cumulative pockets. Replacement volumes are issued as needed.

The *USCS* is a subject compilation of Federal law whose titles and sections are identical to that in the *USC* However, the text is based upon the *Statutes at Large.* Although case annotations are more thorough in the *USCA,* the *USCS* cites the *Code of Federal Regulations* and law reviews, information excluded from the *Code Annotated.*

See also *United States Code.*

United States Code Annotated.

United States Government Manual. Office of The Federal Register. Washington, D.C.: GPO, 1935-annual. Previously entitled: *United States Government Organization Manual.*

The structure of the legislative, judicial and executive branches of the Federal government is outlined. Organization charts, names, addresses and phone numbers, summaries of functions, statutory authorities and sources for further information are cited. The personal name, subject and agency indexes are fairly comprehensive. This reference should be used in conjunction with the *Federal Executive Directory,* a bimonthly publication which notes more current personnel and telephone numbers.

See also *Congressional Staff Directory.*

Federal Executive Directory.

United States Government Publications. Monthly Catalog. Cumulative Personal Author Index 1941-1975. Ed. by Edward Przebienda. Ann Arbor, Michigan: Pierian Press. 1971-1972, vol. 5 published in 1979. 5 vols.

Separate volumes cover 1941-50, 1951-60, 1961-65, 1966-70 and 1971-75. Following authors' names, *Monthly Catalog* year and page or entry numbers are given. Corporate authors are excluded.

See also *Monthly Catalog.*

United States Government Publications, Monthly Catalog. Decennial Cumulative Index 1941-1950.

See *Monthly Catalog of United States Government Publications.*

United States Statutes at Large. National Archives and Records Service. Office of The Federal Register. Washington, D.C.: GPO, 1937-annual. Earlier volumes covering 1789-1936 published irregularly.

The *Statutes at Large* is the official compilation of U.S. law. Each annual issue includes texts of public and private laws, concurrent resolutions and proclamations enacted during that year. The Subject Index lists both subject headings and names of agencies, whereas the Individual Index cites personal names. A Laws Affected table lists existing legislation which was amended or repealed by the current year's *Statutes.*

See also *United States Code.*

Index Section

GENERAL COMPREHENSIVE INDEXES:
CURRENT PUBLICATIONS ISSUED BY ALL AGENCIES

Source	Author	Title	Subject	Report #	Keyword	Comments
American Statistics Index, mid 1963-monthly. (Chapter 7)	✓	✓	✓	✓		Statistical sources are emphasized.
Government Reports Announcements and Index, 1946-semimonthly. (Chapter 9)	✓	✓	✓	✓	✓	Technical reports emphasized.
GPO Sales Publications Reference File (PRF), 1977-bimonthly. (Chapter 2)	✓	✓	✓		✓	Materials available for sale from GPO.
Index To United States Government Periodicals, 1970-monthly. (Chapter 2)	✓		✓			Only index of its kind; cites articles from approximately 180 periodicals.
Monthly Catalog of United States Government Publications, 1895-monthly. (Chapter 2)	✓ since 1974	✓ since 1974	✓	✓ since July 1976	✓ since 1980	Most comprehensive index to U.S. government documents.

GENERAL COMPREHENSIVE INDEXES:
RETROSPECTIVE PUBLICATIONS ISSUED BY ALL AGENCIES

Source	Author	Title	Subject	Report #	Keyword	Comments
Cumulative Subject To The Monthly Catalog, 1900-1971 (Chapter 2)			✓			Most complete retrospective index to the *Monthly Catalog*.
Cumulative Title Index To United States Public Documents, 1789-1976. (Chapter 2)		✓				Only index of its kind.
Exhausted GPO Sales Publications Reference File (EPRF), 1980-annual (1980 edition covers 1972-1978 and 1981 issue covers 1979-mid 1980.) (Chapter 2)	✓	✓	✓		✓	Cites GPO materials no longer available for sale.
Monthly Catalog of United States Government Publications, 1895-monthly. (Chapter 2)	✓ since 1974	✓ since 1974	✓	✓ since July 1976	✓ since 1980	Most complete index to U.S. government publications.
United States Government Publications. Monthly Catalog. Cumulative Personal Author Index, 1941-1975. (Chapter 2)	✓					Only index of its kind.

GENERAL COMPREHENSIVE INDEXES:
CURRENT CONGRESSIONAL PUBLICATIONS

Source	Author	Title	Subject	Report #	Keyword	Comments
See also GENERAL COMPREHENSIVE INDEXES: CURRENT PUBLICATIONS ISSUED BY ALL AGENCIES.						
CIS Index To Publications of The United States Congress, 1970-monthly. (Chapter 4)	✓	✓	✓	✓		Most comprehensive index to Congressional Committee publications.

GENERAL COMPREHENSIVE INDEXES:
RETROSPECTIVE CONGRESSIONAL PUBLICATIONS

Source	Author	Title	Subject	Report #	Keyword	Comments
See also GENERAL COMPREHENSIVE INDEXES: RETROSPECTIVE PUBLICATIONS ISSUED BY ALL AGENCIES.						
CIS U.S. Congressional Committee Hearings Index, early 1800's-1969. (Chapter 5)	✓	✓	✓	✓		When published, will be most comprehensive guide to hearings.
CIS US Congressional Committee Prints Index, 1830's-1969. (Chapter 5)		✓	✓			Most complete index of its type.
CIS US Serial Set Index, 1789-1969. (Chapter 5)			✓	✓	✓	Most complete index of its kind.
Index of Congressional Committee Hearings (Not Confidential In Character), 1869-1978. (Chapter 5)					✓	Index to the Senate Library's Congressional hearings collection.

LEGISLATIVE HISTORIES: RECENT LEGISLATION

Source	Bill #	Report #	Law #	Subject	Popular Names of Acts	Sponsors	Comments
Calendars of The United States House of Representatives and History of Legislation. (Chapter 3)	✓		✓	✓	✓		All issues are cumulative for the entire Congress. Index is printed in Monday issues.
CIS Index To Publications of The United States Congress, 1970-monthly. (Chapter 4)	✓	✓	✓	✓	✓		The most comprehensive guide to Congressional publications. Legislative Histories section is among very few to include hearings.
Congressional Index Service, 1937-weekly. (Chapter 3)	✓		✓	✓		✓	One of the most current sources to consult.
Congressional Record, 1873-daily while Congress is in session. (Chapter 3)	✓		✓	✓	✓	✓	Indexes to daily issues cover two week periods. Chart arranged by law numbers is in bound version of *Daily Digest* (History of Bills Enacted Into Public Law section).
Digest of Public General Bills and Resolutions, 1936-monthly. (Chapter 3)	✓		✓	✓	✓	✓	Detailed abstracts of all bills and public laws are provided.

LEGISLATIVE HISTORIES: RECENT LEGISLATION (Continued)

Source	Bill #	Report #	Law #	Subject	Popular Names of Acts	Sponsors	Comments
Journal of The House. . .; Journal of The . . . Senate, 1789-annual. (Chapter 3)	✓			✓		✓	Official proceedings of Congress
Statutes at Large. See *United States Statutes at Large*, 1937-annual.							
Superintendent of Documents Microfiche Users Guide For Congressional House and Senate Bills, 1979-irregularly while Congress is in session. (Chapter 3)	✓	✓					Only guide available to bills on microfiche.
United States Code Congressional and Administrative News, 1942-semimonthly (monthly when Congress is not in session). (Chapter 3)	✓		✓	✓	✓		Partial, and in some cases, complete texts of Congressional reports are reprinted.
United States Statutes at Large, 1937-annual. (Chapter 6)	✓		✓	✓	✓		Official compilation of Federal law. Legislative histories follow texts of acts.

LEGISLATIVE HISTORIES: RECENT LEGISLATION—SUMMARIES AND ANALYSIS OF BILLS AND ISSUES FACING CONGRESS

Source	Bill #	Report #	Law #	Subject	Popular Names of Acts	Sponsors	Comments
Congressional Quarterly Almanac, 1948-annual. (Chapter 3)	✓	✓	✓	✓	✓	✓	Bill, report and law numbers are cited in both the text and the Public Laws section.
CQ Weekly Report, 1945-weekly. (Chapter 3)	✓	✓	✓	✓	✓	✓	Bill and report numbers are cited far more often than law numbers.
Digest of Public General Bills and Resolutions, 1936-monthly. (Chapter 3)	✓		✓	✓	✓	✓	Detailed abstracts of all bills and public laws are provided.

LEGISLATIVE HISTORIES: RECENT LEGISLATION—SOURCES FOR FURTHER INFORMATION

Source	Bill #	Report #	Law #	Subject	Popular Names of Acts	Sponsors	Comments
Congressional Staff Directory, 1959-annual. (Introduction)							Citations to legislative histories and in some cases, the relevant documentation can often be acquired at no cost by consulting the Congressmen, Senators or committee staffs listed in the *Directory*.

LEGISLATIVE HISTORIES: RETROSPECTIVE LEGISLATION

Source	Bill #	Report #	Law #	Subject	Popular Names of Acts	Sponsors	Comments
See also selected sources listed under COMPILING LEGISLATIVE HISTORIES OF RECENT LEGISLATION.							
CIS U.S. Congressional Committee Hearings Index, earliest hearings-1969. (Chapter 5)	✓	✓		✓	✓		Will be published in its entirety by 1985.
CIS US Congressional Committee Prints Index. . ., earliest prints-1969. (Chapter 5)	✓			✓			Most complete guide to committee prints.
CIS US Serial Set Index, 1789-1969. (Chapter 5)		✓		✓			Most complete guide to the Serial Set.
Congress and The Nation, 1965-quadrennial. (Chapter 3)	✓		✓	✓	✓	✓	First volume covers 1945-1964. Bill and law numbers are not indexed, but are often cited in the text.
Index of Congressional Committee Hearings (Not Confidential In Character), 1869-1978. (Chapter 5)	✓			✓	✓		Subject index is based upon keywords. Popular Names of Acts are indexed when they are reflected in keywords of titles.

LEGISLATION: OFFICIAL COMPILATIONS

Source	Public Law #	Statutes at Large Citation	Popular Names	Subject	Comments
Statutes at Large See *United States Statutes at Large*					
United States Code, 1926-every six years; annual supplements. (Chapter 6)	✓	✓	✓	✓	Only those titles which have been "re-enacted" by Congress are recognized as official compilations.
United States Statutes at Large, 1937-annual; earlier volumes covering 1789-1936 published irregularly. (Chapter 6)	✓	✓	✓	✓	Public and private laws, reorganization plans, concurrent and joint resolutions which have been enacted and Presidential proclamations are cited.

LEGISLATION: SUBJECT CODIFICATIONS

Source	Public Law #	Statutes at Large Citation	Popular Names	Subject	Comments
United States Code, 1926–every 6 years; annual supplements. (Chapter 6)		✓	✓	✓	Limited to laws currently in effect.
United States Code Annotated, 1927–irregular; pocket supplements issued annually. (Chapter 6)	✓	✓	✓	✓	Citations to and abstracts of court decisions at all levels are provided following each section.
United States Code Service, 1972– pocket supplements issued annually. (Chapter 6)	✓	✓	✓	✓	References to relevant CFR sections, court rules, executive orders and law reviews are provided.

LEGISLATION: SUMMARIES AND ABSTRACTS

Source	Public Law #	Statutes at Large Citations	Popular Names	Subject	Comments
Congress and The Nation, 1965-quadrennial. (Chapter 3)	✓		✓	✓	Factual summaries are given.
Congressional Quarterly Almanac, 1948-annual. (Chapter 3)	✓		✓	✓	Brief factual summaries are given. Most emphasis, however, is upon political development of related bills.
CQ Weekly Report. (Chapter 3)			✓	✓	See comments for *Congressional Quarterly Almanac.*
Digest of Public General Bills and Resolutions, 1936-monthly. (Chapter 3)	✓		✓	✓	Detailed abstracts of all bills and public laws are provided.

REGULATIONS: PRIMARY SOURCES

Source	Subject	Agency	Authority cited by		Comments
			USC	Statutes at Large	
Code of Federal Regulations, 1949–annual; first issue published in 1938. (Chapter 6)	✓	✓	✓	✓	Official subject codification of Federal regulations.
Federal Register, 1936–daily except Saturday, Sunday and Federal holidays. (Chapter 6)	✓	✓	✓		Includes Presidential orders and proclamations, notices, interpretations of regulations and other related information, in addition to rules and proposed rules. *USC* citations are given in text. Index provides few subject headings. When they are given, cross references refer users to relevant entries under agencies' names.

REGULATIONS: ABSTRACTS OF REGULATIONS

Source	Subject	Agency	Authority cited by			Comments
			USC	Statutes at Large		
Calendar of Federal Regulations, 1979-semiannual. (Chapter 6)	✓	✓	✓			Proposed and existing rules, alternatives and cost benefit analysis, among additional information are provided.
Federal Register, 1936-daily except Saturday, Sunday and Federal holidays. (Chapter 6)	✓	✓	✓			Preambles to proposed and final regulations summarize the rules and issues involved. *USC* citations are given in text.

REGULATIONS: BACKGROUND INFORMATION ABOUT AGENCIES AND REGULATIONS

Source	Subject	Agency	Authority cited by USC	Authority cited by Statutes at Large	Comments
Calendar of Federal Regulations, 1979-semiannual. (Chapter 6)	✓	✓	✓		Information is presented in a clear, lucid style easily comprehensible to most laymen. *USC* citations are noted in text.
Federal Regulatory Directory, 1979/80-annual. (Chapter 6)	✓	✓	✓	✓	Deals more with functions and responsibilities of agencies than specific regulations. *USC* and *Statutes at Large* citations are noted in text.

REGULATIONS: SOURCES OF FURTHER INFORMATION

Source	Authority cited by				Comments
	Subject	Agency	USC	Statutes at Large	
Code of Federal Regulations; LSA, List of CFS *Sections Affected,* 1977-monthly; published earlier under various titles. (Chapter 6)			✓	✓	Changes and proposed changes to the CFR, which have appeared in the Federal Register, are noted. Major part of guide is arranged by CFR citations, rather than those for the USC or the Statutes at Large.
Federal Register, 1936-daily except Saturday, Sunday and Federal holidays. (Chapter 6)	✓	✓	✓		Agency contacts and phone numbers are noted. USC citations are provided in the text.
Federal Regulatory Directory, 1979/80-annual. (Chapter 6)	✓	✓	✓	✓	Sources of information pertaining to agencies, rather than specific regulations, are noted. These include names, addresses, phone numbers, citations to both government and private publications, and names, addresses and phone numbers of public interest groups. USC and Statutes at Large citations are noted in the text.

INDEX

Agricultural Statistics, 162

Agricultural Statistics Data Finder, 179

American State Papers. Documents, Legislative and Executive of the Congress of the United States, 78

American Statistics Index: A Comprehensive Guide and Index To The Statistical Publications of The U.S. Government, 34-35, 147-56, 166-68, 217-18, 229

American Statistics Index: A Comprehensive Guide and Index To The Statistical Publications of The U.S. Government, Users Guide, 156

American Statistics Index: ASI Search Guide, 156

American Statistics Index Microfiche Library of Statistical Publications of the U.S. Government, 156

American Statistics Index 1974 Annual and Retrospective Edition: A Comprehensive Guide To The Statistical Publications of The U.S. Government, 147

Annual Report To Congress (Department of Energy), 160

ASI Search Guide, see *American Statistics Index: ASI Search Guide*

Basic Information On The Use of The Privacy Act of 1974 and The Freedom of Information Act, 210, 214

Bibliography of Science and Industrial Reports, 186

Bibliography of Technical Reports, 186

Bills—definition, 44

Bureau of The Census Catalog of Publications, 174, 181

Bureau of The Census Catalog of Publications, 1790-1972, 174

Business Statistics, 162

Business Statistics Data Finder, 179

Calendar of Business—Senate of The United States, 47, 59

Calendar of Federal Regulations, 109, 138-41, 217-18, 242-43

Calendars of the United States House of Representatives and History of Legislation, 47-48, 58-59, 218, 223, 233

Catalog of Aeronautical Charts and Related Publications, 198-99

Catalog of Nautical Charts, 198

Catalog of Publications Issued by the Government of the United States, see *Monthly Catalog of United States Government Publications*

Catalog of United States Public Documents, see *Monthly Catalog of United States Government Publications*

Census Bureau Guide To Transportation Statistics, 180

Census Data For Community Action, 178

Census '80: Continuing The Factfinder Tradition, 177

Census '80: Projects For Students, 177

Census of Agriculture, 173-74, 176, 180

Census of Construction Industries, 172, 180

Census of Governments, 174, 180

Census of Manufacturers, 171, 178-79

Census of Mineral Industries, 171, 178-79

Census of Population and Housing, 169-70, 174-76

Census of Retail Trade, 171, 178-79

Census of Service Industries, 172-73, 178-79

Census of Transportation, 172-73, 178-80

Census of Wholesale Trade, 171, 179

CFR, see *Code of Federal Regulations*

CRF Index and Finding Aids, 133-37, 219

CFR Parts Affected, 138; see also *Code of Federal Regulations, LSA, List of CFR Sections Affected*

CFR Parts Affected In This Issue, 138; see also *Code of Federal Regulations, LSA, List of CFR Sections Affected*

Checklist of Hearings Before Congressional Committees Through The Sixty-Seventh Congress, 97

Checklist of U.S. Public Documents, 1789-1976, 31

CIS Congressional Bills, Resolutions and Laws on Microfiche, 80

CIS Five-Year Cumulative Index, 1970-1974, 65

CIS Four-Year Cumulative Index, 1975-1978, 65

CIS Index Search Guide, 74

CIS Index To Publications of The United States Congress, 45-46, 48, 62, 65-76, 78, 217-18, 231, 233

CIS Index User Handbook For Librarians and Researchers Using Congressional Publications, 74

CIS Microfiche Library of United States Congressional Publications, 74

CIS U.S. Congressional Committee Hearings Index, 77, 90-97, 107-08, 218-19, 224, 232, 237

House Journal, see *Journal of the House of Representatives of the United States*

Housing Data Resources: Indicators and Sources of Data For Analyzing Housing and Neighborhood Conditions, 178

How To Find U.S. Statutes and U.S. Code Citations, 142, 223

HUD Statistical Yearbook, 161

Index of Congressional Committee Hearings (Not Confidential In Character) Prior to January 3, 1935 In The United States Senate Library, 77, 86-90, 96, 106, 108, 223, 232, 237

Index To Congressional Committee Hearings In The Library of The House of Representatives Prior to January 1, 1951, 97

Index To Selected 1970 Census Reports, 177-78

Index To The Code of Federal Regulations, 138

Index To The Code of Federal Regulations, 1938-1976, 138

Index To Topographic Maps, 197

Index To United States Government Periodicals, 9, 31-34, 35, 40, 42, 224, 229

Industrial Statistics Data Finder, 179

An Introduction To Congressional Committee Prints and The CIS US Congressional Committee Prints Index From The Earliest Publications Through 1969, 103

Introduction To United States Public Documents, 224

Issues In Federal Statistical Needs Relating to Women, 159-60

Joint Resolutions—definition, 44

Journal of The House of Representatives of The United States, 47-48, 53, 55, 224, 234

Journal of The Senate of The United States of America, 47-48, 53-55, 225, 234

Legislative History of The Privacy Act S. 3418 (Public Law 93-579): Source Book on Privacy, 211, 214

List of Sections Affected, see *Code of Federal Regulations, LSA, List of CFR Sections Affected*

LSA, see *Code of Federal Regulations, LSA, List of CFR Sections Affected*

Map and Chart Catalog 5: United States, Bathymetric Maps and Special Purpose Charts, 198

Map Data Catalog, 199

Map Products and Sources, 199-202

Maps and Atlases (United States and Foreign), 199

Maps For America: Carteographic Products of The U.S. Geological Survey and Others, 199

Microfiche User's Guide for Congressional House and Senate Bills; see *Superintendent of Documents Microfiche Users Guide For Congressional House and Senate Bills*

Minerals Yearbook, 160-61

Mini-Guide To The 1977 Economic Censuses, 178-79

Minority Owned Businesses, 179

Monthly Catalog of United States Government Publications, viii-ix, 9-20, 38-39, 41, 45-46, 48, 78, 217, 221, 225, 228-30

Monthly Catalog of United States Government Publications: Cumulated Index, 1961-1965, 9, 18, 225

Monthly Catalog of United States Government Publications: Cumulated Index, 1966-1970, 9, 18, 225

Monthly Catalog of United States Government Publications: Cumulative Index, 1971-1976, 9, 18, 225

Monthly Catalog of United States Government Publications: Decennial Cumulative Index, 1951-1960, 9, 18, 225

Monthly Catalog of United States Government Publications: Serials Supplement, 9, 34-35, 225

Monthly Catalog, United States Public Documents, see *Monthly Catalog of United States Government Publications*

Monthly Energy Review, 160

Monthly Labor Review, 162

Monthly Product Announcements, 174

Motion Pictures, Films and Audiovisual Information, 204

NASA STI Database, 192

National Clearinghouse For Census Data Services: Address List, 181

The National State Papers of The United States: Part II, Texts of Documents (1789-1817), 78

National Technical Information Service Bibliographic Data File, 191

National Technical Information Service: General Catalog of Information Services No. 7a, 194

National Transportation Statistics, 163

National Travel Survey, 172, 180

National Union Catalog Pre-1956 Imprints, 97

Nautical Chart Catalog 1: United States Atlantic and Gulf Coasts Including Puerto Rico and the Virgin Islands, 198

Nautical Chart Catalog 2: United States Pacific Coast Including Hawaii, Guam and Samoa Islands, 198

Nautical Chart Catalog 3: United States Alaska Including Aleutian Islands, 198

Nautical Chart Catalog 4: United States Great Lakes and Adjacent Waterways 198

Nautical Chart Catalog 5; see *Map and Chart Catalog 5: United States, Bathymetric Maps and Special Purpose Charts*

New Publications of The Geological Survey, 197, 199

1980 Census of Population and Housing: Users Guide, Part A, Text, 177

1980 Census Update, 177

1980 Supplement To Economic Indicators: Historical and Descriptive Background 162

1977 Economic Censuses Publication Program, 179

Nonregulated Motor Carriers and Public Warehousing Survey, 173, 180

NTIS Title Index (Current), 186

NTIS Title Index (Retrospective, 1964-1978), 186

Numerical List and Schedule of Volumes, 77, 84-86, 106, 108, 226

Numerical Listing of Charts and Publications, 198

ORD Publicatitns Summary, 192

Oversight of The Administration of The Federal Freedom of Information Act, 209

Photography, 204

Pocket Data Book USA, 1979, 156-57

PRF, see *GPO Sales Publications Reference File Microform*

PRF Users Manual: A Guide To Using the G.P.O. Sales Publications Reference File, 31

Price List of Maps and Charts For Public Sale, 199

Printed Hearings of The House of Representatives Found Among Its Committee Records In The National Archives of The United States, 1824-1958, 97

Privacy Act Issuances, 213

Proclamations — definitions, 125

Publications of The Geological Survey, 1879-1961, 197

Publications of The Geological Survey, 1962-1970, 197

Publications Reference File, see *GPO Sales Publications Reference File Microform*

Quadrennial Supplement To Cumulative Index of Congressional Committee Hearings (Not Confidential In Character) From Eighty-Sixth Congress (January 7, 1959) Through Eighty-Seventh Congress (January 3, 1963) Together With Selected Committee Prints In The United States Senate Library, 87, 223

Quarterly Update: A Comprehensive Listing of New Audiovisual Materials and Services Offered by The National Audiovisual Center, 203

Readex microprints of the *Monthly Catalog;* see *United States Government Publications (Depository)* and *United States Government Publications (Non-Depository)*

A Reference Guide To The NTIS Bibliographic Data Base, 1980, 194

A Reference List of Audiovisual Materials Produced By The United States Government, 1978, 203

A Reference List of Audiovisual Materials Produced by The United States Government, Supplement, 1980, 203

Reference Manual on Population and Housing Statistics From The Census Bureau, 178

Regulations, 109, 126-28

Regulatory Agendas; see *Semiannual Agendas of Significant Regulations*

Regulatory analyses, 128

Reports — definition, 45-46

Resolutions — definition, 45

Revised Statutes of the United States, Passed at the First Session of the Forty-Third Congress, 1873-74; Embracing the Statutes of the United States, General and Permanent In Their Nature, In Force Dec. 1, 1873, 123, 223

Rules; see Regulations

Scientific and Technical Aerospace Reports, 192-93

Semi-Annual Agendas of Significant Regulations, 128, 141

Senate Executive Documents — definition, 48

Senate Executive Reports — definition, 48

Senate Journal, see *Journal of The Senate of The United States of America*

Serial Set, 77-86, 106-08, 226

Shepard's Acts and Cases by Popular Name, 223

Slip Laws, 43, 109

The Social and Economic Status of The Black Population In The United States: An Historical View, 1790-1978, 157, 160

Social Indicators, III: Selected Data on Social Conditions and Trends In The United States, 157, 159

Sourcebook of Criminal Justice Statistics, 163

STAR; see *Scientific and Technical Aerospace Reports*

State and Metropolitan Area Data Book, 1979: A Statistical Abstract Supplement, 156, 158

State Data Centers, 181

Statistical Abstract of The United States, 156-58

A Statistical Portrait of Women In The United States, 1978, 157, 159

Statistical Reporter, 163, 174, 177

Statutes at Large, see *United States Statutes at Large*

A Student Workbook On The 1970 Census, 177

Subject bibliographies, 24

Superintendent of Documents Microfiche Users Guide For Congressional House and Senate Bills, 61-62, 234

Supplement To The Index of Congressional Committee Hearings Prior To January 3, 1935 Consisting of Hearings Not Catalogued By The U.S. Senate Library With Subject Index From The Twenty-Fifth Congress, 1839 Through The Seventy-Third Congress, 1934, 90

Supplemental Index To Congressional Committee Hearings January 3, 1949 To January 3, 1955, 81st, 82d, and 83d Congresses In The Library of The United States House of Representatives, 97

Survey of Current Business, 162

Truck Inventory and Use Survey, 172, 179-80

Uniform Crime Reports For The United States, 163

United States Code, 109, 111, 116-17, 119-25, 129, 132, 134, 137, 142, 145-46, 217, 219, 223, 226-27, 238-39, 241-44

United States Code Annotated, 109, 116-17, 125, 223, 227, 239

United States Code Congressional and Administrative News, 109, 113-18, 145-46, 223, 227, 234

United States Code Service: Lawyers' Edition, 109, 125, 223, 227, 239

United States Government Manual, viii, 221, 227

United States Government Publications: A Monthly Catalog; see *Monthly Catalog of United States Government Publications*

United States Government Publications (Depository), 19

United States Government Publications. Monthly Catalog. Cumulative Personal Author Index, 1941-1975, 9, 18-19, 225, 228, 230

United States Government Publications, Monthly Catalog: Decennial Cumulative Index, 1941-1950, 9, 18, 225

United States Government Publications (Non-Depository), 19

United States Government Research and Development Reports, 186

United States Government Research Reports, 186

United States Statutes at Large, 109-114, 119, 122, 134-35, 137, 142, 223, 226-28, 234, 238, 243-44

U.S. Congressional Committee Hearings on Microfiche, 87

U.S. Congressional Committee Prints on Microfiche, 45, 97-98

Weekly Compilation of Presidential Documents, 71

Women Owned Businesses, 179

World, United States and Historical Maps, 198